Touchstones

1

Junior Cycle First Year English

CLARE MADDEN

The Educational Company of Ireland

First published 2022
The Educational Company of Ireland
Ballymount Road
Walkinstown
Dublin 12
www.edco.ie
A member of the Smurfit Kappa Group plc

ISBN 978-1-80230-017-8

Editor: Sarah Reece
Proofreader: Judith Paskin
Layout: emc design
Cover design: Slick Fish Design
Cover illustration: János Orbán
Interior design: emc design
Illustrations: Shirley Chiang, Xavier Mula (Beehive Illustration)

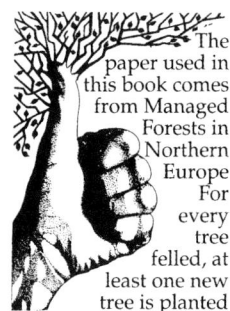

The paper used in this book comes from Managed Forests in Northern Europe For every tree felled, at least one new tree is planted

Author's Acknowledgements
With thanks to:
My husband Ray, my kids and the Madden family for their unwavering support.
My brilliant colleagues at GCC for their help, ideas and encouragement.
My English students, past and present, for inspiring me every day.

The author and publisher would like to thank Eoghan Evesson for his work in this book.

Introduction – Your Guide To Touchstones 1

Welcome to **Touchstones 1**, your **new First Year Junior Cycle English course**.

All **22 First Year learning outcomes** are covered in *Touchstones 1*, with emphasis on the **three strands** of the Junior Cycle English specification: **oral language**, **reading** and **writing**.

A wide variety of exciting and engrossing **texts** will make learning English in First Year a rich and engaging experience, with interesting extracts from fiction, play scripts, non-fiction sources and poems – both old and new – as well as an immersive introduction to the language of Shakespeare.

Scaffolded **activities** will help you gain confidence and develop your skills as a listener, reader, writer, speaker and performer. **Formative** and **summative** **assessment** opportunities, such as retrieval practice and whole-class feedback, are integrated throughout the programme.

The *Touchstones 1* package comprises a **textbook**, an **activity book** and **digital resources**.

Icons

Reading Task	Group Discussion
Writing Task	Linked Activity Book Task
Communicating Task	Reflection
Performing Task	Challenging Vocabulary

Textbook

Touchstones 1 contains six **genre-based** units that offer an enjoyable journey through First Year English. The units include the following features:

Knowledge Organiser:

An at-a-glance guide to all the things you will learn and the skills you will develop in the unit.

Reading:

Tasks to encourage reading for a variety of purposes using a range of strategies.

READING

1 What element of the fairy-tale genre is being played with here?
2 Do you think the wolf is a reliable narrator? Why? Why not?
3 What makes this an entertaining version of the story?

Writing:

Tasks to stretch your writing skills, including for a range of purposes and in a variety of text types.

WRITING

Enjoy watching the short film: edco.ie/rk2t

Then watch it again and write your answers to the questions below.

1 Summarise the plot of the film in one sentence.
2 Write a short paragraph to describe the setting of the film.
3 Write a short paragraph to describe the mise-en-scène and colour palette used in this film.

Communicating:

Tasks to build your oral communication skills.

COMMUNICATING

1 Listen to a reading of the poem: edco.ie/mm73
Complete the personal response grid in your activity book (see page 52). Then divide into small groups and share your ideas.
2 Create a dramatic performance of this poem. Think about which words should be emphasised, what tone of voice you should speak in and what kind of sound effects or backing music you might play in the background.

Vocabulary:

Increase your vocabulary bank by engaging with new challenging words.

PRE-READING TASK: CHALLENGING VOCABULARY

In order to understand a new, challenging word, that word needs to be explored and investigated in a variety of ways. This will help the new word stick in your memory.

Create two sentences that include the word 'sullen' that clearly show your understanding of the word.

Definition:
bad-tempered and sullen

Sullen

Synonyms:
sulky, sour, morose, resentful

Example:
Her boyfriend was annoyed, because she ruined their selfie with her sullen look.

Toolkits:

Scaffolding, ideas and examples to support your learning.

DESCRIBING A THEME PARK ATTRACTION TOOLKIT

The purpose of the descriptions of the most popular rides is to persuade people to want to come and visit the park. Below are some ways a writer could use language to make their descriptions exciting and engaging.

Projects:

Engaging step-by-step projects that can be used to prepare for the Classroom-Based Assessments (CBAs).

Test Your Knowledge:

Assess your knowledge and practise your improved writing skills at the end of each unit.

Shakespeare

Includes an immersive introduction to the language of Shakespeare.

Reading Unit

Includes numerous activities and book reviews to inspire even the most reluctant reader.

What Type Of Reader Are You?

Many different types of reader exist in the world. You may yourself go through all the types in your lifetime or even in the space of a year. There are times in our life when we are reluctant to read and other times when we can't get enough of reading. The important thing to know is that just because you may not be in love with reading right now, doesn't mean you won't fall in love with a book again sometime in the future. Take the quiz opposite to see what type of reader you are at the moment.

Spelling, Punctuation and Grammar

This section helps you consolidate your knowledge of grammar.

SPELLING, PUNCTUATION AND GRAMMAR KNOWLEDGE ORGANISER

Things I need to know

- **Etymology:** The history of a word.
- **Morphology:** The different parts of a word.
- **Synonym:** A word that means the same thing.
- **Antonym:** A word that means the opposite.
- **Prefix:** Letters added to the beginning of a word to make a new word with a different meaning.
- **Suffix:** Letters added to the end of a word to make a new word with a different meaning.
- **Root word:** A word in its most basic form, with no prefix or suffix.
- **Dictionary:** A book where you can find the meaning of words, listed in alphabetical order.
- **Thesaurus:** A book where you can find synonyms of words.

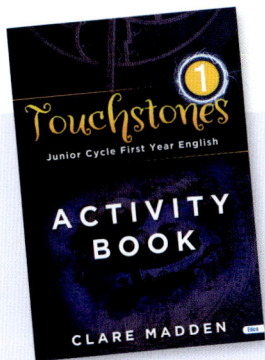

Activity book

Touchstones 1 provides a **scaffolded Activity Book**, with additional material, questions and activities, covering the same unit structure and text extracts, to complement your textbook.

Digital resources

These provide supplementary content to enhance your learning experience. Links to the digital resources, which include PowerPoints, videos and interactive quizzes, are **referenced throughout the textbook**.

You can access the resources via the Touchstones 1 interactive e-book, which is available online at www.edcolearning.ie. Additional resources for teachers include editable planning documents and solutions to activities.

Audio and video resources

Links to **video** and **audio** clips such as poetry readings, short films and podcasts

PowerPoint

Editable PowerPoint presentations provide unit summaries, highlighting key themes and topics in the textbook

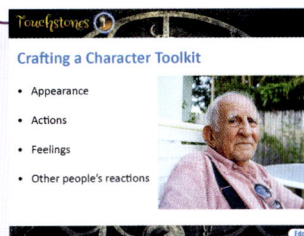

Touchstones 1

Crafting a Character Toolkit

- Appearance
- Actions
- Feelings
- Other people's reactions

Video

Additional support for key English skills

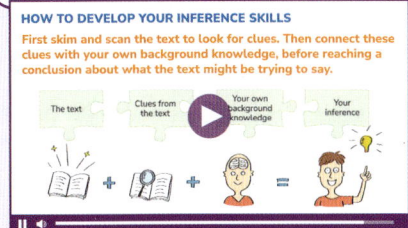

HOW TO DEVELOP YOUR INFERENCE SKILLS

First skim and scan the text to look for clues. Then connect these clues with your own background knowledge, before reaching a conclusion about what the text might be trying to say.

The text | Clues from the text | Your own background knowledge | Your inference

Research links

Useful websites for further research

Interactive website

CONTENTS

Unit 2: Poetry

Unit 2: Poetry

Projects*

Unit 3: Film

Key features

Texts

Projects*

Unit 4: Drama

Unit 5: Shakespeare

Unit 6: Non-Fiction

Unit 7: Reading

pages 246–269

Unit 8: Spelling, Punctuation and Grammar

pages 270–277

*The projects can be used as **learning in focus** units. See the editable plans on **www.edcolearning.ie**.

UNIT 1
FICTION

FICTION KNOWLEDGE ORGANISER

Things I need to know

Plot: the events that happen within the story.

Narrative perspective: the point of view from which the story is told.

First-person perspective: when the story is told by one character in that character's voice. *My I*

Third-person limited narrator: a narrator who is telling the story from one character's point of view, knowing the thoughts and feelings of just this one character. *using he/she*

Third-person omniscient narrator: a narrator who has access to the thoughts and feelings of all the characters in the story.

Setting: where all the action happens. It is the specific place, timeframe and world where the story happens.

Character: the person who appears in the story. The craft of creating a character is called characterisation.

A writer's craft

A writer's purpose is the aim of a piece of writing. It could be to inform, explain, describe or entertain.

Crafting a piece of writing involves thinking about how you will show your reader something instead of just telling them.

Create a setting by appealing to the five senses – sight, touch, hearing, smell and taste.

Create a character by writing about their appearance, actions, feelings or other people's opinions of them.

Redraft a piece of writing at both word and sentence level by skimming and scanning the text, cutting, upgrading and using a dictionary or thesaurus.

Edit a piece of writing by skimming and scanning with a focus on spelling and punctuation, using a dictionary or thesaurus and using a second pair of eyes to check.

Skills I will develop

- Reading texts to understand character, setting and story
- Writing in a variety of text types for different purposes and audiences
- Learning from model texts to improve my own writing skills
- Engaging in class group discussions actively

Projects

- Write A Fractured Fairy Tale: Engaging in the writing process to craft my own short story
- Create A Podcast: Responding imaginatively to a novel by creating and recording a podcast

What do I know?

What do you already know about fiction or stories? Do you know any famous authors? What's your favourite story?

Go to your activity book (see page 7) and complete the fiction knowledge download activity.

What Is Fiction?

PowerPoint

Telling and listening to stories are at the heart of what it means to be human. Fiction is the telling of stories that are in some way imaginary. A writer imagines and creates a world and characters and shares it with their readers. Writers find inspiration for fiction from real life, from old stories, from a person they have met or a place they have visited.

> Some of these things are true and some of them lies. But they are all good stories.
>
> **Hilary Mantel, Wolf Hall**

> Fiction is like a spider's web, attached ever so lightly perhaps, but still attached to life at all four corners.
>
> **Virginia Woolf, A Room of One's Own**

> Writing fiction is the act of weaving a series of lies to arrive at a greater truth.
>
> **Khaled Hosseini**

> Fiction can show you a different world. It can take you somewhere you've never been.
>
> **Neil Gaiman, The View from the Cheap Seats: Selected Nonfiction**

Which of these quotes do you like best? Which quotes do you agree with? Are there any you disagree with?

A good story is crafted through a process that includes brainstorming, planning, drafting, redrafting and editing. The finished product that we pick up from a library or bookshop is the result of a long writing process.

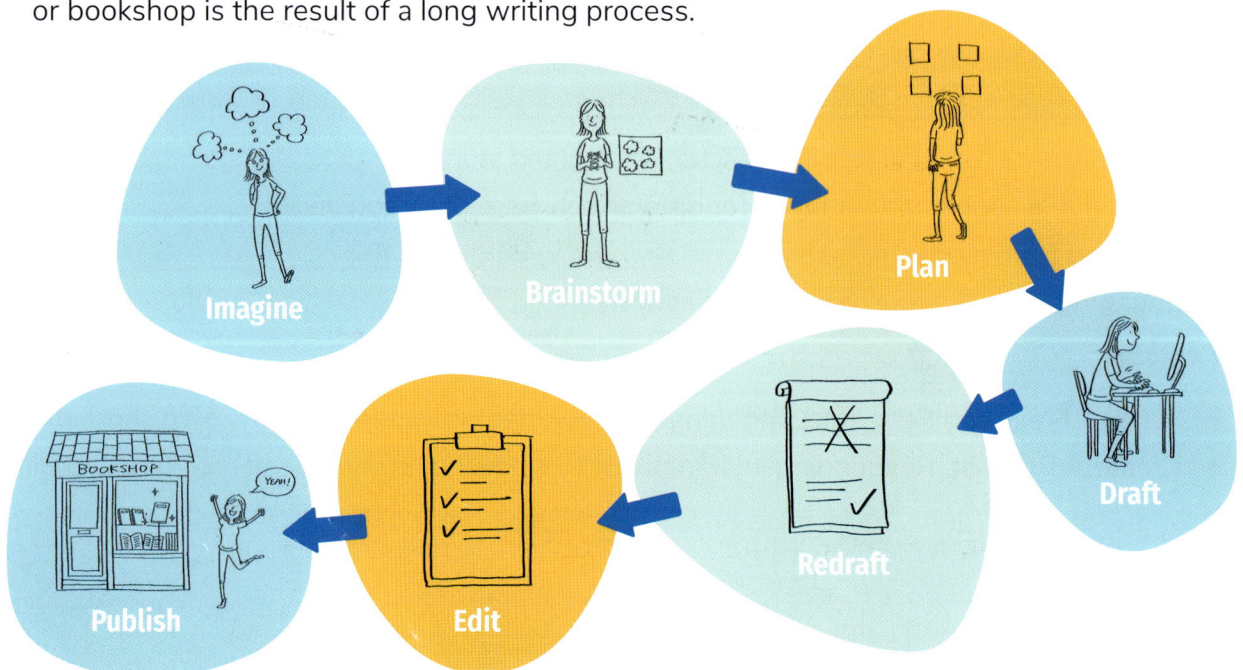

Imagine → Brainstorm → Plan → Draft → Redraft → Edit → Publish

Plot

The plot of a story is the events that happen within the story. Some stories follow a straightforward plot line. The story usually begins with an interesting **opening** where we meet the characters and are introduced to the setting. Next, a **problem** arises that sets the story in motion. The action and tension continues to rise (**rising action**) until we reach the **climactic** moment, the moment when the conflict finally comes to a head. Following this, the action calms down (**falling action**) and finally the conflict is dealt with and **resolved** in some way. In fairy tales, this is the point where everyone lives happily ever after!

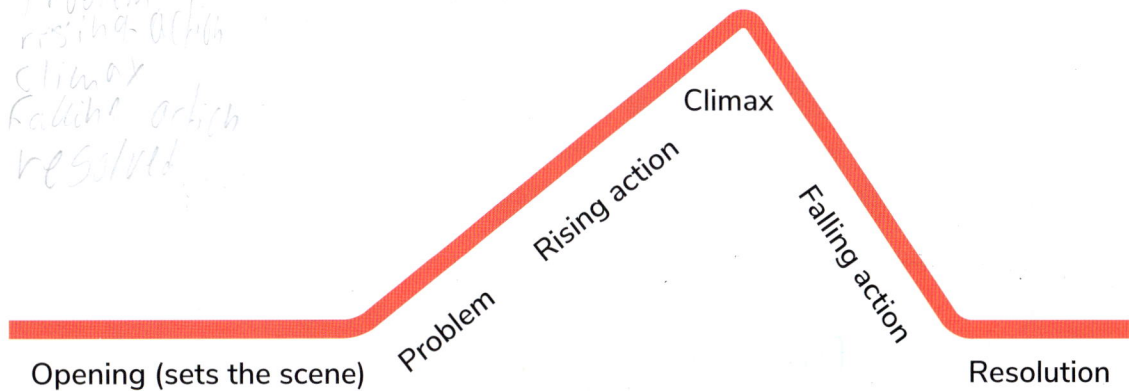

Climax

Rising action

Falling action

Problem

Opening (sets the scene)

Resolution

READING

Look at this list of the plot points from the well-known fairy tale *Jack and the Beanstalk*. They are not in the correct order. In your activity book (see page 7), sort the plot points into the correct order.

(a) Jack meets a man. He sells the cow for magic beans.

(b) Jack and his mum live happily ever after.

(c) Jack goes down the beanstalk.

(d) The next morning, Jack sees the beanstalk and decides to climb it.

(e) The giant follows Jack.

(f) Jack chops down the beanstalk and the giant dies.

(g) Jack is sent to sell the cow.

(h) Jack's mum gets angry and throws the beans out of the window.

(i) Jack enters the castle at the top of the beanstalk.

(j) Jack steals the harp and the hen.

(k) Jack sees a giant and hides.

(l) Setting: Jack's House

(m) Jack sees a singing harp and a hen that lays golden eggs.

(n) The giant falls asleep.

(o) The giant wakes up.

(p) Characters: Jack, Mum, Cow, Man, Giant

Narrative Perspective

The narrative perspective of a story is the point of view from which the story is told. There are a number of narrative perspectives that can be used to tell a story, but the most common are **first person**, **third-person limited** and **third-person omniscient**.

First-person perspective is when the story is told by one character in that character's voice. You can recognise a first-person perspective when a character uses the words 'I' and 'we'.

Third-person limited perspective is when an external narrator is telling the story from one character's point of view. The narrator knows all the thoughts and feelings of this one character, but doesn't know the thoughts and feelings of anyone else.

Third-person omniscient narrators are all-seeing and all-powerful. This type of narrator has access to the thoughts and feelings of all the characters in the story.

First person	Third-person limited	Third-person omniscient
I, Me		
I looked at Grandmother in her big brass bed. She looked different somehow, changed, or aged, or something. Grandmother shifted from side to side in the bed. It looked like she was nervous.	Little Red Riding Hood thought that there was something off about her grandmother today. Her grandmother shifted nervously in the bed. She let out what could only be described as a growl. Little Red Riding Hood blinked in shock.	The wolf licked his lips, salivating at the thought of devouring the little girl. Little Red Riding Hood thought to herself that there was something not entirely right about her grandmother. Meanwhile, the huntsman ran as fast as his legs could carry him, worried that he was far too late.

The narrative perspective affects how believable or reliable you will find a narrator. For example, a story written in the first person from the perspective of a particular character will be less reliable than a story written from the third-person omniscient perspective. A first-person narrator may present themselves in the best possible light and will only tell you their side of the story. They have to infer the thoughts and feelings of other characters, and their viewpoint can be coloured by their attitudes and beliefs. In contrast, a third-person omniscient narrator is able to present the thoughts and feelings of any character, both positive and negative, in order to tell every side of the story.

READING

Read the extracts below, which are written from a variety of narrative perspectives.

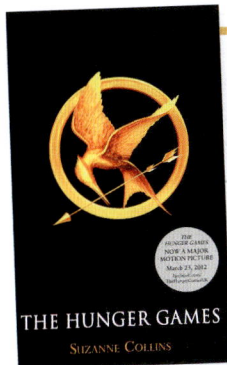

Extract A: The Hunger Games by Suzanne Collins

It's this detail, the untucked blouse forming a ducktail, that brings me back to myself.

'Prim!' The strangled cry comes out of my throat, and my muscles begin to move again. 'Prim!' I don't need to shove through the crowd. The other kids make way immediately allowing me a straight path to the stage. I reach her just as she is about to mount the steps. With one sweep of my arm, I push her behind me.

'I volunteer!' I gasp. 'I volunteer as tribute!' *First person (p)*

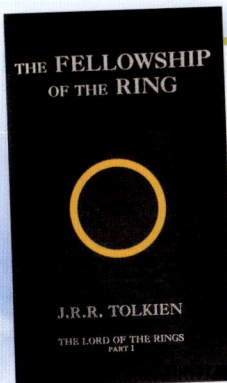

Extract B: The Fellowship of the Ring by J.R.R. Tolkien

A few creatures came and looked at them when the fire had died away. A fox passing through the wood on business of his own stopped several minutes and sniffed.

'Hobbits!' he thought. 'Well, what next? I have heard of strange doings in this land, but I have seldom heard of a Hobbit sleeping out of doors under a tree. Three of them! There's something mighty queer behind this.' He was quite right, but he never found out any more about it. *Third-person (O)*

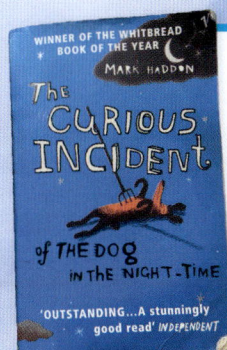

Extract C: The Curious Incident of the Dog in the Night-time by Mark Haddon

This is a murder mystery novel. Siobhan said that I should write something I would want to read myself. Mostly I read books about science and maths. I do not like proper novels. In proper novels people say things like, 'I am veined with iron, with silver and with streaks of common mud. I cannot contract into the firm fist which those clench who do not depend on stimulus.' What does this mean? I do not know. Nor does Father. Nor do Siobhan or Mr Jeavons. I have asked them. *Third person — Limited*

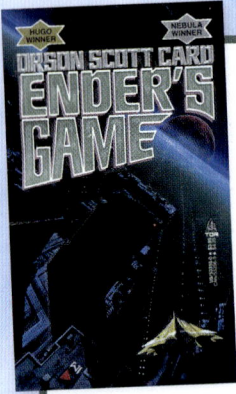

Extract D: *Ender's Game* by Orson Scott Card

But Ender knew, even as he thought it, that Peter wouldn't leave him alone. There was something in Peter's eyes, when he was in his mad mood, and whenever Ender saw that look, that glint, he knew that the one thing Peter would not do was leave him alone. I'm practicing piano, Ender. Come turn the pages for me. Oh, is the monitor boy too busy to help his brother? Is he too smart? Got to go kill some buggers, astronaut? No, no, I don't want your help. *Third-person (O)*

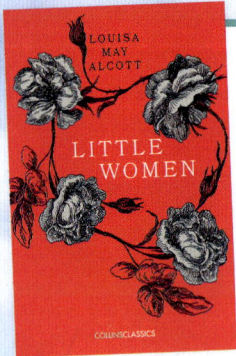

Extract E: *Little Women* by Louisa May Alcott

While these things were happening at home, Amy was having hard times at Aunt March's. She felt her exile deeply, and for the first time in her life, realized how much she was beloved and petted at home. Aunt March never petted any one; she did not approve of it, but she meant to be kind, for the well-behaved little girl pleased her very much, and Aunt March had a soft place in her old heart for her nephew's children, though she didn't think it proper to confess it. *First person (P)*

READING

1 Complete the narrative perspective task in your activity book (see page 7).
2 Choose one of the extracts above and rewrite it in a different perspective. Swap your copy with the person next to you and see if they can figure out what perspective you've written from. Do you think the change in perspective has made the extract better or worse? Why?
3 Do you think that the narrators in extracts A, B, C and D are reliable? How do you know? Could there be something they are leaving out?
4 Pretend you are a writer about to sit down to write a new story. Create a list of the pros and cons for the three different narrative perspectives. What would be the advantages and disadvantages of writing in each perspective?

COMMUNICATING: GROUP DISCUSSION

1 Can you think of any stories you have read that had a narrative perspective that stood out to you for any reason?
2 Looking at the extracts above, which of these stories would you most like to read and why?
3 Which of these stories would you least like to read and why?

Setting

The setting of a story is where all the action happens. It is the specific place, timeframe and world where the story happens. The setting of a text tells the reader a lot about who holds the power in a story and who will have none. It can give an insight into the relationships between characters and influence how a character thinks and feels. It can tell us about the environment of the world and the impact this might have on the characters. Settings can be like our normal everyday world or can be completely fictional depending on the story.

READING

Read the three extracts below, which are taken from well-known novels that use the five senses to craft engaging settings.

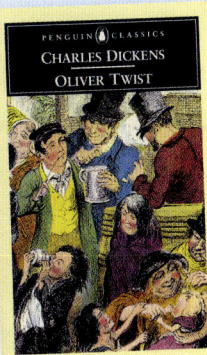

Extract A: Oliver Twist by Charles Dickens

The public-houses, with gas-lights burning inside, were already open. By degrees, other shops began to be unclosed, and a few scattered people were met with. Then, came straggling groups of labourers going to their work; then, men and women with fish-baskets on their heads; donkey-carts laden with vegetables; chaise-carts filled with livestock or whole carcasses of meat; milk-women with pails; an unbroken concourse of people trudging out with various supplies to the eastern suburbs of the town. As they approached the City, the noise and traffic gradually increased; when they threaded the streets between Shoreditch and Smithfield, it had swelled into a roar of sound and bustle.

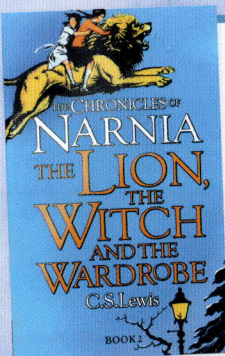

Extract B: The Lion, the Witch and the Wardrobe by C.S. Lewis

Next moment she found that what was rubbing against her face and hands was no longer soft fur but something hard and rough and even prickly. 'Why, it is just like branches of trees!' exclaimed Lucy. And then she saw that there was a light ahead of her; not a few inches away where the back of the wardrobe ought to have been, but a long way off. Something cold and soft was falling on her. A moment later she found that she was standing in the middle of a wood at night-time with snow under her feet and snowflakes falling through the air.

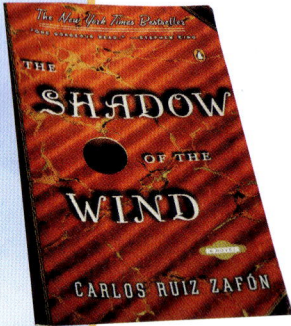

Extract C: The Shadow of the Wind by Carlos Ruiz Zafón

A reef of clouds and lightning raced across the skies from the sea … My hands were shaking, and my mind wasn't far behind. I looked up and saw the storm spilling like rivers of blackened blood from the clouds, blotting out the moon and covering the roofs of the city in darkness. I tried to speed up, but I was consumed with fear and walked with leaden feet, chased by the rain. I took refuge under the canopy of a newspaper kiosk, trying to collect my thoughts and decide what to do next. A clap of thunder roared close by, and I felt the ground shake under my feet … On the flooding pavements the streetlamps blinked, then went out like candles snuffed by the wind. There wasn't a soul to be seen in the streets, and the darkness of the blackout spread with a fetid smell that rose from the sewers.

smelly

READING

1 Complete the five senses task in your activity book (see page 9).

2 Choose one of the extracts above and say what you think the author's purpose was in creating that setting. What were they trying to tell the reader?

3 Rewrite your chosen extract with a different purpose in mind. For example, you could rewrite the extract from *The Shadow of the Wind* and attempt to create a peaceful setting instead of a terrifying one.

COMMUNICATING

Describe a place you have been to the person next to you. It could be from a local area or your favourite place, or maybe somewhere you've been on holiday. Your aim should be to use the five senses to make the person feel like they have actually been to this place.

WRITING SKILLS: CRAFTING A SETTING

Read through the two settings created below. The purpose of both pieces of writing is to describe a war-torn city. Identify which is a better piece of writing and discuss the reasons why.

▶ Video

SETTING A

There were guns firing everywhere. The sky was black with smoke from the fires in the buildings. The footpath was piled with rubble and debris from all the bombs. There were dead bodies everywhere.

SETTING B

An eerie silence descended on the city. Time to catch its breath before the volley of gunfire drowns it once again. The remains of once majestic buildings are discarded on the bloody footpaths.

SETTING A tells the reader everything about the scene all at once, so they are not left wondering anything. It reads like a factual account, so the reader doesn't have to do any work imagining the scene and doesn't have to try connecting the dots through the hints the writer has suggested. As a result there is no atmosphere created and the reader may lose interest and concentration.

vibe

SETTING B is a much better piece of writing because it creates an atmosphere that invites the reader into the world the writer has created. The reader is dropped subtle hints about the world of the text and must connect the dots and imagine the scene for themselves.

Setting B	Suggests to the reader
Eerie silence	The silence is unusual and is only temporary.
Time to catch its breath	The city is a living thing.
Once majestic buildings	The city was once amazing.
Bloody footpaths	People have died here.

Good writers create settings by keeping in mind two things: **purpose** and **crafting**.
Purpose: What atmosphere and mood does the writer want to convey? Peaceful? Sinister? Terrifying? Homely?

Crafting: How will I craft this piece of writing by giving subtle clues and not telling the reader everything at once about the world of the text?

CRAFTING A SETTING TOOLKIT

One of the ways a writer can craft an engaging setting is through using the **five senses** to make a reader feel like they are transported to the world of the story. Below are some interesting ways a writer could use the senses to engage the reader in the world of the text.

Smell	See	Hear	Touch	Taste
What does it not smell like? *Strangely, the stable did not smell like horses. It did not smell like hay or manure or hard work.*	**Describe specific colours or use colour as a symbol** *The woman's ashen grey face told them all they needed to know.*	**Describe the sound first, then reveal its source** *A loud banging echoed around the dungeon; the prisoner was awake again.*	**Describe specific textures in detail** *The chair was decorated in a circus of stains, each with their own distinctive texture.*	**Taste something that is a smell** *Gasping for air, she swallowed the filthy smog and ashes.*
Link the smell to a memory *The salty sea air wafted through the window and Sarah remembered summer at her grandmother's.*	**Describe how the light affects things in the setting** *The rickety table was illuminated by a stream of light sneaking in through a tear in the blind.*	**A sound that is unexpected or surprising for the setting** *A gunshot cut through the birdsong and trees.*	**Describe the temperature of people or things** *The floor was ice cold like a frozen lake.*	**Taste is subjective. Use taste to reveal something about a character.** *The steak was barely cooked, but she ate it without flinching.*
Link the smell to an emotion *She walked into the kitchen to the smell of fresh bread baking; she had to swallow her grief quickly.*	**Zoom in and describe specific details of objects within the scene** *The necklace on the dresser was broken and rusting.*	**Describe a sound but do not reveal exactly what it is** *Something rumbled in the distance; it sounded hungry, angry and louder with every second.*	**Describe the vibrations of something** *The room was buzzing; it seemed alive.*	**Reveal something about a character by revealing a taste craving** *He needed to feed. Something big and juicy.*
Use nouns or verbs to describe a smell *She smelled like home.*	**Link what you see to emotions** *The doll's house was arranged meticulously. Her heart broke in two at the sight of it.*	**Describe a sound that a character has imagined** *Someone was calling her, softly and gently. She would go into the night and find it.*	**Link touch to a memory or emotion** *He touched the soft velvet curtain and was immediately transported back to his childhood.*	**Link the taste to a memory or emotion** *The melting mashed potato reminded her of Granny.*

COMMUNICATING: GROUP DISCUSSION

In small groups, look at the three settings pictured below. Choose the one that most appeals to you. Describe the setting in the picture by using the toolkit on page 12. First choose a sense to engage, then choose a way to engage it. Finally, apply it to the picture you have chosen. Each member of the group should take a turn adding to the oral picture description.

WRITING

First choose three tools from the toolkit opposite to help you craft a setting. Now select one of the purposes from the list below. Write a short paragraph to describe your setting. An example has been completed for you.

Craft a setting that is...		
peaceful and relaxing	sinister and unsettling	amusing
romantic	unusual and different	joyful and uplifting

Example

Purpose: Craft a setting that is sinister and unsettling.

Toolkit choices:

- Describe a sound but do not reveal exactly what it is.
- What does it not smell like?
- Describe specific colours or use colour as a symbol.

Slowly, Sarah opened the door to the enclosed garden. She was not met with the smell of flowers, grass or earth. This was a different kind of smell; one she was familiar with but could not, or would not, name. The trees hung limp, their leaves a pale grey. There was not a flower nor an insect to be seen. Then it started again. She followed the low humming, determined, no matter what the consequences, to find its source.

Edit your paragraph

Skim and scan your setting paragraph and ensure you have used capital letters and end punctuation correctly. Turn to page 272 to check the rules.

Character

A character is the person who appears in the story. The craft of creating a character is called **characterisation**. Often one of the most absorbing things about a story is the characters. A writer has crafted an excellent character if they have made you, the reader, care about the person. You know the writer has hooked you if you stay up late reading because you simply had to find out what happened to a character at the end of a story.

READING

Read the extracts below from some well-known stories that display expert character crafting.

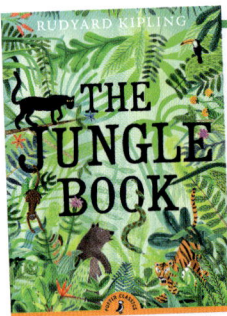

Extract A: *The Jungle Book* by Rudyard Kipling

A black shadow dropped down into the circle. It was Bagheera the Black Panther, inky black all over, but with the panther markings showing up in certain lights like the pattern of watered silk. Everybody knew Bagheera, and nobody cared to cross his path, for he was as cunning as Tabaqui, as bold as the wild buffalo, and as reckless as the wounded elephant. But he had a voice as soft as wild honey dripping from a tree, and a skin softer than down.

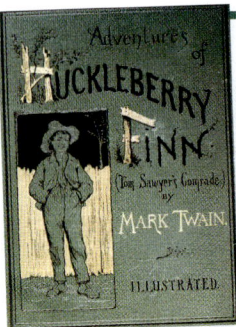

Extract B: *The Adventures of Huckleberry Finn* by Mark Twain

He was most fifty, and he looked it. His hair was long and tangled and greasy, and hung down, and you could see his eyes shining through like he was behind vines. It was all black, no gray; so was his long, mixed-up whiskers. There warn't no color in his face, where his face showed; it was white; not like another man's white, but a white to make a body sick, a white to make a body's flesh crawl – a tree-toad white, a fish-belly white. As for his clothes – just rags, that was all. He had one ankle resting on t'other knee; the boot on that foot was busted, and two of his toes stuck through, and he worked them now and then. His hat was laying on the floor – an old black slouch with the top caved in, like a lid.

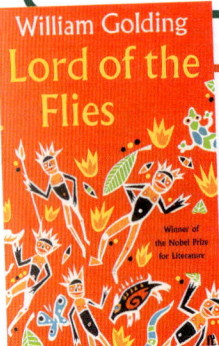

Extract C: *Lord of the Flies* by William Golding

Inside the floating cloak he was tall, thin, and bony; and his hair was red beneath the black cap. His face was crumpled and freckled, and ugly without silliness.

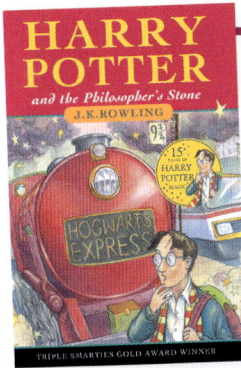

Extract D: Harry Potter and the Philosopher's Stone by J.K. Rowling

A giant of a man was standing in the doorway. His face was almost completely hidden by a long, shaggy mane of hair and a wild, tangled beard, but you could make out his eyes, glinting like black beetles under all the hair.

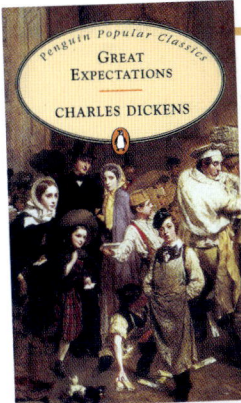

Extract E: Great Expectations by Charles Dickens

My sister, Mrs. Joe, with black hair and eyes, had such a prevailing redness of skin that I sometimes used to wonder whether it was possible she washed herself with a nutmeg-grater instead of soap. She was tall and bony, and almost always wore a coarse apron, fastened over her figure behind with two loops, and having a square impregnable bib in front, that was stuck full of pins and needles.

COMMUNICATING: GROUP DISCUSSION

1 Which of the characters in these extracts would you like to meet and why?
2 Can you think of any character from any story that you were really engaged with? Why do you think that was?
3 Can you think of any character in any text you have come across that you had absolutely no interest in? Why do you think this was?

READING

Complete the character task in your activity book (see page 10).

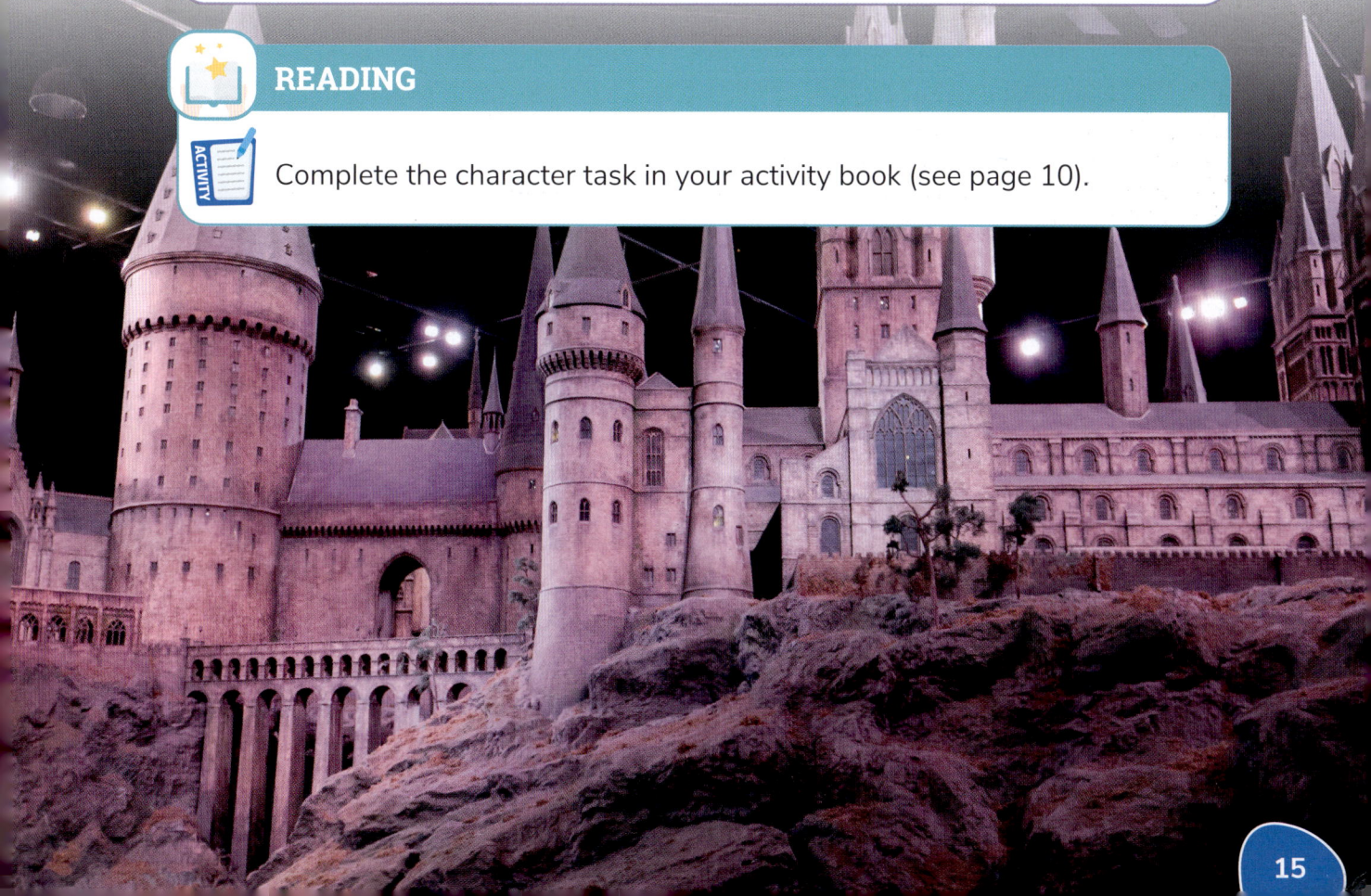

WRITING SKILLS: CRAFTING A CHARACTER

Read the descriptions of the two characters below. Identify which is a better piece of writing and discuss the reasons why.

▶ Video

CHARACTER A

The evil man came into the room and everyone was scared. He had black clothes, black hair and even black eyes.

CHARACTER B

The man slipped through the doorway silently, with the skill of someone practised in the art of sneaking. His eyes were pools of endless darkness and his thin lips seemed frozen in a straight line. The hairs on the back of my neck stood up before I saw him. It was as if my body sensed something before I laid eyes on him.

Character A is revealed as an evil villain immediately and the description of his appearance gives away his character's purpose without the reader having to do any thinking at all. This takes away the element of suspense and surprise in the story and may lead to the reader losing interest.

Character B is a much better piece of writing as the character and his motivations are revealed to the reader slowly and subtly. The reader is certain this is a sinister character but not sure why and how. The reader must do a bit of work thinking about the character and will therefore be interested in reading on to pick up more and more clues.

Character B	This suggests to the reader
Someone practised in the art of sneaking	He does underhand things.
Pools of endless darkness	There is something sinister about him.
Thin lips seemed frozen in a straight line	He does not ever smile or talk.
Hairs on the back of my neck stood up	He scares other people.

Just like when creating a setting, a good writer must create interesting characters by keeping in mind two things: **purpose** and **crafting**.

Purpose: What is the purpose of each character? Are they the hero? The villain? The love interest? The sidekick?

Crafting: How will I craft this piece of writing by giving subtle clues and not telling the reader everything about the character?

CRAFTING A CHARACTER TOOLKIT

There are several ways you can craft a character. Below are some interesting ideas to start you off. You can describe the person's appearance, actions, feelings or other people's opinions about or reactions to the character.

Appearance	Actions	Feelings	Other people's reactions
Describe their eyes or mouth in detail: colour, movement, anything unusual *Lily's eyes smiled back. Big pools of sparkling blue, uncoloured by the evils of the world she would have to live in.*	**How the character or a part of the character moves strangely, revealing something about them** *Looking down at his hands, she realised that she had never seen them shaped any other way than in a tight fist.*	**Angry: biting lip, red face, sweaty, pacing back and forth, heart beating quickly** *Fuming, she stumbled back upstairs. Her cheeks burned with rage and she bit her lip so hard she began to bleed.*	**The character's relationship with their family** *Not one of the O'Connors turned to look at Eoghan when he walked into the room. It was as if he was a ghost or, worse still, like he did not exist at all.*
Describe the clothes they are wearing in detail: where they bought them, the fabric texture, the condition of them *Violet swept into the room draped in a luxurious fur coat that must have cost more than my entire house.*	**A strange action the character does repeatedly that reveals something about them** *His leg never stopped moving. At times he placed his hand on his knee to steady it, but it was futile.*	**Embarrassed: red face or cheeks, wanting to disappear, covering face, teary-eyed, flushed red all over** *Alice stepped back behind her sister, bending her head to look at the floor again. She did not want them to see the flames engulfing her cheeks.*	**How others react when the character enters the scene** *A cold breeze blew through the room suddenly, and they knew he was coming. They braced themselves with every shred of bravery they could muster.*
Describe their voice in detail: tone, pitch, other characters' reaction to it *Ms Naylor's voice was like honey. As soon as she began to speak, I knew it would be fine.*	**How a character does not react to a situation** *Bombs rained down, so near them, they could taste the gunpowder. He continued reading his newspaper, unperturbed.*	**Bored: watching clock, slouching, sighing, rolling eyes, tapping something, staring into space** *Tapping his pencil on the blank page, Alfie sighed again, and again.*	**The character's relationship with others with less power than them** *Mrs Spillane barely looked at them. It was as if they did not exist. And maybe in her bitter mind, they did not.*
Describe their hands: nails, cleanliness, scars, veins, worn, nail varnish *Her hands betrayed her age, despite the flaming red nails and the extravagant rings.*	**How a character can do something nobody else can do** *I never saw her leave a room without every man, woman and child falling in love with her.*	**Shy: looking down, speaking too low, lack of eye contact, blushing, hands in pockets, fidgeting, hiding** *Conor never looked her in the eye. He rooted his hands in his pockets as if he were anchoring himself.*	**How other characters notice or do not notice the character** *Maybelline scrubbed, swept, wiped, polished and dusted, shielded by the invisibility cloak of her race.*

COMMUNICATING

In small groups, look at the three characters pictured below. Choose the one that most appeals to you. Describe the character by using the toolkit on page 17. First choose your character's actions, appearance, emotions or other people's opinions of them. Next, choose a way to express this and apply it to your character. Each member of the group should take a turn adding to the oral picture description.

WRITING

First choose three tools from the toolkit on page 17 to help you craft a character. Now select one of the purposes from the list below. Write a short paragraph to describe your character. An example has been completed for you.

Craft a character who is...		
the hero's love interest	brave but impatient	powerful but cruel
the unwilling hero	a respected leader	a rebel

Example

Purpose: Craft a character who is a rebel.

Toolkit choices:

- Bored: watching clock, slouching, sighing, rolling eyes, tapping something, staring into space.
- Describe the clothes they are wearing in detail; where they bought them, the fabric texture, the condition of them.
- How other characters notice or do not notice the character.

Chase lounged lazily on the chair at the back of the classroom, one eye on the clock and another on the door. His untucked shirt, his missing tie and his non-regulation biker boots under his stone-grey trousers set him apart from the others. He noticed that the first thing a teacher did when they entered the room was to scan the back of the room for his presence. He smiled to himself when he saw a flash of fear on their face.

Edit your paragraph

Skim and scan your character paragraph and ensure you have used capital letters and end punctuation correctly. Turn to page 272 to check the rules.

Epic Poems

An epic poem is a lengthy, narrative work of poetry, usually describing daring feats and heroic deeds. In Ancient Greece, poets would learn epic poems by heart and entertain crowds by reciting them.

The Iliad by Homer

PRE-READING: COMMUNICATING

Which of the statements below do you agree with? Which ones do you disagree with? Give reasons for your answers.

- All military personnel are heroes.
- A hero sacrifices himself – or herself – for their cause.
- One person's hero is another person's villain.
- There is no heroism without suffering.
- An ordinary life is the most heroic one.

CHALLENGING VOCABULARY

ACTIVITY

Read the following four words that appear in the text below. Then complete the vocabulary task in your activity book (see page 11).

Immortal

Definition: living forever; never dying or decaying

Synonyms: undying, deathless, eternal

Example: The pharaohs were considered gods, and therefore immortal.

Avenge

Definition: inflict harm or punishment in return for an injury or wrong done to oneself or another

Synonyms: take revenge, extract retribution

Example: He made a plan to avenge his father's murder.

Cunning

Definition:
having or showing skill in achieving one's ends, often by deceit or evasion

Synonyms:
devious, sly, knowing, wily, crafty

Example:
She was a rather cunning teenager, well able to get whatever she wanted.

Appease

Definition:
try to stop someone being angry by giving them what they want

Synonyms:
placate, pacify, satisfy

Example:
The company changed its rules to appease the discontented workers.

All about *The Iliad*

Homer lived around 800BC and is renowned as one of the greatest storytellers of all time. His epic poem *The Iliad* came from the oral storytelling tradition, where long poems and stories were passed from generation to generation by word of mouth. The original poem is twenty-four books long and is an account of the epic ten-year war between the Trojans and the Greeks, featuring Greek myths, great battles and plenty of drama. The war began when Paris, one of the Trojan princes, stole Helen, the wife of Meneleus, one of the Greek kings. This edited extract from the story takes place near the end of the war.

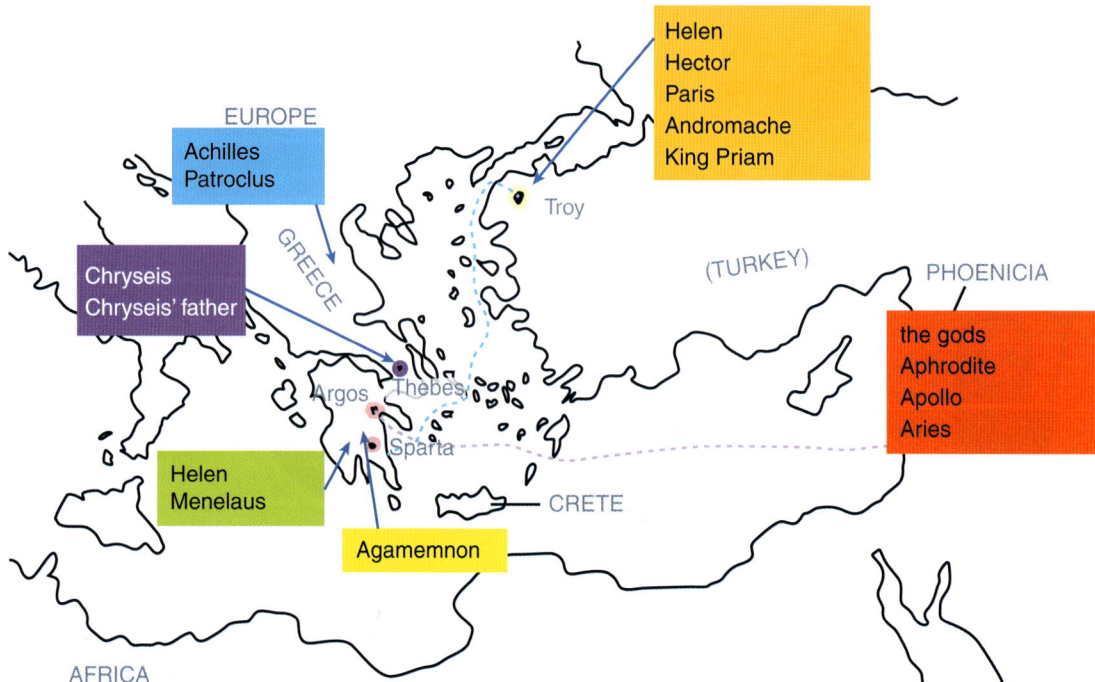

EUROPE

Achilles
Patroclus

GREECE

Chryseis
Chryseis' father

Helen
Menelaus

Agamemnon

Argos Thebes
Sparta

Troy

Helen
Hector
Paris
Andromache
King Priam

(TURKEY)

PHOENICIA

the gods
Aphrodite
Apollo
Aries

CRETE

AFRICA

Part 1: Agamemnon and Achilles disagree

Each of the great cities of Greece sent an army to join the war against the Trojans – each, that is, except for one: the city of Thebes refused to join the war, saying that it had no quarrel with the far away Trojans, and so the Greek King Agamemnon ('Aga-mem-non') decided to teach the Thebans a lesson. He ordered his men to destroy their beautiful city and take its treasure – and that is what they did. While the ruined city of Thebes was still burning, the greatest of the Greek warriors shared out the prizes of war.

King Agamemnon chose for himself one of the captives – a beautiful young girl called Chryseis ('Cry-see-is'), a priest's daughter. Agamemnon told her that she must live with him from now on and be his slave. The girl wept bitterly and begged to be returned to her father, but King Agamemnon had a cruel heart and was unmoved by her tears.

The Greek ships returned to Troy, where the army had set up a vast camp on the beach not far from the city. One evening, the good old priest, who was the father of Chryseis, arrived at the camp and asked to meet King Agamemnon and all the greatest of the Greeks.

He said, 'Oh Agamemnon, leader of men, may the gods grant your wish to destroy the magnificent city of Troy, and may all the Greeks return home safely in their black ships, but grant me this favour: free my daughter and accept in her place a gift of great treasure that I have brought for you.'

The Greek army cheered the old man for his generous offer, and for the love that he had shown for his daughter, but Agamemnon flew into a rage. 'Old man,' said he, 'let me not find you hanging about our ships, nor coming here again. I will not free your lovely daughter. She shall grow old in my house, in Argos, far from her home. So get out of my sight right now, or it will be the worse for you!'

The priest was afraid and swiftly left, but later that evening he knelt down on the shore of the resounding sea and prayed to the immortal god, Apollo of the silver bow. Apollo heard the good old man's prayer for just revenge, and he took up his silver bow and fired arrows into the Greek camp. The arrows of Apollo brought disease, and many of the Greek soldiers fell ill.

By far the greatest of the Greek warriors was Achilles ('A-kill-ees'). He was faster and stronger than any man alive, and also very proud.

When Achilles saw the Greek soldiers dying of disease, he called a meeting of all the generals and spoke as follows, 'Noble Agamemnon, though you are our leader, I must speak the truth. It was wrong to threaten the priest, a good old man who came to you with a generous offer. The gods are angry with us for what you did, and matters must be put right. You must return the lovely Chryseis to her father.'

King Agamemnon was surprised to hear such words, as he was not at all used to being told what to do. 'Great Achilles,' he said, 'brave and strong you may be, but I am king, and I shall do what I like and you shall know your place!'

To which Achilles replied, 'You are too greedy! Why should all the Greeks suffer for your evil ways? I, for one, am not going to follow a leader like you into battle.'

Now King Agamemnon was absolutely furious but he also understood that something must be done to appease the gods and stop the plague that was destroying his army, and so the next day he ordered a boat to take the young girl back to her father, but he also sent messengers to the tent of Achilles and ordered him to hand over his own slave girl. From that moment on, the pride of Achilles was so hurt that he refused to take part in the battle for Troy, but instead stayed inside his tent and sulked while the Greeks went out and fought.

Part 2: Menelaus fights Paris

Soon after, the Trojans opened the great doors of their city and their army marched out – like a flock of wild birds swooping back and forth and calling with screeching voices.

Now the finest warrior among the Trojans was Prince Hector. He was the brother of Paris, but he was quite different in character. Hector was brave and noble, while Paris loved fine clothes and parties and enjoyed his riches to the full.

As they rode out to battle, Hector said to his brother, 'Paris, it is for your sake that thousands of brave soldiers will die today. It is only because you ran away with the Greek Queen Helen that this great army has arrived at our gates with the aim of destroying our beautiful city, killing all the men, and carrying off the women and children as slaves. It would be better had you not been born, my brother.'

When he heard this, Paris felt ashamed, and to make amends he drove his chariot out in front the Trojan army and towards the enemy. In his fiercest voice, Paris called out to the Greeks to send forth their bravest warrior, and to fight him in single combat to decide the war – so that others need not suffer.

On the Greek side, King Menelaus ('Menel-a-us') hated Paris more than any other man alive, so Menelaus jumped out of his chariot and said, 'I will gladly fight Paris, and kill him with my spear which is made of ash wood and tipped with cruel bronze.'

When Paris heard this, he was so frightened that he coiled back like a man who has seen a snake, and he shrank into the protection of his men. Great laughter arose from the Greek army, and the Trojans were furious with Prince Paris for bringing shame on them. Then Paris began to worry that if the beautiful Helen heard about his running away, she would not love him anymore. So he gathered his courage, and went out once more in front of the army, and again shouted out to the Greeks, 'I call on you men to lay your swords and spears on the ground while King Menelaus and I fight one another – hero against hero.'

Menelaus did not give Paris time to change his mind. He hurled his spear at him so that it broke his shield, but just missed his body. Paris fell backwards, and soon Menelaus was on him, dragging him by the plume of his helmet towards the Greek army. However, the Goddess of Love, Aphrodite, who was fond of Paris, saw what was happening and came to his aid disguised as a cloud. She scooped him into her lovely arms, and whisked him back to his Palace where the fair and fragrant Helen was waiting for him. So the Greeks and the Trojans fought each other in battle.

Many brave soldiers were killed and wounded on both sides, but as long as Achilles refused to help the Greeks, the Trojans were stronger and drove the Greeks back to their camp. At night, a thousand campfires glowed upon the plain, and by the light of each fire there sat fifty men while the horses chomped oats and corn beside their chariots and waited for dawn to come.

Part 3: Patroclus spurs Achilles into battle

The Greeks begged the great warrior Achilles to come out and fight, but still he refused to join the battle. His best friend, Patroclus, came up with a cunning plan. He secretly put on the magnificent armour of Achilles and went out into the battle, looking exactly like the great hero. He knew that when the Greeks saw him, they would gain courage at the sight of Achilles and fight with redoubled strength, and when the Trojans saw him, they would think that the warrior they most feared had returned, and would lose heart. When the Trojans saw Patroclus dressed like Achilles, Prince Hector flew at him with his spear and killed him. Only then did he discover that it was not Achilles whom he had killed, but Patroclus.

When the mighty Achilles heard that his best friend had been killed by Hector, his anger and sorrow were great in equal measure, and he stood up before a meeting of the Greek army and said, 'As you know, King Agamemnon has insulted me and I have every right not to fight in this stupid war; but now things have changed. My best friend has been killed by Prince Hector of Troy. It is for the sake of Patroclus, who was dearer to me than any other man, that I will take up the fight and avenge his death.'

When the Greek army heard this, they all cheered and threw their helmets in the air, for they knew that with Achilles on their side, victory could be theirs.

When Prince Hector saw that Achilles stood once again at the head of the Greek army, he knew that there was only one thing for it. He must go out and fight Achilles and decide the fate of Troy.

Hector rode out before the gates of Troy. Achilles, seeing him, started to run with all his might towards Hector, ready to hurl his spear at his hated enemy. Hector jumped from his chariot and stood firm, waiting to meet Achilles, but secretly he thought to himself, 'What if I were to lay down my shield and helmet, lean my spear against the wall and go straight up to noble Achilles? What if I were to promise to hand back Helen, who was the cause of all this war, and let the Greeks take half of all the treasure in the city? But why argue with myself in this way? Were I to go up to him now, he would show me no mercy.'

As he pondered, the swift-footed Achilles charged up to him as if he were Aries himself, the plumed God of battle. The bronze tip of Achilles' spear gleamed around him like the rays of the rising sun. Fear came over Hector and he turned and ran, while Achilles darted after him with his utmost speed. As a mountain hawk, the swiftest of birds, swoops down upon some trembling white dove, that is how Achilles made straight for Hector with all his might, while Hector fled around the city walls as fast as his legs could carry him.

Achilles chased Hector three times around the walls of Troy until at last Hector turned and fought. First Achilles threw his spear at Hector and missed. Hector then threw his spear at Achilles and hit his shield, but did not break it. They fell on each with clashing bronze swords, and Achilles, for he was the stronger hero, killed Hector.

When they heard the sad news, all the women of Troy wept for the loss of their greatest hero, but none wept more than his wife, Andromache.

Part 4: The death of Achilles

Now that the finest hero of the Trojans was dead, the Greek army thought that they would soon win the war. King Priam of Troy greatly grieved the loss of his bravest son, and feared that the city would soon be defeated, but this is not how things turned out – well, not yet – for Apollo, the winged god of the silver bow, again decided to help the Trojans. One day, in the midst of battle, he came up to Prince Paris and said to him, 'Hail Paris, Prince of Troy. Lift up your bow and fire an arrow into the Greek army. I will guide its point into Achilles and kill him.'

When he heard this, Prince Paris replied, 'Almighty Apollo, I will gladly do as you ask, but will I not just waste my arrow? Everyone knows that when Achilles was a baby, his mother dipped him in the River Styx that runs through the Underworld – no weapon can wound him, for the waters of the River Styx make a man immortal.'

Apollo replied, 'Paris, you speak the truth, but the gods gave the great Achilles a choice – he could lead a short and glorious life, or a long and boring one. He chose glory and so his life must be short.'

So Paris dipped his arrow in deadly poison and fired it into the air. Its poisoned tip drove into Achilles' heel – for when Achilles' mother had dipped him in the river of the underworld, she had held him by his heel, and no water had touched it. Achilles fell from his chariot. His great body lay on the ground, dead.

And that is the story of how the Greeks and the Trojans fought for nine years without either side gaining victory. Many brave warriors died on either side, and many tears were shed over lost sons and lost friends.

READING

1 Choose six words that summarise this story. The words do not have to link together in a sentence. For example: kings, warriors, jealousy.

2 The main plot points of the story are listed below, but not in the correct order. In your activity book (see page 12), sort them into the correct order.

(a) Achilles reasons with Agamemnon, who returns Chryseis to her father.

(b) Achilles joins the battle to avenge his best friend.

(c) King Agamemnon steals Chryseis as his slave.

(d) Menelaus fights Paris, who is saved by Aphrodite.

(e) Agamemnon punishes Achilles by taking his favourite slave girl.

(f) Achilles refuses to fight for the Greeks.

(g) Chryseis' father pleads to have her returned. Agamemnon refuses.

(h) Hector shames Paris into seeking single combat with the Greeks.

(i) Paris kills Achilles.

(j) Hector kills Patroclus.

(k) Agamemmnon destroys the city of Thebes.

(l) Achilles fights and kills Hector.

(m) Patroclus rides into battle in Achilles' armour.

(n) Apollo tells Paris about Achilles' choice of a short and glorious life.

3 What is the climax of the story? Is there more than one?

4 Complete the quote quest task in your activity book (see page 12).

5 Complete the character map task in your activity book (see page 13), drawing in the relationships and connections between all of the characters in the story.

6 Complete the hero of heroes task in your activity book (see page 14).

7 What characteristic is valued more than anything else in the world of the text? Do you agree that this is the most important and valuable characteristic that someone should have?

8 Look at the following phrases containing adverbs taken from *The Iliad*. First pick out the adverb in each phrase. Then rewrite the phrase using a synonym for that adverb (see page 277 for more on adverbs).

The priest was afraid and swiftly left	Secretly he thought to himself

9 Complete the extended writing activity in your activity book (see page 15).

WRITING

Write four sentences, each one containing one of the new words you have learned from *The Iliad*.

immortal	avenge	cunning	appease

COMMUNICATING

The Iliad comes from the oral tradition of storytelling. Professional poets and storytellers learned the whole epic poem by heart and recited it as a form of entertainment. As a class, prepare to do an oral retelling of the story of Achilles.

- Divide the story up between everyone in the class.
- Everyone should have a small section of story to learn by heart.
- Arrange the classroom in a circle and sit in the order of the story.
- Each person has a chance to tell their part of the story.
- Don't worry about getting the words completely accurate. The great poets who retold *The Iliad* never recited it word for word. They knew the main plot points, but often improvised as they worked their way through the story.

A good storyteller:

- speaks clearly and slowly so that everyone understands what is being said
- makes eye contact with their audience, inviting everyone into the story
- knows when to pause for audience reaction
- uses hand gestures and facial expressions when telling a story.

Short Stories

A short story is a piece of fiction that is shorter than a novel and can be read in one sitting. Nevertheless, a short story has the ability to make a large impact on a reader and can often inspire them or transport them to another world.

The Secret Life of Walter Mitty by James Thurber

PRE-READING: COMMUNICATING: GROUP DISCUSSION

1 Do you daydream?
2 What situations do you find yourself daydreaming in?
3 Do you ever find objects from the real world making their way into your daydreams?
4 Does something trigger or influence your daydreams?
5 Do you imagine yourself as the hero or the villain in your daydreams?

? CHALLENGING VOCABULARY

Read the following four words that appear in the story below. Once you feel you know the words and their meanings, use your thesaurus to come up with two synonyms for each of these challenging words.

---

words that mean the same thing

Definition: a chaotic situation

Synonyms: bedlam, chaos, disorder, mayhem

Pandemonium

Example: Pandemonium broke out during the Trump rally as supporters stormed the Capitol building.

where the polititions were.

---

to suggest something about someone

Definition: to provoke gradual doubt in someone or something

Synonyms: give an impression, hint, allude to

Insinuating

Example: He insinuated that the leader was corrupt.

Inscrutable

Definition: impossible to understand or interpret

Synonyms: enigmatic, unreadable, mysterious

Example: The ancient scroll was completely inscrutable.

Insolent

cheeky or disrespectful

Definition: showing a rude and arrogant lack of respect

Synonyms: saucy, cheeky, ill-mannered, disrespectful

Example: The teacher frowned at the insolent tone of her student's voice.

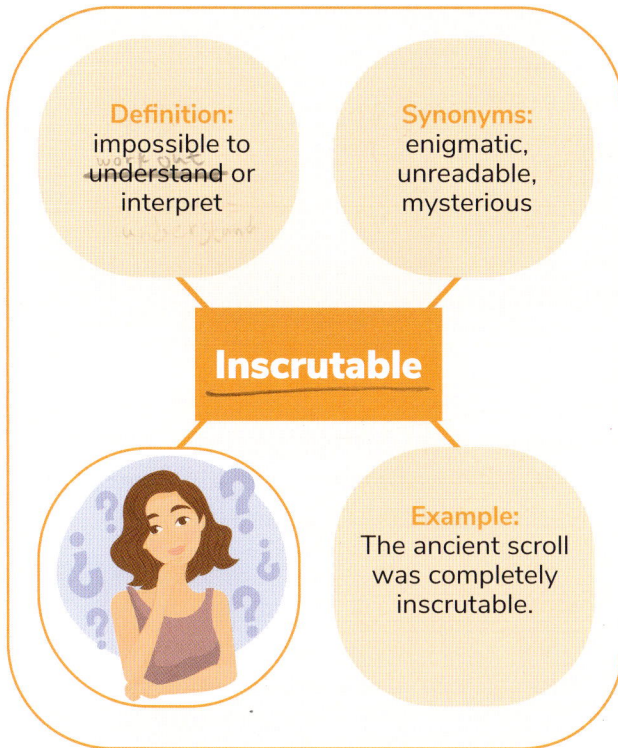

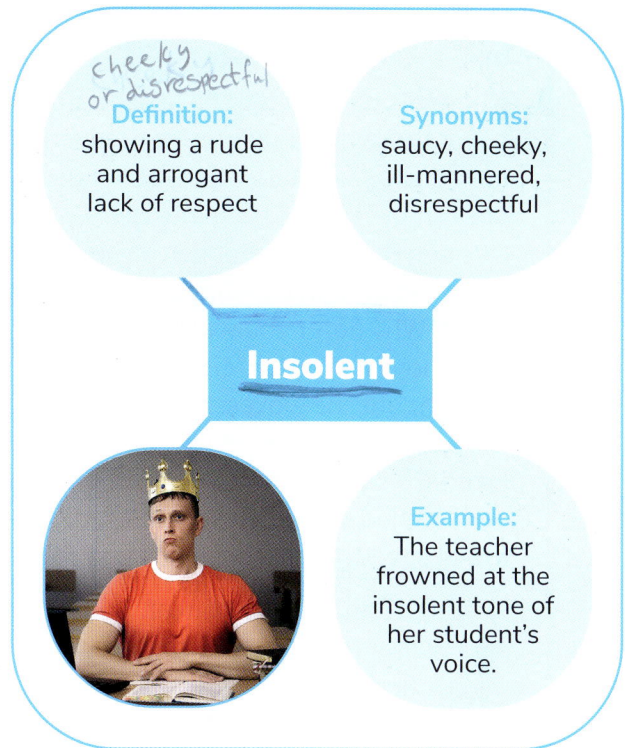

All about *The Secret Life of Walter Mitty*

This short story first appeared in *The New Yorker* in 1939 and is now one of the world's best-loved and famous short stories. This story has appeared in numerous short-story anthologies and was made into a stage play and film in 2013.

colection

'We're going through!' The Commander's voice was like thin ice breaking. He wore his full-dress uniform, with the heavily braided white cap pulled down rakishly over one cold gray eye. 'We can't make it, sir. It's spoiling for a hurricane, if you ask me.' 'I'm not asking you, Lieutenant Berg,' said the Commander. 'Throw on the power lights! Rev her up to 8,500! We're going through!' The pounding of the cylinders increased: ta-pocketa-pocketa-pocketa-*pocketa-pocketa*. The Commander stared at the ice forming on the pilot window. He walked over and twisted a row of complicated dials. 'Switch on No. 8 auxiliary!' he shouted. 'Switch on No. 8 auxiliary!' repeated Lieutenant Berg. 'Full strength in No. 3 turret!' shouted the Commander. 'Full strength in No. 3 turret!' The crew, bending to their various tasks in the huge, hurtling eight-engined Navy hydroplane, looked at each other and grinned. 'The Old Man'll get us through,' they said to one another. 'The Old Man ain't afraid of Hell!' ... 'Not so fast! You're driving too fast!' said Mrs Mitty. 'What are you driving so fast for?'

'Hmm?' said Walter Mitty. He looked at his wife, in the seat beside him, with shocked astonishment. She seemed grossly unfamiliar, like a strange woman who had yelled at him in a crowd. 'You were up to fifty-five,' she said. 'You know I don't like to go more than forty. You were up to fifty-five.' Walter Mitty drove on toward Waterbury in silence, the roaring of the SN202 through the worst storm in twenty years of Navy flying fading in the remote, intimate airways of his mind. 'You're tensed up again,' said Mrs Mitty. 'It's one of your days. I wish you'd let Dr Renshaw look you over.'

Walter Mitty stopped the car in front of the building where his wife went to have her hair done. 'Remember to get those overshoes while I'm having my hair done,' she said. 'I don't need overshoes,' said Mitty. She put her mirror back into her bag. 'We've been all through that,' she said, getting out of the car. 'You're not a young man any longer.' He raced the engine a little. 'Why don't you wear your gloves? Have you lost your gloves?' Walter Mitty reached in a pocket and brought out the gloves. He put them on, but after she had turned and gone into the building and he had driven on to a red light, he took them off again. 'Pick it up, brother!' snapped a cop as the light changed, and Mitty hastily pulled on his gloves and lurched ahead. He drove around the streets aimlessly for a time, and then he drove past the hospital on his way to the parking lot.

... 'It's the millionaire banker, Wellington McMillan,' said the pretty nurse. 'Yes?' said Walter Mitty, removing his gloves slowly. 'Who has the case?' 'Dr Renshaw and Dr Benbow, but there are two specialists here, Dr Remington from New York and Dr Pritchard-Mitford from London. He flew over.' A door opened down a long, cool corridor and Dr Renshaw came out. He looked distraught and haggard. 'Hello, Mitty,' he said. 'We're having the devil's own time with McMillan, the millionaire banker and close personal friend of Roosevelt. Obstreosis of the ductal tract. Tertiary. Wish you'd take a look at him.' 'Glad to,' said Mitty.

In the operating room there were whispered introductions: 'Dr Remington, Dr Mitty. Dr Pritchard-Mitford, Dr Mitty.' 'I've read your book on streptothricosis,' said Pritchard-Mitford, shaking hands. 'A brilliant performance, sir.' 'Thank you,' said Walter Mitty. 'Didn't know you were in the States, Mitty,' grumbled Remington. 'Coals to Newcastle, bringing Mitford and me up here for a tertiary.' 'You are very kind,' said Mitty. A huge, complicated machine, connected to the operating table, with many tubes and wires, began at this moment to go pocketa-pocketa-pocketa. 'The new anaesthetizer is giving way!' shouted an interne. 'There is no one in the East who knows how to fix it!' 'Quiet, man!' said Mitty, in a low, cool voice. He sprang to the machine, which was now going pocketa-pocketa-queep-pocketa-queep. He began fingering delicately a row of glistening dials. 'Give me a fountain pen!' he snapped. Someone handed him a fountain pen. He pulled a faulty piston out of the machine and inserted the pen in its place. 'That will hold for ten minutes,' he said. 'Get on with the operation.' A nurse hurried over and whispered to Renshaw, and Mitty saw the man turn pale. 'Coreopsis has set in,' said Renshaw nervously. 'If you would take over, Mitty?' Mitty looked at him and at the craven figure of Benbow, who drank, and at the grave, uncertain faces of the two great specialists. 'If you wish,' he said. They slipped a white gown on him; he adjusted a mask and drew on thin gloves; nurses handed him shining...

'Back it up, Mac! Look out for that Buick!' Walter Mitty jammed on the brakes. 'Wrong lane, Mac,' said the parking-lot attendant, looking at Mitty closely. 'Gee. Yeh,' muttered Mitty. He began cautiously to back out of the lane marked 'Exit Only.' 'Leave her sit there,' said the attendant. 'I'll put her away.' Mitty got out of the car. 'Hey, better leave the key.' 'Oh,' said Mitty, handing the man the ignition key. The attendant vaulted into the car, backed it up with insolent skill, and put it where it belonged.

They're so damn cocky, thought Walter Mitty, walking along Main Street; they think they know everything. Once he had tried to take his chains off, outside New Milford, and he had got them wound around the axles. A man had had to come out in a wrecking car and unwind them, a young, grinning garageman. Since then Mrs Mitty always made him drive to a garage to have the chains taken off. The next time, he thought, I'll wear my right arm in a sling; they won't grin at me then. I'll have my right arm in a sling and they'll see I couldn't possibly take the chains off myself. He kicked at the slush on the sidewalk. 'Overshoes,' he said to himself, and he began looking for a shoe store.

When he came out into the street again, with the overshoes in a box under his arm, Walter Mitty began to wonder what the other thing was his wife had told him to get. She had told him, twice, before they set out from their house for Waterbury. In a way he hated these weekly trips to town – he was always getting something wrong. Kleenex, he thought, Squibb's, razor blades? No. Toothpaste, toothbrush, bicarbonate, carborundum, initiative and referendum? He gave it up. But she would remember it. 'Where's the what's-its-name?' she would ask. 'Don't tell me you forgot the what's-its-name.' A newsboy went by shouting something about the Waterbury trial.

... 'Perhaps this will refresh your memory.' The District Attorney suddenly thrust a heavy automatic at the quiet figure on the witness stand. 'Have you ever seen this before?' Walter Mitty took the gun and examined it expertly. 'This is my Webley-Vickers 50.80,' he said calmly. An excited buzz ran around the courtroom. The Judge rapped for order. 'You are a crack shot with any sort of firearms, I believe?' said the District Attorney, insinuatingly. 'Objection!' shouted Mitty's attorney. 'We have shown that the defendant could not have fired the shot. We have shown that he wore his right arm in a sling on the night of the fourteenth of July.' Walter Mitty raised his hand briefly and the bickering attorneys were stilled. 'With any known make of gun,' he said evenly, 'I could have killed Gregory Fitzhurst at three hundred feet *with my left hand*.' Pandemonium broke loose in the courtroom. A woman's scream rose above the bedlam and suddenly a lovely, dark-haired girl was in Walter Mitty's arms. The District Attorney struck at her savagely. Without rising from his chair, Mitty let the man have it on the point of the chin. 'You miserable cur!' ...

'Puppy biscuit,' said Walter Mitty. He stopped walking and the buildings of Waterbury rose up out of the misty courtroom and surrounded him again. A woman who was passing laughed. 'He said "Puppy biscuit",' she said to her companion. 'That man said "Puppy biscuit" to himself.' Walter Mitty hurried on. He went into an A & P, not the first one he came to but a smaller one farther up the street. 'I want some biscuit for small, young dogs,' he said to the clerk. 'Any special brand, sir?' The greatest pistol shot in the world thought a moment. 'It says "Puppies Bark for It" on the box,' said Walter Mitty.

His wife would be through at the hairdresser's in fifteen minutes, Mitty saw in looking at his watch, unless they had trouble drying it; sometimes they had trouble drying it. She didn't like to get to the hotel first; she would want him to be there waiting for her as usual. He found a big leather chair in the lobby, facing a window, and he put the overshoes and the puppy biscuit on the floor beside it. He picked up an old copy of *Liberty* and sank down into the chair. 'Can Germany Conquer the World Through the Air?' Walter Mitty looked at the pictures of bombing planes and of ruined streets.

... 'The cannonading has got the wind up in young Raleigh, sir,' said the sergeant. Captain Mitty looked up at him through touselled hair. 'Get him to bed,' he said wearily. 'With the others. I'll fly alone.' 'But you can't, sir,' said the sergeant anxiously. 'It takes two men to handle that bomber and the Archies are pounding hell out of the air. Von Richtman's circus is between here and Saulier.' 'Somebody's got to get that ammunition dump,' said Mitty. 'I'm going over. Spot of brandy?' He poured a drink for the sergeant and one for himself. War thundered and whined around the dugout and battered at the door. There was a rending of wood and splinters flew through the room. 'A bit of a near thing,' said Captain Mitty carelessly. 'The box barrage is closing in,' said the sergeant. 'We only live once, Sergeant,' said Mitty, with his faint, fleeting smile. 'Or do we?' He poured another brandy and tossed it off. 'I never see a man could hold his brandy like you, sir,' said the sergeant. 'Begging your pardon, sir.' Captain Mitty stood up and strapped on his huge Webley-Vickers automatic. 'It's forty kilometres through hell, sir,' said the sergeant. Mitty finished one last brandy. 'After all,' he said softly, 'what isn't?' The pounding of the cannon increased; there was the rat-tat-tatting of machine guns, and from somewhere came the menacing pocketa-pocketa-pocketa of the new flame-throwers. Walter Mitty walked to the door of the dugout humming 'Auprès de Ma Blonde'. He turned and waved to the sergeant. 'Cheerio!' he said ...

Something struck his shoulder. 'I've been looking all over this hotel for you,' said Mrs Mitty. 'Why do you have to hide in this old chair? How did you expect me to find you?' 'Things close in,' said Walter Mitty vaguely. 'What?' Mrs Mitty said. 'Did you get the what's-its-name? The puppy biscuit? What's in that box?' 'Overshoes,' said Mitty. 'Couldn't you have put them on in the store?' 'I was thinking,' said Walter Mitty. 'Does it ever occur to you that I am sometimes thinking?' She looked at him. 'I'm going to take your temperature when I get you home,' she said.

They went out through the revolving doors that made a faintly derisive whistling sound when you pushed them. It was two blocks to the parking lot. At the drugstore on the corner she said, 'Wait here for me. I forgot something. I won't be a minute.' She was more than a minute. Walter Mitty lighted a cigarette. It began to rain, rain with sleet in it. He stood up against the wall of the drugstore, smoking ... He put his shoulders back and his heels together. 'To hell with the handkerchief,' said Walter Mitty scornfully. He took one last drag on his cigarette and snapped it away. Then, with that faint, fleeting smile playing about his lips, he faced the firing squad; erect and motionless, proud and disdainful, Walter Mitty the Undefeated, inscrutable to the last.

READING

1 Summarise the story by completing the following sentences:

Walter Mitty's real life is ....
....
....

Walter Mitty's imaginary life is ....
....
....
....

2 Examine the plot and settings of the story by completing the spark and pull task in your activity book (see page 16).

3 Complete the quote quest task in your activity book (see page 16).

4 What narrative perspective is the story written from? How do you know?

5 From the list of characteristics below, which would you apply to Walter Mitty, Walter Mitty's wife and the imaginary Walter Mitty? Fill in the table in your activity book (see page 17), then complete the sentences.

weak	carefree	controlling	forgetful	courageous
condescending	imaginative	powerful	nagging	unfulfilled
strong	domineering	ineffective	heroic	bossy

6 Compare the two versions of Walter Mitty using the comparison organiser in your activity book (see page 18).

7 Why do you think Walter Mitty creates such brave and strong versions of himself in his own imagination? Give a reason for your answer.

8 The two lists of adverbs below were used to describe the actions of Walter and the actions of all the imaginary Walters. Which list belongs to which? What do you think the author was trying to show the reader through his use of adverbs (see page 277 for more on adverbs)?

List A	List B
hastily	rakishly
aimlessly	delicately
cautiously	expertly
vaguely	carelessly
	softly

9 Choose one of the sentence starters below and write a short paragraph to answer the following question:

What, in your opinion, is the message of this short story?

The message of this story is that...		
imagination is a powerful tool	it is important to treat people with respect	you should live your life to the fullest in the real world

WRITING

Write four sentences, each one containing one of the new words you have learned from *The Secret Life of Walter Mitty*.

pandemonium	insinuating	inscrutable	insolent

PROJECT:
Write A Fractured Fairy Tale

What Is A Fractured Fairy Tale?

A fractured fairy tale is a story from the fairy-tale genre that has in some way been flipped, reimagined or restructured. You can create a fractured fairy tale by being creative with any of the elements of the fairy-tale genre.

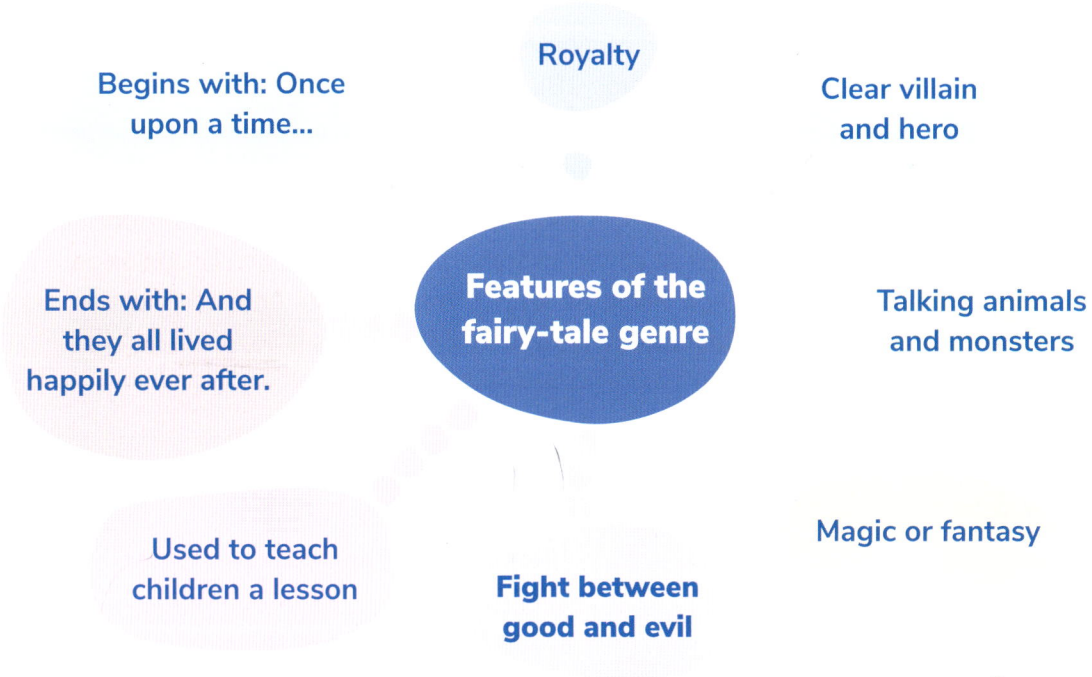

Royalty

Begins with: Once upon a time...

Clear villain and hero

Ends with: And they all lived happily ever after.

Features of the fairy-tale genre

Talking animals and monsters

Used to teach children a lesson

Fight between good and evil

Magic or fantasy

To fracture a fairy tale, you could do one of the following:

Action	Example
Change the character traits of the characters	The woodsman is not brave and runs away from the big bad wolf
Have well-known fairy-tale characters meet	Shrek
Change the narrative perspective	Describe the three little pigs from the wolf's perspective
Change the problem in the story	The wolf in Little Red Riding Hood is lonely and just wants to make some friends
Change the resolution in the story	Prince Charming ends up marrying one of the ugly sisters
Write a different ending	The frog princess actually hates being a princess and wants to be a frog again

Read this famous fractured fairy tale based on the story of *The Three Little Pigs*.

The True Story of the Three Little Pigs by John Scieszka

Everybody knows the story of the Three Little Pigs. Or at least they think they do. But I'll let you in on a little secret. Nobody knows the real story, because nobody has ever heard my side of the story.

I'm the wolf. Alexander T. Wolf. You can call me Al. I don't know how this whole Big Bad Wolf thing got started, but it's all wrong.

Maybe it's because of our diet. Hey, it's not my fault if wolves eat cute little animals like bunnies and sheep and pigs. That's just the way we are. If cheeseburgers were cute, folks would probably think you were Big and Bad, too.

But like I was saying, the whole Big Bad Wolf thing is all wrong. The real story is about a sneeze and a cup of sugar.

Way back in Once Upon a Time, I was making a birthday cake for my dear old granny. I had a terrible sneezing cold. I ran out of sugar.

So I walked down the street to ask my neighbor for a cup of sugar. Now this neighbor was a pig. And he wasn't too bright, either.

He had built his whole house out of straw. Can you believe it? I mean who in his right mind would build a house of straw?

So of course the minute I knocked on the door, it fell right in. I didn't want to just walk into someone else's house.

So I called, 'Little Pig, Little Pig, are you in?' No answer.

I was just about to go home without the cup of sugar for my dear old granny's birthday cake. That's when my nose started to itch. I felt a sneeze coming on. Well I huffed. And I snuffed.

And I sneezed a great sneeze.

And you know what? That whole darn straw house fell down. And right in the middle of the pile of straw was the First Little Pig – dead as a doornail. He had been home the whole time.

It seemed a shame to leave a perfectly good ham dinner lying there in the straw. So I ate it up. Think of it as a big cheeseburger just lying there.

I was feeling a little better. But I still didn't have my cup of sugar. So I went to the next neighbor's house. This neighbor was the First Little Pig's brother. He was a little smarter, but not much. He had built his house of sticks.

I rang the bell on the stick house. Nobody answered. I called, 'Mr Pig, Mr Pig, are you in?' He yelled back, 'Go away wolf. You can't come in. I'm shaving the hairs on my chinny chin chin.'

I had just grabbed the doorknob when I felt another sneeze coming on. I huffed. And I snuffed. And I tried to cover my mouth, but I sneezed a great sneeze.

And you're not going to believe it, but this guy's house fell down just like his brother's. When the dust cleared, there was the Second Little Pig – dead as a doornail. Wolf's honor.

Now you know how food will spoil if you just leave it out in the open. So I did the only thing there was to do. I had dinner again. Think of it as a second helping. I was getting awfully full. But my cold was feeling a little better. And I still didn't have that cup of sugar for my dear old granny's birthday cake.

So I went to the next house. This guy was the First and Second Little Pigs' brother. He must have been the brains of the family. He had built his house of bricks.

I knocked on the brick house. No answer. I called, 'Mr Pig, Mr Pig, are you in?' And do you know what that rude little porker answered? 'Get out of here, Wolf. Don't bother me again.'

Talk about impolite! He probably had a whole sack full of sugar. And he wouldn't give me even one little cup for my dear sweet old granny's birthday cake. What a pig! I was just about to go home and maybe make a nice birthday card instead of a cake, when I felt my cold coming on. I huffed. And I snuffed. And I sneezed once again. Then the Third Little Pig yelled, 'And your old granny can sit on a pin!'

Now I'm usually a pretty calm fellow. But when somebody talks about my granny like that, I go a little crazy. When the cops drove up, of course I was trying to break down this Pig's door. And the whole time I was huffing and puffing and sneezing and making a real scene.

The rest, as they say, is history. The news reporters found out about the two pigs I had for dinner. They figured a sick guy going to borrow a cup of sugar didn't sound very exciting. So they jazzed up the story with all that 'Huff and puff and blow your house down'. And they made me the Big Bad Wolf. That's it. The real story. I was framed. But maybe you could loan me a cup of sugar.

READING

1 What element of the fairy-tale genre is being played with here?

2 Do you think the wolf is a reliable narrator? Why? Why not?

3 What makes this an entertaining version of the story?

COMMUNICATING: GROUP DISCUSSION

Watch this advertisement for the *Guardian* newspaper, which flips the fairy tale on its head:

edco.ie/d75d

1 What element of the fairy-tale genre is being flipped here?

2 Which retelling of the three little pigs did you prefer? Give a reason why?

3 Do you think this was a good idea for an advertisement for a newspaper? Give a reason for your answer.

PROJECT BRIEF

Write an entertaining fractured fairy tale for a young adult fiction audience.

To be successful in this piece of writing, you will need to:

- experiment creatively with the fairy-tale genre
- maintain a clear and convincing narrative perspective
- choose interesting words and sentence types to make your writing entertaining
- describe an engaging setting and craft interesting characters
- use dialogue creatively and make sure it's punctuated correctly.

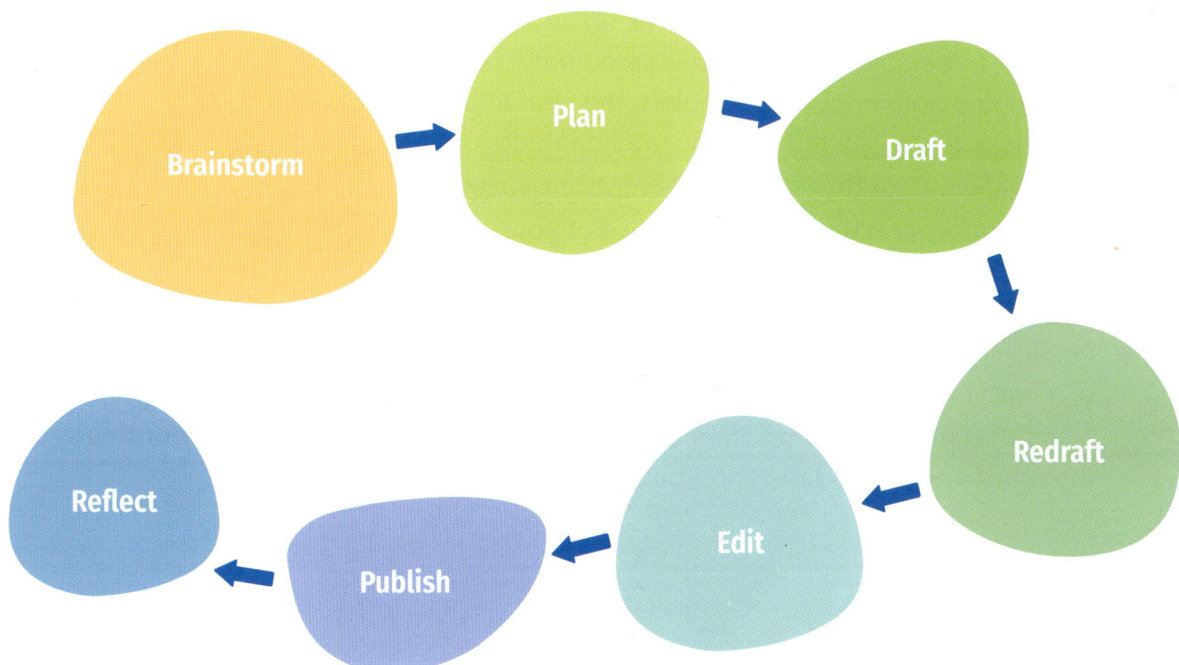

Brainstorm → Plan → Draft → Redraft → Edit → Publish → Reflect

Brainstorm

1 In your activity book (see page 18), list all of the fairy tales that you know well. List the main characters in these stories and what you think is the most interesting thing about the plot or the characters. Who is the villain? Who is the hero? Who is an interesting side character you think deserves more investigation?

2 Look through your list and think about what or who stands out as a possible interesting story.

3 Pitch your story idea in one sentence. For example: The big bad wolf actually just has really bad allergies.

Plan It

1 **Plot:** Using the plot graphic organiser in your activity book (see page 19), plan out the plot of your story. Do not overcomplicate your story and remember that it must in some way resemble the original fairy tale.

2 **Setting:** Think about the purpose of your setting. This will affect how you write about your setting.

- Do you want the setting to be similar to the original story?
- Do you want to remain faithful to the original setting apart from one or two unsettling details?
- Do you want to move the setting of the fairy tale to explore how your characters would fare in a different world? For example: How would the woodsman cope living in an apartment in New York?
- Do you want to make your setting peaceful, dangerous, sinister, unnerving?

Draw a sketch of your story and label the setting of your story in your activity book (see page 19). Look at the crafting a setting toolkit on page 12 and think about how you will show your reader the things you want them to know about the setting.

3 **Characters:** Now it's time to think about the characters for your story.

- Choose one main character to focus on and one or two minor characters. In order to be able to write about your character, you must get to know your main character very well. Complete the character creation task in your activity book (see page 20) and imagine your character as a real living person.
- Next, think about the three main points you want to get across to your reader about your character and the purpose of your character. Is your character spoilt, sneaky and rude? Is your character the hero or the villain? Is your character evil or good underneath it all?
- Finally, look at the crafting a character toolkit on page 17 and think about how you will show your reader these things about your character. For example, you could describe the clothes they are wearing in detail, where they bought them, the fabric texture and the condition of them.

Draft It

Using your planning materials, write the first draft of your story. Just get the bones of the story down and don't worry about making it perfect at this point. A first draft is where you let your ideas flow and you put into words all of the work you have done in your brainstorming and planning.

Redraft It

Redrafting is one of the most important stages of the writing process. This is the stage where you spot mistakes, plot holes and places where you could improve.

You could first read through your piece focusing on how the piece of writing seems at word level. Here you could look for words you've overused, words that seem boring, words that don't fit with the genre you are writing in.

Then you could look through your piece focusing on the sentence level. Here you could look at the types of sentences you have used or perhaps overused. Below is some advice for you to follow to make the redrafting process easier and more effective.

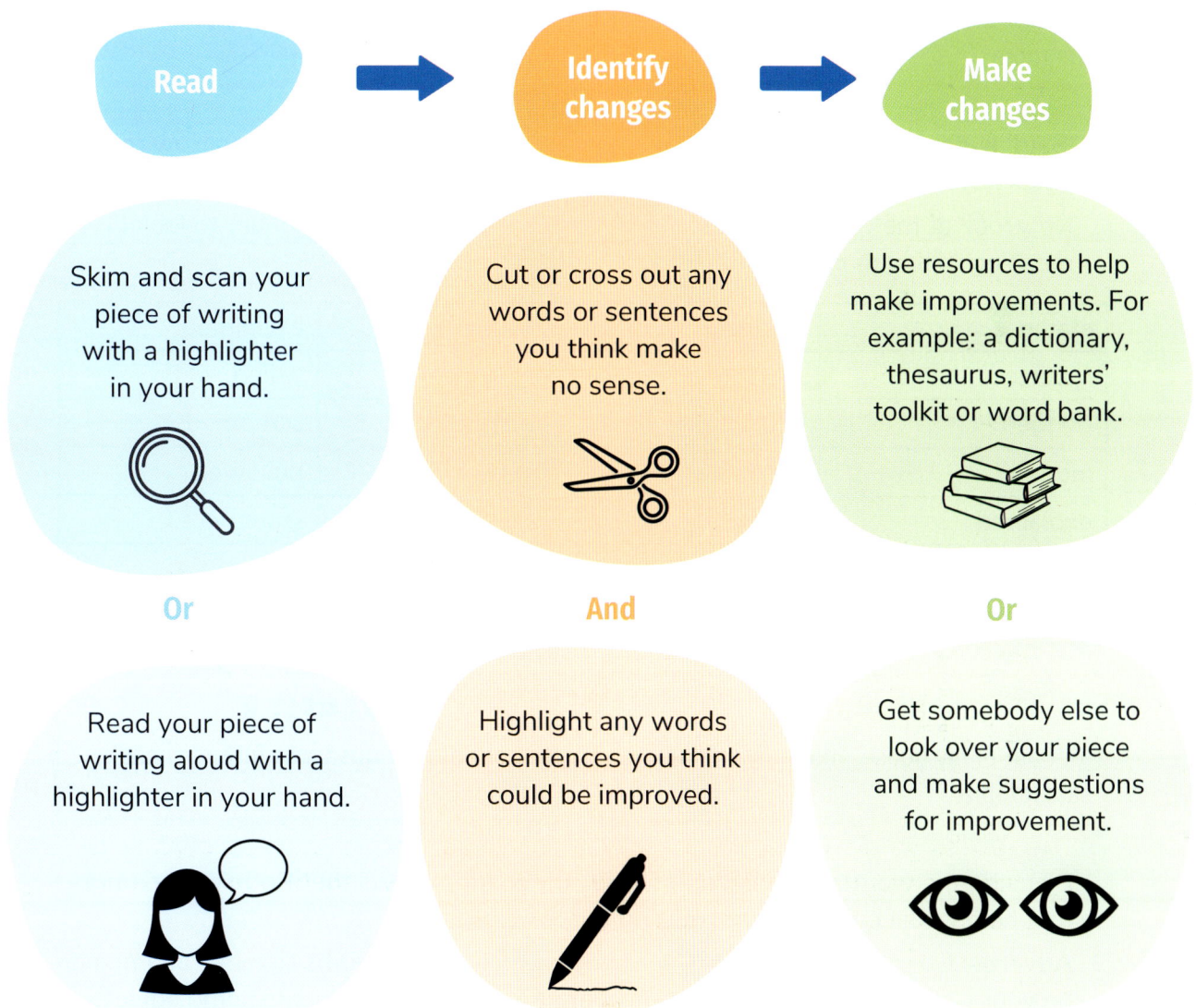

Read → **Identify changes** → **Make changes**

Skim and scan your piece of writing with a highlighter in your hand.

Cut or cross out any words or sentences you think make no sense.

Use resources to help make improvements. For example: a dictionary, thesaurus, writers' toolkit or word bank.

Or

And

Or

Read your piece of writing aloud with a highlighter in your hand.

Highlight any words or sentences you think could be improved.

Get somebody else to look over your piece and make suggestions for improvement.

Redrafting at word level

The first way you can look at your piece of writing is at word level. Below are a number of resources you could use to improve the words you have used in your piece of writing.

1 **Fairy-tale word bank:** The word bank below is full of exciting vocabulary that you may want to use in your story. Use a dictionary to look up the meaning of any words you don't know.

malevolent	potion	diabolical	thwarted
villain	sorcery	chivalrous	wrathful
tragedy	concoction	gallant	gnarled
cantankerous	vindictive	prophesy	mesmerising
nimble	devious	serene	benevolent

Are there any words you have used in your draft that you could upgrade with one from the word bank? Look at the example below.

EXAMPLE A

The thin man was an evil presence in the room.

EXAMPLE B

The thin man was a malevolent presence in the room.

2 **'Said' is dead:** Look through any dialogue you have used in your story. How many times have you used the word 'said'? Highlight each time you've used 'said'.

Now look at the word bank below full of alternatives. Use a dictionary to look up the meaning of any of the words you don't understand.

stated	laughed	whispered	exclaimed
reported	marvelled	muttered	yelled
begged	demanded	pondered	screamed
inquired	cried	dictated	bellowed
explained	insisted	commanded	stammered

Can you substitute 'said' with another word that will add more to the story? Look at the example below.

EXAMPLE A

'Get out of my house, you filthy animal!' said Robbie.

EXAMPLE B

'Get out of my house, you filthy animal!' spat Robbie.

By using the word 'spat' instead of 'said', the reader knows that Robbie is so angry that he has lost control and is spitting out his words.

3 **Adverbs:** Go to page 277 and look at how you can use adverbs to make an impact on your writing. Is there anywhere in your story that you could add some adverbs to make your writing more interesting?

Redrafting at sentence level

▶ Video

To make a piece of writing really engaging, you need to vary the length and type of sentences you use.

There are multiple different types of sentences that you use when you are writing. You may have come across the following in primary school: simple, compound and complex sentences. Using a variety of sentence types will make your writing more interesting to read (see page 40).

Look at the two pieces of writing below and think about which one is more interesting.

EXAMPLE A

The whole family drove down to the beach together. Everyone got out of the car and walked to the edge of the sea. They threw the ashes into the sea. The whole family walked back to the car and drove back home.

EXAMPLE B

They went together.

Devastated, they drove the long and winding road to the deserted beach. It was a cold, windy, slow walk to the water's edge.

Joey tipped over the urn: hands shaking, tears flowing, body aching.

They returned home, together.

Example A is repetitive, as all of the sentences are the same type and length. Every sentence just lets the reader know the bare bones of the plot.

Example B is more interesting because there is a great variety in sentence type and length. The reader is intrigued, because the plot and the characters' emotions and reactions to the plot are interwoven.

SUPER SENTENCE TOOLKIT

Below are five ways of constructing sentences that you could use to vary your writing and to make it more interesting for your reader.

Sentence type	Rules	Example 1	Example 2
Short and dramatic	Three to four words max	He never came back.	She was gone.
Emotion and action	Start with an emotion, finish with the action	Devastated, he carried on walking.	Overjoyed, she skipped down the stairs.
Tell – use three	Tell the emotion and three ways of physically showing that emotion	She was terrified: hands shaking, lips trembling, brow sweating.	Harry was furious: fists clenched, teeth gritted, cheeks burning.
A two-action sentence	Start with an action word, finish with an action	Lifting his head, the dog sniffed the air.	Circling the house, the man sang to himself.
List	Three to four adjectives followed by the noun	It was a long, dark, leafy lane.	She had a cold, cruel, heartless cackle.

Now look through your own piece of writing. Highlight any sections where you think you've repeated the same types of sentence over and over again. Upgrade some of your sentences using the toolkit.

> You should now redraft your piece of writing to include all of the changes you have made.

Edit It

At the editing stage, you will not be doing a whole rewrite. This is the point in the writing process when you are making sure there are no spelling or punctuation mistakes. It is too difficult to look for every single possible mistake at once. A focused skim and scan, therefore, with pen in hand, looking through your piece of writing for one thing at a time, is a much better way to approach editing.

Capital letters and end punctuation

One of the most important things to get right when editing a piece of work is to get the start and end of each sentence correct. This has a big effect on your reader, as they will know when one sentence ends and another begins.

Look at the rules of capital letters and full stops on page 272. Skim and scan each sentence you have written and make changes if necessary.

Punctuating dialogue

In a narrative story, a writer may use a lot of dialogue. Look at the rules for writing dialogue and the examples on page 275. Skim and scan your piece of writing and make any punctuation edits that you need to.

> Your piece of writing is now ready for publication in whatever way your teacher has decided.

REFLECTION

1 Why do you think fairy tales have stood the test of time? What makes them appealing to generation after generation?

2 Do you enjoy writing fiction? Why? Why not?

3 Which stage of the writing process did you find easiest and why?

4 Which stage of the writing process did you find hardest and why? What could you do to make it easier next time round?

5 What insight have you gained into what it must be like to write a 200-page novel from this writing experience?

PROJECT:
Create A Podcast

What Is A Podcast?

A podcast is like a radio show, but it is not usually recorded live. Podcasts are recorded, then put up online so that listeners can listen to them at a time of their own choosing. They are usually based on a topic, theme or story and contain a variety of the following features and characteristics:

- a host (or hosts)
- interviews with experts, special guests, celebrities, commentators, sports people, etc.
- advertisements
- conversations between host and guest or a panel of guests or between hosts
- discussion of details of investigations or sports events
- music snippets, intro music and exit music
- audience questions (if live podcast)
- vox pops – snippets of interviews from people stopped on the street to give an opinion.

COMMUNICATING

Choose one of the following three podcasts to listen to:

1 *Who Would Win?* A podcast that debates who would win in a fight between a host of characters from comics, films and books. Episodes feature discussions such as who would win in Batman vs. Yoda, Mad Max vs. Rick Grimes and Captain America vs. Darth Vader. Each week there is a different set of combatants and a new guest judge. edco.ie/kefm

2 *Stuff You Should Know.* A podcast that discusses events or people you should know in an entertaining fashion. Topics range from Rosa Parks and 'Mary Had a Little Lamb' to true crime. edco.ie/h4kn

3 *Radiolab.* A podcast that investigates the most unusual and jaw-dropping stories from all around the world. Topics range from mysterious meat allergies to a ceremony to launch a new cryptocurrency. edco.ie/x7b2

Choose one episode that appeals to you and listen for a minimum of ten minutes. Then answer the questions below.

1 List the features of a podcast that appear in the podcast.
2 What is entertaining about the podcast?
3 What is appealing about the podcast?
4 Would you be interested in listening to more of that podcast. Why? Why not?

PROJECT BRIEF

Create an entertaining podcast for a teenage audience about a text you have studied in English class.

To be successful in your project, your podcast should:

- be informative, educational and entertaining, and appeal to your teenage audience
- explore interesting and relevant details about your chosen text
- experiment imaginatively with the features and characteristics of a podcast.

Plan It

Your podcast script should be three to four minutes long in total and its purpose is to explore the text you are studying.

1 First you need to decide on the host of your show. Will you have one or two hosts? Who will your host be? Could it be someone from the text? Could it be someone related to the text in some way?

2 Below is a list of possible ideas for your podcast that you may like to include.

an **advertisement** from a sponsor that relates to one of the themes or symbols from the text

a catchy and memorable **name** for your podcast, linked to your text

intro music to start your podcast and exit music to end your podcast that is linked to the text

a **song snippet** that is thematically relevant to the text

an **interview** with a character about a specific event in the text

an **interview** with a character about another character in the text

a **conversation** between two characters in the text

an **interview** with a character about a central theme from the text

an **interview** with the text's author about a central theme from the text, or their inspiration for the text, or their reasons for their choice of narrative perspective/narrative voice

a **news story** about a related real world historical event relevant to the text or an event from the world of the text

a **poem or rap** about a central theme or major event in the text

a **vox pop** from the world of the text after a particular event in the text or about an issue in the text

3 Think about how you are going to structure your podcast. Your podcast should have an introduction at the beginning and a sign off at the end. You should try to include at least three segments from the suggested list of ideas on page 43. You should link one segment to another, possibly through music or an advertisement.

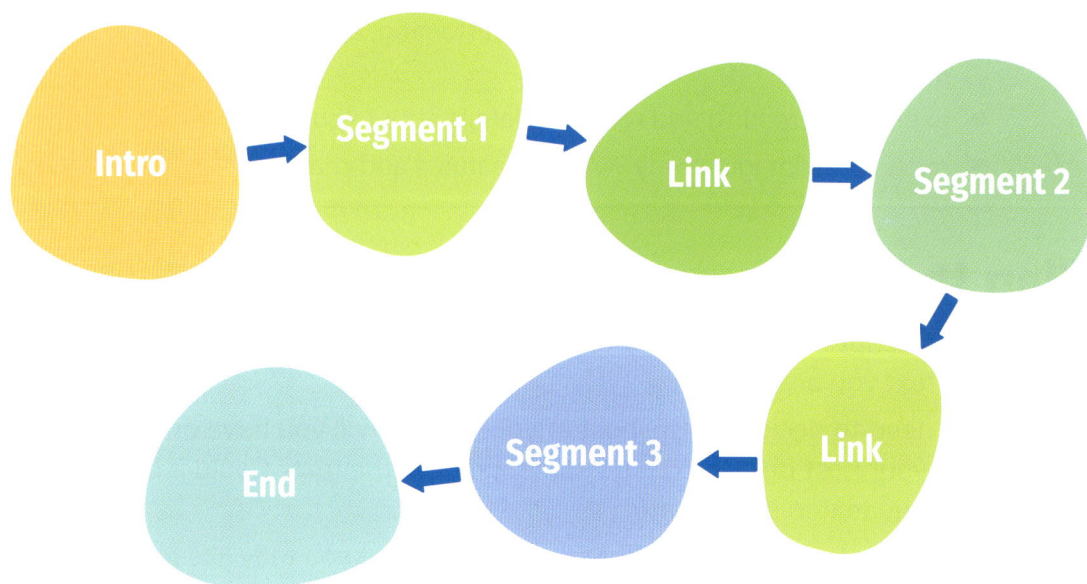

Intro → Segment 1 → Link → Segment 2 → Link → Segment 3 → End

Script It

Using your planning to guide you, get your ideas down on paper. Remember to structure the podcast into sections and that the script should be laid out as in the example below, with the speaker identified on the left and what they are going to say on the right. Any music or sound effects should be written in italics or a different pen colour.

Intro music

Host: In today's podcast, we will get to the bottom of the mystery that we have been obsessing about.

Host 2: Yes, today is an episode you won't want to miss...

Redraft It

Look back at the success criteria in the project brief box on page 43. Is there anything you have left out? Is there anything you need to work on some more?

Look through your script and check if there are any opportunities to show off your knowledge of the text. Could you use some of the place names from the text? Could you advertise any of the businesses in the text?

Remember the purpose of the podcast is to inform teenagers about the text in an entertaining way.

Record It

- Have your script in front of you before you start.
- You can choose to try to record the script in one sitting or record it section by section, then edit it with an editing app afterwards.
- Depending on your devices, explore some of the free software for recording and editing podcasts: Audacity, GarageBand, Soundtrap and Zoom.
- You could record your podcast using your smartphone, or you might prefer to set up a microphone, which is sometimes easier if you are conducting an interview.
- Find a quiet place, ideally a small room for the best sound quality.
- Don't worry if you mess it up; just delete the recording and start again.

REFLECTION

1 What did you like about the podcast?

2 What about the podcast appealed to a teenage audience?

3 What do you think people learned about your text from listening to your podcast?

4 How would you improve this podcast if you were to start from the beginning again?

Test Your Knowledge

1 **What is first-person narrative perspective?**

   a) When the story is being told by one character in that character's voice and uses the words 'I' and 'we'

   b) When an external narrator is telling the story from one character's point of view and the narrator knows all the thoughts and feelings of this one character, but doesn't know the thoughts and feelings of anyone else

   c) The all-seeing, all-powerful narrator

   d) How believable or reliable you find a narrator

2 **What is the setting of a story?**

   a) The positive things that happen in the story

   b) The people that appear in it

   c) The person telling the story

   d) The specific place, timeframe and world the story takes place in

3 **In a story the plot is…:**

   a) The events of the story

   b) A graph

   c) The highlight of a story

   d) The ending of a story

4 **What is a reliable narrator?**

   a) A narrator that uses the first-person perspective

   b) A narrator that you believe is being truthful about everything in the story

   c) A narrator that knows everything

   d) A narrator that manipulates readers into thinking well of some characters and badly of other characters

5 **An .... narrator has access to the thoughts, feelings and actions of all of the characters in the story.**

6 **A third-person .... narrative perspective is one where the narrator has full access to the thoughts and feelings of one character, but no one else.**

7 **Match the narrative perspectives with their correct definitions.**

Narrative perspective	Definition
First-person narrative perspective	When a narrator has access to the thoughts and feelings of all the characters in the story
Third-person limited perspective	When an external narrator is telling the story from one character's point of view
Omniscient narrative perspective	When the story is being told by one character in that character's voice

8 Match the plot parts with their correct definitions.

Plot part	Definition
Rising action	Where everyone lives happily ever after
Opening	The tension rises and the problems multiply
Climax	Where the scene is set and characters are introduced
Falling action	A difficult situation is introduced to set the story in motion
Problem	The point of maximum drama and action
Resolution	The action slows down

9 How would you pick out an unreliable narrator?

10 What advice would you give a writer trying to create an interesting setting?

11 What advice would you give a writer trying to create an interesting character?

12 Give an example of an interesting setting and interesting character from a story you have read.

13 Thinking back on all you have learned in this unit, try the personal dictionary task on pages 22–23 of your activity book.

Practise Your Writing Skills

1 Use one of these story starters to write the opening paragraph to a fictional story.

- I had never seen a dragon before that day in the forest. It was not at all what I expected...
- Astra had never planned on being on another planet. Luckily, she had a...
- His cold hand opened the door. I knew what he had come here for...
- Heir to the throne. Now that is something I never thought I would say...
- Hurtling towards earth, he has a sneaking suspicion that he might die this time. But...

2 Use one of these prompts to write a paragraph, introducing and describing a character.

- An alien trying to pass as a human
- A former Disney child star who still thinks they are famous
- An old wizard who just wants to retire
- An enthusiastic cowboy desperate to be a hero
- An intimidating king who rules with an iron fist

Interactive website

Go to **www.edco.ie/touchstones1** for interactive activities based on this unit.

UNIT 2
POETRY

POETRY KNOWLEDGE ORGANISER

Things I need to know

- **Structure:** how a poem is built. Poems are constructed by assembling syllables, words, line and stanzas.

- **Speaker:** the voice of the poem.

- **Rhyme:** rhyming words sound the same. A rhyme scheme is the pattern of rhyme in a poem.

- **Rhythm:** the beat or pace of the poem. The rhythm can be found by looking at the stressed and unstressed syllables in the words.

- **Subject:** the topic, person or place that the poem is about.

- **Theme:** the underlying message or idea of the poem – what it's really about.

- **Tone:** the attitude and feelings of the poet expressed through their poem.

- **Mood:** how the reader feels after reading the poem.

- **Simile:** a language technique where the poet compares two things using 'like' or 'as'.

- **Metaphor:** a language technique where the poet compares two different things and, as a result, reveals their similarities.

- **Personification:** a language technique where non-human things are given human characteristics.

- **Alliteration:** repeating the same letter or sound at the beginning of closely connected words.

- **Assonance:** repeating similar vowel sounds in a series of words or phrases.

- **Onomatopoeia:** when a word sounds like what it describes.

- **Annotation:** when a reader makes notes on a text by flagging or highlighting important details.

- **Quotation:** a phrase or line taken directly from the text.

- **Inference:** finding exact clues in the text and using your own background knowledge to come up with an idea not stated obviously in the text.

Skills I will develop

- Learning to interpret and respond to poetry
- Reading poems to understand and appreciate language choices
- Using reading strategies to understand and appreciate poetry
- Writing in a variety of text types for different purposes
- Engaging in class group discussions actively

Projects

- Perform A Rap: Creating a unique group choral reading of a rap
- The Poet's Toolbox: Researching, planning and creating a poetic techniques booklet
- Spoken Word Poetry: Experiencing, appreciating and creating spoken word poetry

What do I know?

What do you already know about poetry? Do you know any poems? Do you know any poets? Do you have a favourite poem?

Go to your activity book (see page 24) and complete the poetry knowledge download activity.

What Is Poetry?

PowerPoint

Poetry has existed and been part of human life since before history started to be written down and recorded. Poets were employed by rulers to create and perform poems so that laws, battles, family histories and legends would be remembered. Poetry was passed from generation to generation by word of mouth. Nowadays, poetry exists in many different forms: written, spoken word, performance and slam poetry, and even film poems.

> Poetry is when an emotion has found its thought and the thought has found words.
> **Robert Frost**

> Poetry: the best words in the best order.
> **Samuel Taylor Coleridge**

> It's an empty basket; you put your life into it and make something out of that.
> **Mary Oliver**

> Poetry is a deal of joy and pain and wonder, with a dash of the dictionary.
> **Khalil Gibran, Sand and Foam**

Poetry means different things to different people. Which of these definitions of poetry by four famous poets do you like best? Which quotes do you agree with? Are there any you disagree with?

READING TASK

Read the four extracts below. The titles and authors have been removed.

1	2
I leant upon a coppice gate When Frost was spectre-grey, And Winter's dregs made desolate The weakening eye of day.	Float like a butterfly, sting like a bee. The hands can't hit what the eyes can't see.
3 Introducing the new Apple iPerson complete with multitouch doesn't it feel good to touch? doesn't it feel good to touch? compatible with your iPod and iPad doesn't it feel good to touch? doesn't it feel good to touch?	**4** In black kitchens they foul the food, walk on our bodies as we sleep over oceans of pirate flags. Skull and crossbones, they crunch like candy. When we die they will eat us, unless we kill them first. Invest in better mousetraps. Take no prisoners on board ship, to rock the boat, to violate our beds with pestilence.

COMMUNICATING: GROUP DISCUSSION

Looking at the extracts opposite, discuss the questions below.

1 Which texts do you consider to be a poem? Why?

2 Which texts do you not consider to be a poem? Why?

3 Is there anything all four texts have in common?

4 Is there anything about any of them that stands out to you as being unusual?

5 Has looking at these four texts changed your own view of what a poem is?

It may surprise you that all four of the texts opposite are poetry texts. Poetry comes in many different shapes and sizes.

Text 1 is a more traditional poem, called 'The Darkling Thrush' by Thomas Hardy.

Text 2 is a poetic phrase that the greatest boxer of all time, Muhammad Ali, used to describe his fighting style.

Text 3 is a transcribed slam poem called Touchscreen by Marshall 'Soulful' Jones.

Text 4 is a prose poem called '[Kills Bugs Dead.]' by Harryette Mullen.

WRITING

A group of friendly aliens have just arrived on our planet. You are in charge of explaining life on earth to them. One of your tasks is to explain poetry to them. Write a short paragraph explaining poetry for your alien audience.

Writing Tips

- You should use clear informative language for your explanation – keep it simple.
- You should write about why people like poetry or what poetry has been used for throughout human history.
- You could give them an example of a line or two of poetry that you know yourself.

Building A Poem: Structure

Poems are created by assembling **syllables**, words, lines and **stanzas**. You already know what words and lines are. A **syllable** is a part of a word. You may be familiar with the term 'verse' from primary school. In secondary school, a verse is called a **stanza**. It is like a paragraph in poetry.

Poets sometimes use a specific structure to build their poems, such as a haiku, a sonnet or a limerick. Some poets choose to use no structure and some poets use a combination of structure and no structure.

Each choice a poet makes about the design and shape of their poems can create a specific effect. For example, a poet may choose to build a poem in the shape of a leaf, to highlight the beauty of nature, or a poet may choose not to structure a poem at all, to get across a message about freedom.

Syllables + **Words** + **Lines** + **Stanzas** = **Poem**

READING

Below are three poems, each built with a different structure. Read the poems, then answer the questions below.

Limerick	Haiku	Free verse
'There was a small dog from Dubai' – author unknown	'The Old Pond' by Matsuo Bashō	'Risk' by Anonymous
There was a small dog from Dubai Who wanted to know how to fly, He ran round his yard, And barked very hard, And floated right up to the sky.	An old silent pond, A frog jumps into the pond, splash! Silence again.	And then the day came, when the risk to remain tight in a bud was more painful than the risk it took to blossom.

1   Which of the poems, do you think, has a set of rules for structure?

2   Choose one of the poems and figure out what the structure rules are. Look at how many lines there are and how many syllables are in each line.

3   Which of these poems does not have a set of rules for structure?

4   Choose one of the three poems and suggest why you think the poet made the choice to structure the poem in that way.

5   Which poem do you prefer and why?

Building A Poem: The Speaker

The speaker of a poem is, in simple terms, the voice of the poem. A poem can be written from a specific perspective, in the same way as a story or novel. A poet can choose to write from a male or female perspective, an old or young person's perspective, a rich or poor person's perspective.

A poet can choose to write from a first-person, second-person or third-person perspective. First-person perspective is when the poem is written from the perspective of the poet themselves. As in fiction (see page 6), this is usually easy to spot as the poet uses the words 'I' and 'we'. Second-person perspective is when the poem's reader is being addressed and the poet uses the words 'you' or 'your'. Third-person perspective is when the poem is written by an all-seeing observer, and the words 'he', 'she' or 'they' are used.

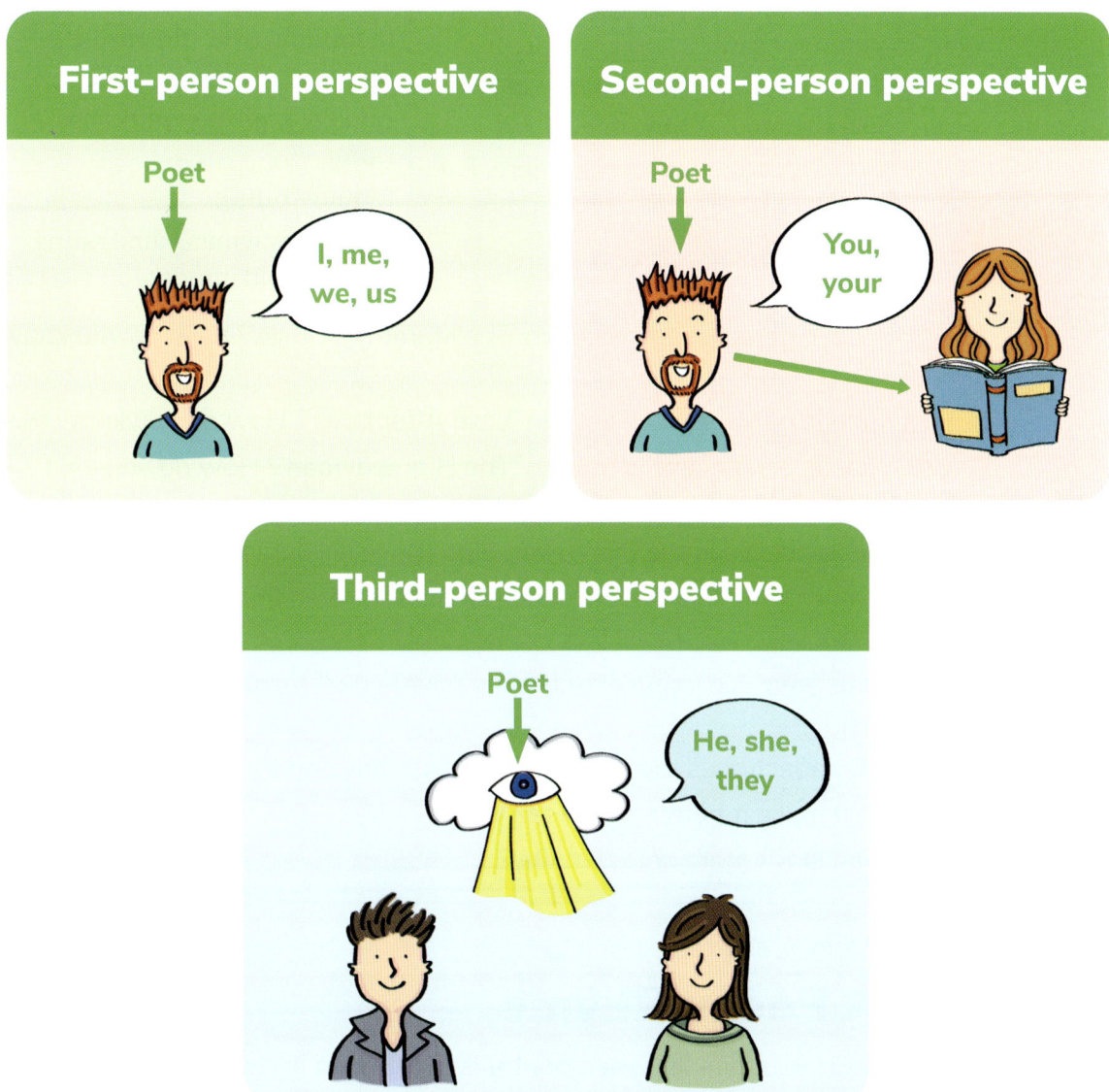

First-person perspective

Poet

I, me, we, us

Second-person perspective

Poet

You, your

Third-person perspective

Poet

He, she, they

The choices a poet makes regarding a poem's perspective have an impact on how the reader will perceive the poem. For example, a poet may elect to write a poem from a first-person perspective to demonstrate a closeness or understanding of an issue or event. A poet may choose to write from a second-person perspective to show the reader something or may opt to write from a third-person perspective to distance themselves from the message of the poem.

READING

Read these three poems, which are all examples of different poetic perspectives, then complete the tasks below.

From 'The Mummy's Smile' by Shelby K. Irons	From 'Love After Love' by Derek Walcott	From 'The Highwayman' by Alfred Noyes
I still remember the sun on my bones. I ate pomegranates and barley cakes. I wore a necklace of purple stones. And sometimes I saw a crocodile Slither silently into the Nile.	The time will come when, with elation you will greet yourself arriving at your own door, in your own mirror and each will smile at the other's welcome, and say, sit here. Eat.	The wind was a torrent of darkness among the gusty trees. The moon was a ghostly galleon tossed upon cloudy seas. The road was a ribbon of moonlight over the purple moor, And the highwayman came riding— Riding—riding— The highwayman came riding, up to the old inn-door.

1 What poetic perspective is used in 'The Mummy's Smile'? How do you know this?

2 What poetic perspective is used in 'Love After Love'? How do you know this?

3 What poetic perspective is used in 'The Highwayman'? How do you know this?

4 Which perspective in the three examples above is your favourite and why?

5 Choose one of the three poems and rewrite the verse from a totally different perspective.

6 Read your rewritten poem aloud to the person next to you, and discuss the following:

- What impact does the change in speaker have on the poem?
- Does it make it better or worse? Why?
- Do you like it more or less? Why?

Building A Poem: Rhyme

One of the first things you think of when poetry is mentioned is rhyme. As a child, you may well have grown up listening to nursery rhymes and might still know some off by heart. There are many ways that a poet can experiment with rhyme. A poet can rhyme words at the end of lines or choose to rhyme words internally within the line. Some poems have a specific rhyme scheme, which is like the plan of a poem. It has fixed places where the poem should rhyme and this pattern is repeated throughout.

Although rhyme is an important part of poetry, a poem does not have to rhyme to be considered a poem. These types of poems are called free verse.

Rhyme: words that sound alike

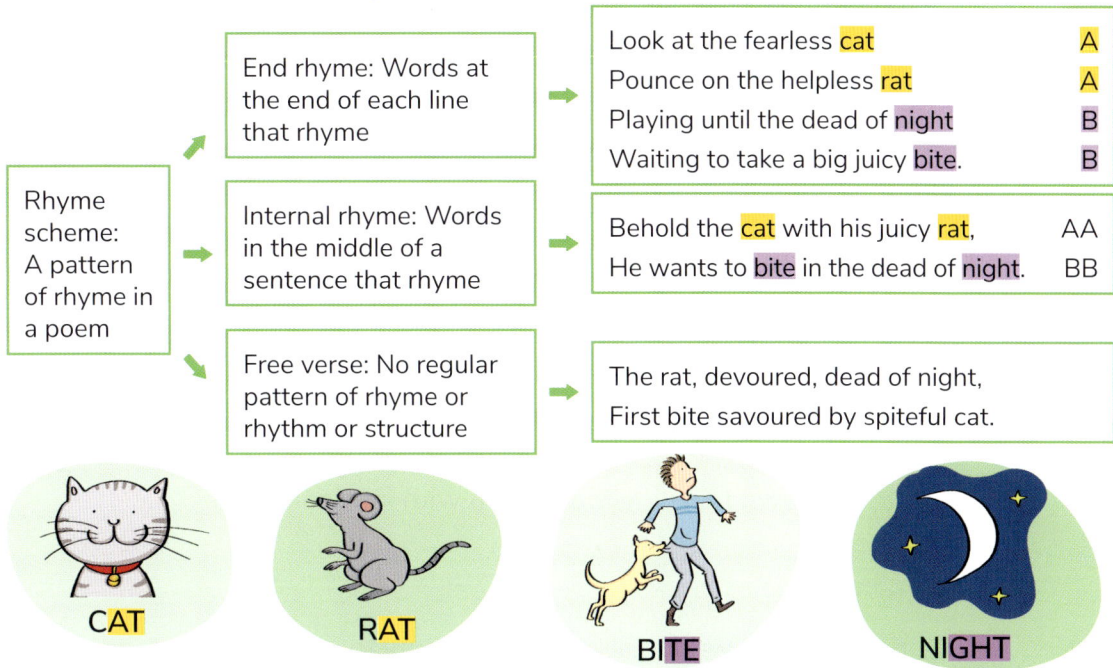

End rhyme: Words at the end of each line that rhyme	Look at the fearless cat — A Pounce on the helpless rat — A Playing until the dead of night — B Waiting to take a big juicy bite. — B

Rhyme scheme: A pattern of rhyme in a poem

Internal rhyme: Words in the middle of a sentence that rhyme	Behold the cat with his juicy rat, — AA He wants to bite in the dead of night. — BB

Free verse: No regular pattern of rhyme or rhythm or structure	The rat, devoured, dead of night, First bite savoured by spiteful cat.

CAT RAT BITE NIGHT

READING

Read these poems, then answer the questions below.

From Macbeth by William Shakespeare	'Twinkle Twinkle Little Star' by Jane Taylor
Round about the cauldron go; In the poison'd entrails throw. Toad, that under cold stone Days and nights has thirty-one Swelter'd venom sleeping got, Boil thou first i' the charmed pot. Double, double toil and trouble; Fire burn and cauldron bubble.	Twinkle, twinkle, little star, How I wonder what you are! Up above the world so high, Like a diamond in the sky.
From 'The Rime of the Ancient Mariner' by Samuel Taylor Coleridge	**'Fog' by Carl Sandburg**
In mist or cloud, on mast or shroud, It perched for vespers nine; Whiles all the night, through fog-smoke white, Glimmered the white Moon-shine.	The fog comes on little cat feet. It sits looking over harbour and city on silent haunches and then moves on.

1 Which poems rhyme at the end of the lines?
2 Which poems have internal rhyme?
3 Choose a poem and try to figure out the poem's rhyme scheme.
4 Which poems do not rhyme at all?
5 What do you call a poem that does not follow any rhyme scheme?
6 Do you prefer poems that rhyme or poems that don't rhyme? Why?

WRITING: FOOD POEM

This fun poem is about the joy of food. The poem makes use of internal rhyme, which you can see underlined here.

> ### Delicious Dishes – Anon
>
> Ice-<u>cream</u> makes you <u>scream</u>
> Apple <u>crumble</u> makes you <u>rumble</u>
> Birthday <u>cake</u> makes your tummy <u>ache</u>
> Curry <u>chips</u> fly through your <u>lips</u>.

Now write your own four-line food poem with internal rhyme.

Writing Tips

- Before you start writing, it might be helpful to write a list of foods and then brainstorm some accompanying rhyming words.
- Create your lines for your poem.
- Use rhymezone.com to help with your rhymes if you get stuck.

WRITING: ANTI-NURSERY RHYME

An anti-nursery rhyme is a humorous version of a traditional nursery rhyme that keeps the same structure and rhyme scheme as the original. Here is an example showing 'Old Mother Hubbard' in its traditional version and turned into an anti-nursery rhyme.

Traditional Nursery Rhyme	Anti-Nursery Rhyme
There was an old woman who lived in a <u>shoe</u>. She had so many children, she didn't know what to <u>do</u>. She gave them some broth without any <u>bread</u>; And whipped them all soundly and put them to <u>bed</u>.	There was an old woman who lived in a <u>box</u>. It didn't have windows or doorknobs or <u>locks</u>. She wanted to travel the world and <u>so</u> She mailed her house where she wanted to <u>go</u>.

Now create your own anti-nursery rhyme.

Writing Tips

- First choose a traditional nursery rhyme and write it down.
- Then pick out the words that rhyme, underline them and think about how to change them.
- Can you change any other words to make the new version humorous?

WRITING: ALPHABET RHYME

An alphabet rhyme is a poem where each line starts with a letter from the alphabet. The last word in each line should rhyme. See the rhyme below for an example.

Alphabet Rhyme

A was an apple, a shiny thing
B was a boxer, who'd rather sing
C was a cord, a long thin string
D was a…

Now create your own alphabet poem with as long a rhyme pattern as possible. Each line should start with a letter of the alphabet. You must keep the same end rhyme at the end of each line.

Writing Tips

- Be strategic with the end rhyming sound you choose. Think about using an end rhyme that has lots of possible rhyming words, such as 'cat': rat, mat, hat.
- Use the same line format as in the example:
  .... was a .... , a ....
- See how far down the alphabet you can get before you get stuck.
- You could use rhymezone.com to help.

CONSTRUCTION BY
LITTLE OLD LADY
WHO WANTS TO
LIVE IN A SHOE

Building A Poem: Rhythm

Creating a **rhythm** for a poem is another important consideration for a poet. But what is rhythm in poetry? Think of a song you like. What is it about that song that makes you tap your feet or want to dance? It is the rhythm of the song. The beat and pace of a poem create its rhythm. Rhythm is generated in a poem by stressed and unstressed syllables.

The choices a poet makes when they are creating a rhythm in a poem are usually guided by specific reasons. For example, the rhythm of a poem may get faster and faster over time to create a sense of panic. Or perhaps a poem's rhythm slows down to show the end of something. Some poets choose not to have a specific rhythm to their poems or just to have some sections of their poems with a specific rhythm.

Rhythm: The beat or pace of a poem

The rhythm of a poem can be found by looking at the stressed and unstressed syllables in words.

Syllable: Part of a word

1 syllable	Fair	Stressed
2 syllables	Be-hold	
3 syllables	Ba-na-na	Unstressed
4 syllables	Un-der-wa-ter	

'There was an Old Man with a Beard' by Edward Lear

There was an Old Man with a beard	8 syllables
Who said, 'It is just as I feared!	8 syllables
Two Owls and a Hen	5 syllables
Four Larks and a Wren,	5 syllables
Have all built their nest in my beard.	8 syllables

COMMUNICATING

Each of the four texts opposite has a specific rhythm that is created through line length and stressed and unstressed syllables. To investigate rhythm, read the texts aloud. You could do this in small groups or pairs. Then discuss the questions below.

1 'The Tyger': Do you notice anything about the stressed and unstressed syllables in the lines of this text?

2 'Folsom Prison Blues': Does the rhythm of this text remind you of anything?

3 The Gruffalo: What do you notice about the rhythm of the text? What possible reason is there for the author's choice of rhythm?

4 'A Visit from St Nicholas': Think about the night before Christmas when you were a young child. What emotion is the writer trying to get across to the reader here through the rhythm of the text?

'The Tyger' by William Blake	'Folsom Prison Blues' by Johnny Cash
Tyger Tyger, burning bright, In the forests of the night; What immortal hand or eye, Could frame thy fearful symmetry? In what distant deeps or skies. Burnt the fire of thine eyes? On what wings dare he aspire? What the hand, dare seize the fire?	I hear the train a comin', it's rolling 'round the bend And I ain't seen the sunshine since I don't know when I'm stuck in Folsom prison, and time keeps draggin' on But that train keeps a rollin' on down to San Antone When I was just a baby my mama told me, 'Son Always be a good boy, don't ever play with guns' But I shot a man in Reno just to watch him die When I hear that whistle blowing, I hang my head and cry.
From *The Gruffalo* by Julia Donaldson	From 'A Visit from St Nicholas' by Clement Clarke Moore
A mouse took a stroll through the deep dark wood. A fox saw the mouse and the mouse looked good. 'Where are you going to, little brown mouse? Come and have lunch in my underground house.' 'It's terribly kind of you, Fox, but no – I'm going to have lunch with a gruffalo.' 'A gruffalo? What's a gruffalo?' 'A gruffalo! Why, didn't you know? He has terrible tusks, and terrible claws, And terrible teeth in his terrible jaws.' 'Where are you meeting him?' 'Here, by these rocks, And his favourite food is roasted fox.'	'Twas the night before Christmas, when all through the house Not a creature was stirring, not even a mouse; The stockings were hung by the chimney with care, In hopes that St. Nicholas soon would be there; The children were nestled all snug in their beds; While visions of sugar-plums danced in their heads; And mamma in her 'kerchief, and I in my cap, Had just settled down for a long winter's nap...

Poetry Skills: Annotation

▶ Video

Annotation means writing your observations and ideas onto the poem itself. A reader might annotate a text by making notes on the page and highlighting important details while reading, to help them understand and make sense of a text. Annotation is a really important skill to develop as you study poetry.

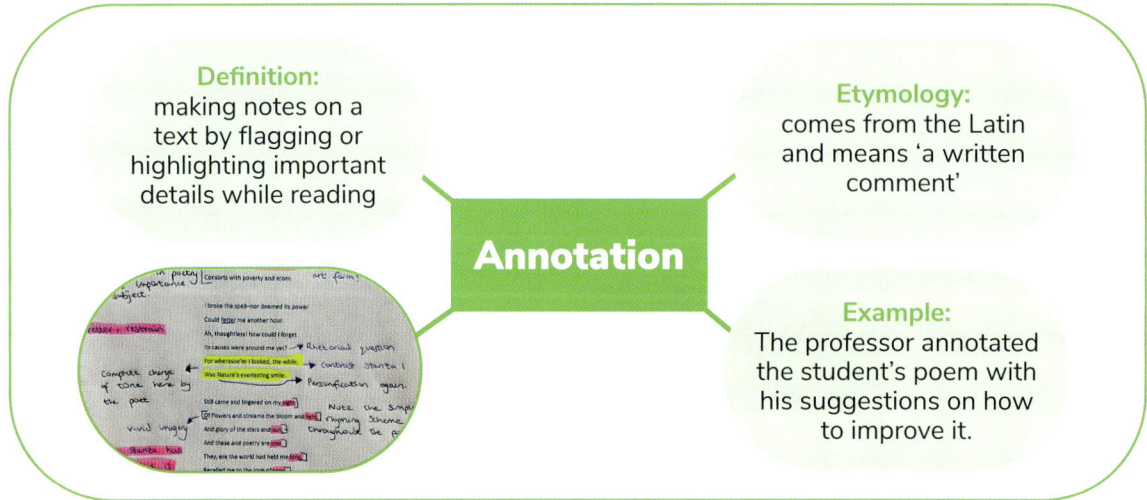

Definition:
making notes on a text by flagging or highlighting important details while reading

Annotation

Etymology:
comes from the Latin and means 'a written comment'

Example:
The professor annotated the student's poem with his suggestions on how to improve it.

Why annotate?

Sometimes after reading a poem, you may be unsure what the poet is trying to say. Annotating a poem is a reading strategy that will help you understand the techniques that went into building the poem and the message the poet is trying to put across. It allows you to understand and keep track of important details and ideas and helps you prepare to discuss or write about a poem.

1	Pick out a technique and highlight it in the poem.	You are my sunshine, my only sunshine. You make me happy when skies are grey. You'll never know, dear, how much I love you. Please don't take my sunshine away.
2	Draw an arrow out to the margin from the highlighted section and identify the technique.	You are my sunshine, my only sunshine. You make me happy when skies are grey. You'll never know, dear, how much I love you. Please don't take my sunshine away. → End rhyme
3	Draw a further arrow outwards and make a comment on the technique. What might it mean? What might it suggest?	You are my sunshine, my only sunshine. You make me happy when skies are grey. You'll never know, dear, how much I love you. Please don't take my sunshine away. → End rhyme → Sing-song rhythm

'From Above' by Cale Young Rice

? PRE-READING TASK: CHALLENGING VOCABULARY

In order to understand a new, challenging word, that word needs to be explored and investigated in a variety of ways. This will help the new word stick in your memory.

Create two sentences that include the word 'sullen' that clearly show your understanding of the word.

Definition:
bad-tempered and sulky

Synonyms:
sulky, sour, morose, resentful

Sullen

Example:
Her boyfriend was annoyed, because she ruined their selfie with her sullen look.

All about 'From Above'

Cale Young Rice was an American poet and dramatist writing in the early twentieth century. His poem 'From Above' has a very specific structure, rhythm and rhyme. He wrote this poem to show how sometimes you can feel in a completely different mood to the mood of your surroundings.

'From Above' by Cale Young Rice

What do I care if the trees are bare
  And the hills are dark
  And the skies are gray.

What do I care for chill in the air
  For crows that cark
  At the rough wind's way.

What do I care for the dead leaves there –
  Or the sullen road
  By the sullen wood.

There's heart in my heart
  To bear my load!
  So enough, the day is good!

READING

ACTIVITY

1 Summarise the poem in six words. The words do not have to make a sentence.

2 Practise your annotation skills in your activity book (see page 25) by trying to figure out the speaker, structure, rhythm and rhyme of the poem.

3 Who is the speaker in this poem?

4 What do you notice about the structure of the poem?

5 What do you notice about the rhyme in this poem?

6 What do you notice about the rhythm of the poem?

7 Finish this sentence: The poet's use of the word sullen makes the road and wood seem ....

8 List the punctuation marks used in the poem. What is the effect of the use of the exclamation marks in the last two lines of the poem?

9 Did you like or dislike the poem? Give one reason for your answer.

COMMUNICATING

In small groups, prepare a reading of this poem. Think carefully about who should read each line or each stanza. Think about any words or lines that everyone should read together. You could record your poetry reading using a voice-recording app or perform it for your class.

WRITING

Can you think of a time when your own mood was at odds with your surroundings? Perhaps you were in a bad mood at a party or in a really giddy mood during an ordinary class at school. Write a paragraph describing that time.

Writing Tips

- Identify the place you were and the mood you were in.
- Jot down what was different about these two things.
- You could begin your paragraph with the sentence: 'Have you ever felt at odds with where you are?'

'We Real Cool' by Gwendolyn Brooks

1 Describe what is happening in this picture.
2 Where do you think these teenagers should be?
3 What do you think they are talking about?
4 What do you think they might do for the rest of the day?
5 Do you think they do this regularly?
6 Listen to a reading of the poem: edco.ie/6vxs
7 What did you find appealing about Gwendolyn Brooks' reading of her poem?
8 If you were to choose an actor to read this poem for a poetry video, who would you choose and why?

All about 'We Real Cool'

Gwendolyn Brooks was a highly regarded African-American author and poet. A lot of her work deals with issues of prejudice, racism and civil rights. She was the first black author to win the Pulitzer Prize for Poetry. Brooks wrote this poem in 1959 after coming across a group of young African-American men playing pool at a pool hall, instead of being in school. She wondered how they felt about themselves. The Golden Shovel is the name of the pool hall.

'We Real Cool' by Gwendolyn Brooks

THE POOL PLAYERS.
SEVEN AT THE GOLDEN SHOVEL.

We real cool. We
Left school. We

Lurk late. We
Strike straight. We

Sing sin. We
Thin gin. We

Jazz June. We
Die soon.

READING

ACTIVITY

1 Summarise what the poet thinks the young men feel about themselves in six words. The words do not have to make a sentence.

2 Practise your annotation skills in your activity book (see page 26), using the prompt boxes to guide you.

3 Who is the speaker in this poem?

4 What do you notice about the structure of this poem? Look at the pattern of syllables, words, lines and stanzas.

5 What do you notice about the rhyme and rhythm in this poem?

6 How do you know that the poet thinks differently to the young men? Which line specifically leads you to think this?

7 What is unusual about the punctuation in this poem? Why do you think the poet decided to do this?

8 Does this poem connect in any way to any other text you have studied? How does it connect?

WRITING

ACTIVITY

Write your own version of 'We Real Cool'. Use the writing frame in your activity book (see page 27) to help you structure your poem if you like.

Writing Tips

- Think about what teenagers in your area might do instead of going to school. How would they fill their day? How do you think they feel about themselves? What do you think might become of them?
- Make sure the words you choose reflect the slang used in your area.

'Refugees' by Brian Bilston

PRE-READING: COMMUNICATING

70.8 million forcibly displaced people worldwide

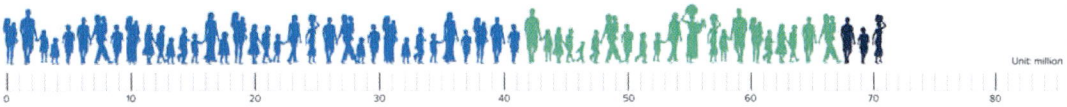

Unit: million

0 10 20 30 40 50 60 70 80

Internally Displaced People
41.3 million

Refugees
25.9 million
20.4 million under UNHCR's mandate
5.5 million Palestinian refugees under UNRWA's mandate

Asylum-seekers
3.5 million

Where the world's displaced people are being hosted

80%

About 80 per cent of refugees live in countries neighbouring their countries of origin

57% of UNHCR refugees came from three countries

6.7M Syria
2.7M Afghanistan
2.3M South Sudan

341,800 new asylum seekers
The greatest number of new asylum applications in 2018 was from Venezuelans

Top refugee-hosting countries

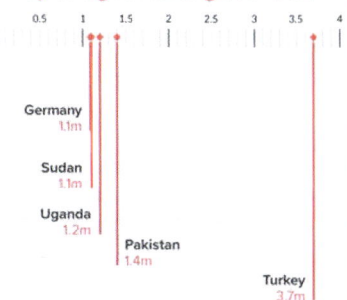

0.5 1 1.5 2 2.5 3 3.5 4

Germany 1.1m
Sudan 1.1m
Uganda 1.2m
Pakistan 1.4m
Turkey 3.7m

UNHCR has data on
3.9 million stateless people
but there are thought to be millions more

92,400 refugees resettled

37,000 people
a day forced to flee their homes because of conflict and persecution

16,803 personnel
UNHCR employs 16,803 people worldwide (as of 31 May 2019)

134 countries
We work in 134 countries (as of 31 May 2019)

We are funded almost entirely by voluntary contributions, with 86 per cent from governments and the European Union and 10 per cent from private donors

1 Do any of these photos shock you? Why? Why not?

2 Which country, do you think, hosts the most refugees in the world?

3 What is the reason for it being the top hosting country?

4 If you look at the top three countries of origin for refugees what, do you think, is the biggest reason people become refugees?

5 What do you think being 'internally displaced' means?

6 Do you agree or disagree with the statement: 'A place should only belong to those who are born there.' Why? Why not?

7 Watch the animated version of the poem: edco.ie/8v8a

8 What did you think was powerful about the animation?

All about 'Refugees'

Brian Bilston is a British poet who has become known as 'the Poet Laureate of Twitter'. He tweets his humorous and topical poetry to his followers. Brian Bilston is an alias; the real identity of the poet remains a mystery. When Brian Bilston tweeted his poem 'Refugees', it was retweeted tens of thousands of times and reprinted in newspapers and magazines all over the world.

This poem is a palindrome poem: a poem that can be read both forwards and backwards.

'Refugees' by Brian Bilston

They have no need of our help
So do not tell me
These haggard faces could belong to you or me
Should life have dealt a different hand
We need to see them for who they really are
Chancers and scroungers
Layabouts and loungers
With bombs up their sleeves
Cut-throats and thieves
They are not
Welcome here
We should make them
Go back to where they came from
They cannot
Share our food
Share our homes
Share our countries
Instead let us
Build a wall to keep them out
It is not okay to say
These are people just like us
A place should only belong to those who are born there
Do not be so stupid to think that
The world can be looked at another way

(now read from bottom to top)

[Handwritten annotations: repetition – things that repeat again; second person; subject – the thing/person/place the poem is about; Speaker; assonance; alliteration / end rhyme; Theme – Racism, xenophobia, sharing, kindness → main issue; enjambment; personification – human emotion; repetition; simile; Rhyme – End rhyme, Rhyming couple]

READING

1 In one sentence, summarise the poem read forwards. Then summarise the poem read backwards in another sentence.

2 Practise your annotation skills in your activity book (see page 28), using the prompt boxes to guide you.

3 What is the difference between the speaker of the poem read fowards and the speaker of the poem read backwards?

4 How did you feel at the end of the poem read forwards and at the end of the poem read backwards?

5 What do you think the poet is trying to teach us by structuring the poem as a palindrome?

6 What do you notice about this poem's rhythm and rhyme?

7 The poet uses a variety of stereotypical slang words in the poem. List these words. Why do you think the poet chose to use these informal slang words?

8 List all the adjectives used to describe the refugees. What picture does this list of adjectives paint?

9 Choose a line in the poem and upgrade one of the words. Rewrite the line of the poem using your new word. Explain why you think it is a better choice of word.

10 Does this poem link to any other text you have studied? (It could link because of the theme, subject, tone, language used or for any other reason.)

WRITING

Often when refugees leave their homes, they can only bring what they can carry in a backpack. Imagine you have to leave your home and have packed a bag. Write a paragraph where you describe what you have packed in your bag and explain why you have included these items.

Writing Tips

● Think about what you would need if you were going to travel thousands of miles, through dangerous territories. What might be important to bring and what might not be important?

● You could start your paragraph with the sentence: 'Today, I packed my bag and left my home'.

Subject And Theme

People write poetry for a variety of different reasons. Sometimes poets want to express their feelings and thoughts on a topic, place or person. People also write poetry to entertain their readers or to describe something beautiful or revolting they have experienced. To better understand a poem, it is useful to realise that a poem usually has a **subject** that is obvious on the surface. If you dig a bit deeper, however, every poem has an underlying message or idea, which is called the **theme**.

Subject ➡ The thing/person/place that the poem is about. ➡

Theme ➡ The underlying message or idea expressed in the poem – what the poem is *really* about. ➡

When it rains on your parade, look up rather than down. Without the rain there would be no rainbow.

Subject: the weather

Theme: always have hope, as hardships also bring beautiful things to our lives

---

READING

Nursery rhymes might well have been your first introduction to poetry. On the surface, each nursery rhyme deals with a particular subject, but if you think and dig a bit deeper, the theme of the rhyme is uncovered. What do you think the subject and theme are of each of these nursery rhymes?

'Humpty Dumpty' *Subject = Humpty*	'Ring a Ring o' Roses'
Humpty Dumpty sat on a wall, Humpty Dumpty had a great fall; All the king's horses and all the king's men Couldn't put Humpty together again.	Ring a ring o' roses → *connection* A pocketful of posies → *Joyful* A-tishoo, a-tishoo → *Black Death* We all fall down.
'Rock-a-bye Baby' *baby*	'Jack and Jill' *People*
Rock-a-bye baby, on the treetops, When the wind blows, the cradle will rock, When the bough breaks, the cradle will fall, And down will come baby, cradle and all.	Jack and Jill went up the hill To fetch a pail of water. Jack fell down and broke his crown, And Jill came tumbling after. *friend ship*

Theme Pach. Reponsibilities somethimes what is booken cannot be fixed

subject Baby falling

theme love Danger loneliness

Many nursery rhymes have dark histories. Choose one nursery rhyme and research where it came from.

Tone And Mood

A poet expresses their attitude and feelings about their subject and theme through their tone in a poem. A poet could choose an optimistic or pessimistic tone or perhaps a bitter or judgemental tone. This then affects the reader of the poem and creates a mood. The mood a reader feels is directly connected to the tone a poet adopts.

Tone: the attitude a poet expresses through their poem

Mood: how the reader feels after reading the poem

Below are some examples of the different types of tones poets use and the types of moods a reader may be in after reading poetry.

Tones

Celebratory: feelings of happiness and pride	Objective: an unbiased view; able to leave personal judgments aside	Judgmental: authoritative and often having critical opinions	Humorous: showing funny, comical, amusing opinions	Compassionate: showing sympathy and concern for others
Heart-warming: positive, emotional and sensitive view of the topic	Critical: finding fault with the actions or views of others	Optimistic: being hopeful, cheerful and positive about the topic	Pessimistic: seeing the worst side of things; no hope	Detached: aloof and objective
Serious/ Solemn: not funny; very earnest	Appreciative: grateful; thankful	Cautionary: giving a warning; raising an alarm	Condescending: looking down on; pouring scorn on	Bitter: showing hurt and resentment

Moods

Calm	Envious	Disappointed	Cheerful	Terrified
Enraged	Uplifted	Depressed	Empowered	Gloomy
Anxious	Guilty	Ashamed	Surprised	Uncomfortable

READING

Read these extracts from two poems that each have a distinct tone. Then answer the questions below.

From 'The Road Not Taken' by Robert Frost

I shall be telling this with a sigh
Somewhere ages and ages hence:
Two roads diverged in a wood, and I–
I took the one less traveled by,
And that has made all the difference.

From 'Still I Rise' by Maya Angelou

You may write me down in history
With your bitter, twisted lies,
You may trod me in the very dirt
But still, like dust, I'll rise.

1 Can you identify the tone of 'The Road Not Taken'?

2 Why do you think this?

3 What do you think the mood of the reader would be after reading the poem?

4 Can you identify the tone of 'Still I Rise'?

5 Why do you think this?

6 What do you think the mood of the reader would be after reading the poem?

7 Choose one of the poems above and edit it to change the tone. This may mean just changing two or three words.

8 Read your rewritten version to your partner. How have the edits changed the poem?

9 Do you prefer the poem now or before the edits? Why?

COMMUNICATING

Below is an extract from a song famously recorded by Louis Armstrong, which you may already be familiar with. Sometimes the tone in which something is delivered can completely change the writing's effect on the mood of the audience or the reader. In groups of four, take turns reading the extract out loud as if you are making a speech. Each of you should choose a different tone from the list below to deliver your speech in.

Sarcastic	Detached	Optimistic	Serious/Solemn

The three people listening in each group (the audience) should note down what mood they were left in after listening to each speech.

'Oh What A Wonderful World' by Bob Thiele and David Weiss

I see trees so green, red roses too
I see them bloom for me and you.
And I think to myself what a wonderful world.
I see skies so blue and clouds so white.
The bright blessed day, the dark sacred night.
And I think to myself what a wonderful world.
The colors of the rainbow so pretty in the sky
Are also on the faces of people going by.
I see friends shaking hands saying how do you do.
They're really saying I love you.
I hear babies crying, I watch them grow.
They'll learn much more than I'll ever know.
And I think to myself what a wonderful world.
Yes I think to myself what a wonderful world
Yes I think to myself what a wonderful world.

Quotations

▶ Video

One of the new things about English in secondary school is learning the skill of referencing a text or quoting from a text. A **quotation** is a phrase or line taken directly and copied exactly from a text – whether it's a poem, novel, play or a non-fiction text.

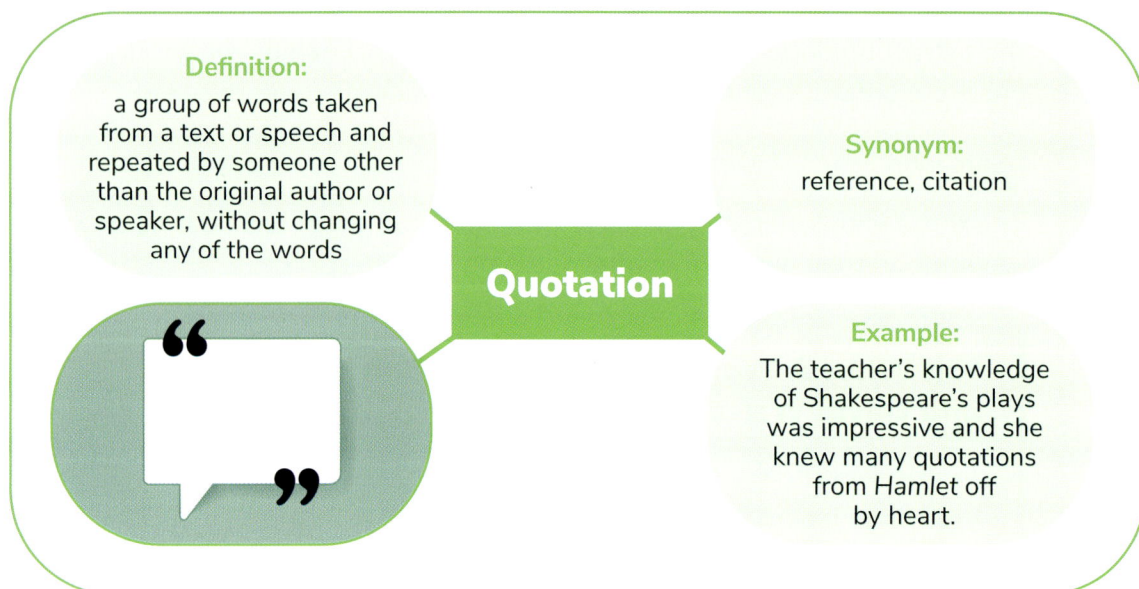

Definition:
a group of words taken from a text or speech and repeated by someone other than the original author or speaker, without changing any of the words

Quotation

Synonym:
reference, citation

Example:
The teacher's knowledge of Shakespeare's plays was impressive and she knew many quotations from *Hamlet* off by heart.

Why use quotations?

Showing your supporting evidence by using a quote shows that you have read into the deeper meaning of the text and can prove that your reading of the text is correct.

Steps to choosing a quotation	'Still I Rise' by Maya Angelou (see page 70)
1 Work out what the question is asking you to do or demonstrate.	Is the speaker of the poem victorious in the end?
2 Skim and scan the text to find a quotation that proves your point.	'You may write me down in history With your bitter, twisted lies, You may trod me in the very dirt But still, like dust, I'll rise.'
3 Only quote what you need. Cut out the parts that don't support what you are trying to say.	'trod' 'dirt' 'rise'
4 Work your quote into a sentence by embedding it.	The speaker of the poem is victorious in the end. Despite the fact that she is 'trod' into the 'dirt' by someone, she is sure she will 'rise' again.

'First They Came' by Martin Niemöller

PRE-READING: READING

Use the internet or other non-fiction reference books to research the answers to the questions below.

1 Find out the meaning of the following terms: communist, socialist and trade unionist.

2 What groups of people were targeted by the Nazis and sent to concentration camps?

3 What happened to the property and possessions of the people that the Nazis came for?

4 How many German citizens lost their lives during the Holocaust?

All about 'First They Came'

Martin Niemöller (1892–1984) was an important church leader in Germany during Nazi rule. He began to speak out against Hitler and the Nazis when he saw what was happening to his community. Niemöller spent the last seven years of Nazi rule in concentration camps and survived to tell his story upon his release. He is best remembered for his post-war confession, found in this piece of prose poetry.

'First They Came' by Martin Niemöller

First they came for the Communists
And I did not speak out
Because I was not a Communist.

Then they came for the Socialists
And I did not speak out
Because I was not a Socialist.

Then they came for the trade unionists
And I did not speak out
Because I was not a trade unionist.

Then they came for the Jews
And I did not speak out
Because I was not a Jew.

Then they came for me
And there was no one left
To speak out for me.

READING

1 Summarise the poem by choosing the most important word in each stanza and making a list.

2 Who is the speaker in this poem? What narrative perspective is being used and how do you know?

3 What is the subject of the poem?

4 What is the theme of the poem?

5 Complete the quote quest task in your activity book (see page 29) to practise choosing appropriate quotations, embedding them and punctuating them.

6 How would you describe the tone of this poem? Look back at page 69 to see if the tone of this poem matches any of the tones described there.

7 Compare how the poem makes you feel at the beginning and at the end. What mood are you in at the end of the first stanza compared to at the end of the last stanza?

8 Each stanza uses only one punctuation mark. Choose one stanza and edit the punctuation. Add in an exclamation mark, a comma or a second full stop. What impact does your punctuation edit have on the text?

9 Does this poem remind you of any other text you have studied?

COMMUNICATING

Watch the dramatic reading of 'First They Came': edco.ie/8qcg

In small groups create a choral reading of the poem. A choral reading is a group reading, where different people in a group take different lines to read and sometimes everyone reads a line or two together. How you read and deliver the poem completely depends on the point you are trying to get across to your audience. You could record this choral reading on a voice-recording app or perform it for the rest of your class.

WRITING

Write your own version of 'First They Came'. First think about all of the injustices you have seen but done nothing about. They need not be things that are a big deal; they are more likely to be things that you regretted not doing anything about that stuck with you afterwards.

Writing Tips

● There is a writing frame in your activity book (see page 30) to help you write the poem.

'Back in the Playground Blues' by Adrian Mitchell

PRE-READING: COMMUNICATING

Sometimes the title of a poem can tell us a lot about the poem's theme. Look in detail at the title of this poem.

1 What hints does the title give about the content of the poem?

2 Listen to a reading of this poem: edco.ie/es97
   Then complete the personal response grid in your activity book (see page 31).

3 Finally, share your thoughts with your partner.

All about 'Back in the Playground Blues'

Adrian Mitchell (1932–2008) was a British poet, playwright and novelist. He used his poetry to speak out against injustices and corruption and was very involved with the anti-nuclear movement. He famously wrote in the preface of his poetry books: 'None of the work in this book is to be used in connection with any examination whatsoever.'

'Back in the Playground Blues' by Adrian Mitchell

I dreamed I was back in the playground, I was about four feet high
Yes I dreamed I was back in the playground, standing about four feet high
Well the playground was three miles long and the playground was five miles wide

It was broken black tarmac with a high wire fence all around
Broken black dusty tarmac with a high fence running all around
And it had a special name to it, they called it The Killing Ground

Got a mother and a father they're one thousand years away
The rulers of the Killing Ground are coming out to play
Everybody thinking: 'Who they going to play with today?'

  Well you get it for being Jewish
  And you get it for being black
  You get it for being chicken
  And you get it for fighting back
  You get it for being big and fat
  Get it for being small
  Oh those who get it get it and get it
  For any damn thing at all

Sometimes they take a beetle, tear off its six legs one by one
Beetle on its black back, rocking in the lunchtime sun
But a beetle can't beg for mercy, a beetle's not half the fun

I heard a deep voice talking, it had that iceberg sound
'It prepares them for Life' – but I have never found
Any place in my life worse than The Killing Ground.

READING

1 Write a short paragraph that summarises the poem. You could start with something like this: There was a little boy who...

2 Who is the speaker in the poem? How do you know?

3 What is the subject of the poem?

4 Complete the quote quest task in your activity book (see page 32) to practise choosing, embedding and punctuating quotes.

5 How would you describe the tone of this poem? Look back at page 69 to see if the tone of this poem matches any of the tones described there.

6 What mood were you in after hearing this poem? Look back at page 69 to see if the mood of this poem matches any of the moods described there.

7 Look closely at how the poet describes the playground in the extract below. List the words or phrases that are unexpected about this description. Why are they unexpected? What place does this description remind you of?

> Well the playground was three miles long and the playground was five miles wide
>
> It was broken black tarmac with a high wire fence all around
> Broken black dusty tarmac with a high fence running all around
> And it had a special name to it, they called it The Killing Ground

8 Complete the editing task in your activity book (see page 33).

9 Explain why you think the poet chose to capitalise the phrase 'The Killing Ground'.

10 What do you think the poem is trying to teach us?

11 Can you make any link between this poem and any other text you have studied?

WRITING

We now live in a time where a large amount of bullying occurs online, on social media or via text messages. Write a conversation between a bully and their victim in the form of text messages. You should base your conversation on the actions of the characters in this poem.

Writing Tips

• Use the text message layout in your activity book (see page 33) to help you write the conversation.

'Mid-Term Break' by Seamus Heaney

PRE-READING: COMMUNICATING

1 What do you know about the traditions of funerals in Ireland?
2 Listen to 'Tears in Heaven' by Eric Clapton: edco.ie/chdb
3 What emotions or feelings is the song trying to convey to the person listening?
4 Listen to 'See You Again' by Wiz Kalifa: edco.ie/8wd3
5 What is the message in this song about grief and loss?
6 Listen to Seamus Heaney reading 'Mid-Term Break': edco.ie/yv6m
   Then complete the personal response quad in your activity book (see page 34). Then share your thoughts with your partner.

All about 'Mid-Term Break'

Seamus Heaney is one of Ireland's most well-loved and respected poets. This poem was written by Heaney about the loss of his brother, who was hit by a car and killed when he was only four years old.

'Mid-Term Break' by Seamus Heaney

I sat all morning in the college sick bay
Counting bells knelling classes to a close.
At two o'clock our neighbours drove me home.

In the porch I met my father crying—
He had always taken funerals in his stride—
And Big Jim Evans saying it was a hard blow.

The baby cooed and laughed and rocked the pram
When I came in, and I was embarrassed
By old men standing up to shake my hand

And tell me they were 'sorry for my trouble'.
Whispers informed strangers I was the eldest,
Away at school, as my mother held my hand

In hers and coughed out angry tearless sighs.
At ten o'clock the ambulance arrived
With the corpse, stanched and bandaged by the nurses.

Next morning I went up into the room. Snowdrops
And candles soothed the bedside; I saw him
For the first time in six weeks. Paler now,

Wearing a poppy bruise on his left temple,
He lay in the four-foot box as in his cot.
No gaudy scars, the bumper knocked him clear.

A four-foot box, a foot for every year.

[Handwritten annotations: setting; foreshadowing → funeral foreshadowing; double entrance; unusual feeling; innocence (Theme); where we find out a family person passed away; emotion bank – sad, conflicted, confused; author feelings; End-rhyme and Rhyming couplet; Tone Theme Mood]

READING

ACTIVITY

1 Complete the summary activity in your activity book (see pages 35–36).

2 Who is the speaker in the poem? How do you know?

3 What is the subject of the poem?

4 How did you feel at the end of the poem? Why?

5 How would you describe the tone of the poem?

6 Complete the quote quest task in your activity book (see pages 36–37) to practise your quotation skills.

7 What is the most effective word in the poem that the poet uses to describe his grief, in your opinion? Why did you choose that word?

8 What do you think is the theme of this poem?

9 The poet uses a dash in the following lines:

> In the porch I met my father crying—
> He had always taken funerals in his stride—

Why do you think the poet has chosen this punctuation mark for these lines?

10 Does this poem connect to any other text you have studied?

WRITING

During times of hardship, communities tend to pull together and support each other, just like the community in this poem support the poet's family in their grief. Think about a time where you have heard about or experienced a community pulling together and helping each other out. Describe what happened in a short paragraph.

Writing Tips

- If you can't think of anything, you could use the internet to search for news stories about communities supporting each other around the world in times of need.

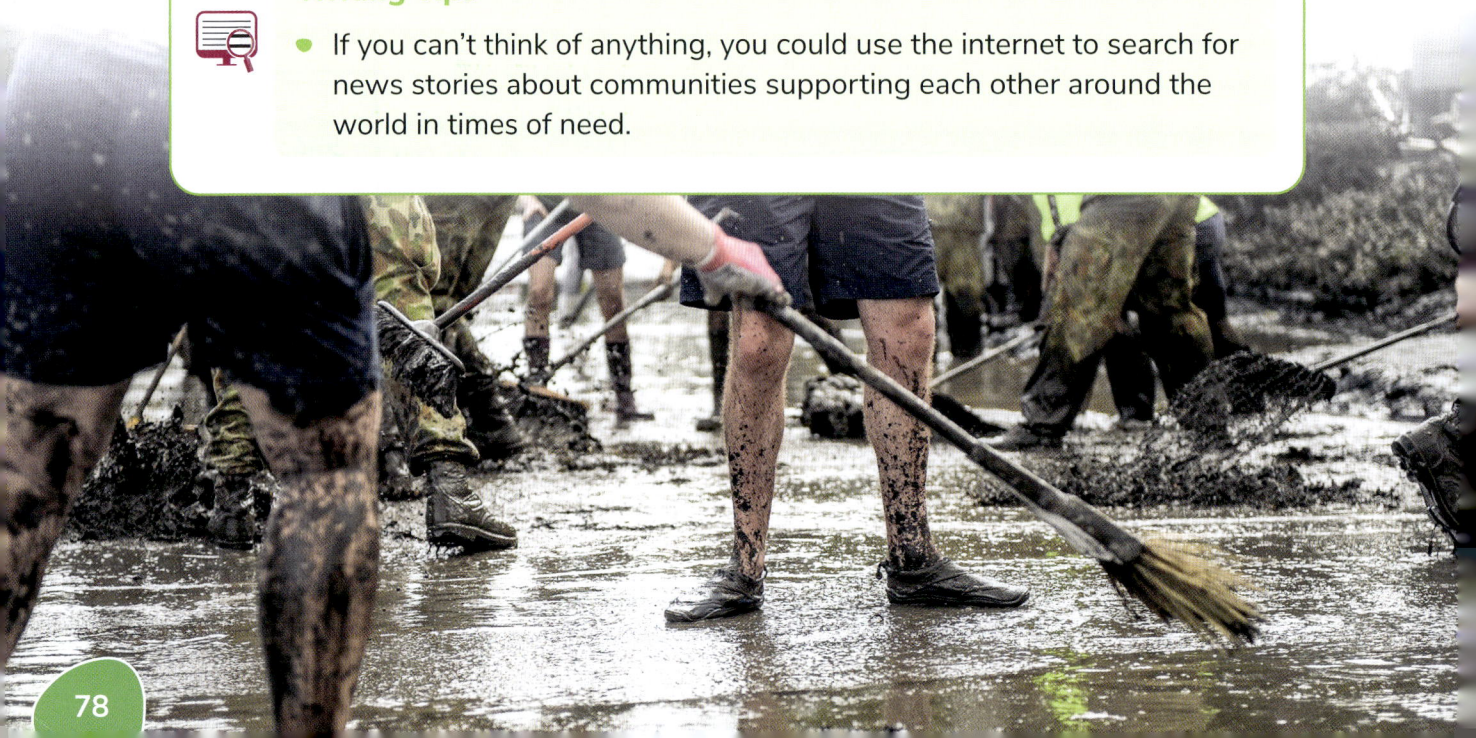

Painting With Words

Poets are excellent at painting a picture for their readers with words. Some poems use words so creatively that the reader can feel like they are walking in the poet's footsteps, experiencing the same event or feeling as them. There are many techniques poets use to create this experience, such as similes, metaphors and personification.

What is a simile?

A simile is a technique in language where the author compares two things using 'like' or 'as'.

Etymology

The word 'simile' comes from fourteenth-century Latin and it means 'like' or 'similar'.

Examples

As cute as a kitten	As happy as a clam	As light as a feather
As blind as a bat	As cold as ice	As hard as nails
She runs like a cheetah	He fights like a lion	She cried like a baby
Your eyes are like sunshine	He eats like a pig	He swam like a fish

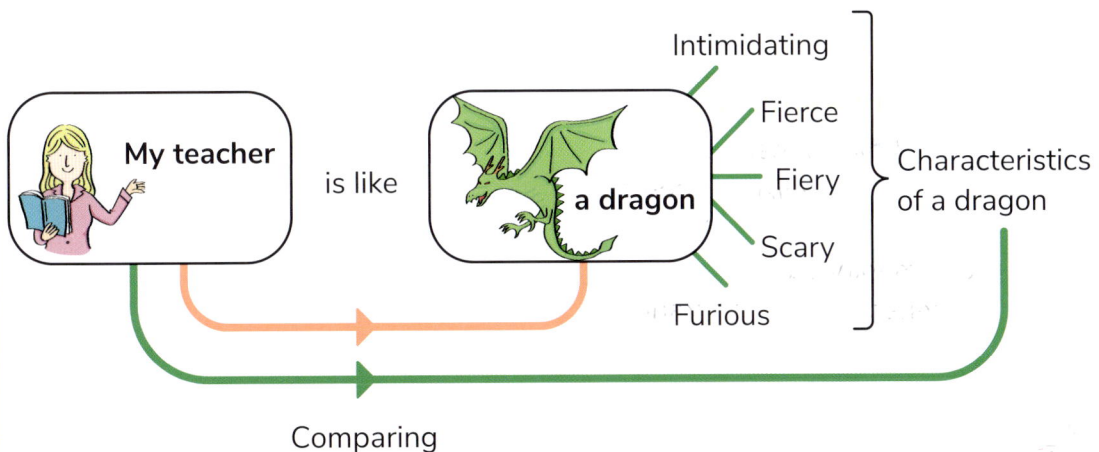

What is a metaphor?

A metaphor is a type of language technique where the author compares two different things and, as a result, reveals their similarities.

Etymology

The word 'metaphor' comes from Ancient Greek and means 'to transfer' or 'carry over'.

Examples

The snow is a white blanket	He is a shining star	The classroom is a zoo
The alligator's teeth are white daggers	She is a peacock	My teacher is a dragon
Laughter is the music of the soul	America is a melting pot	Her lovely voice was music to his ears

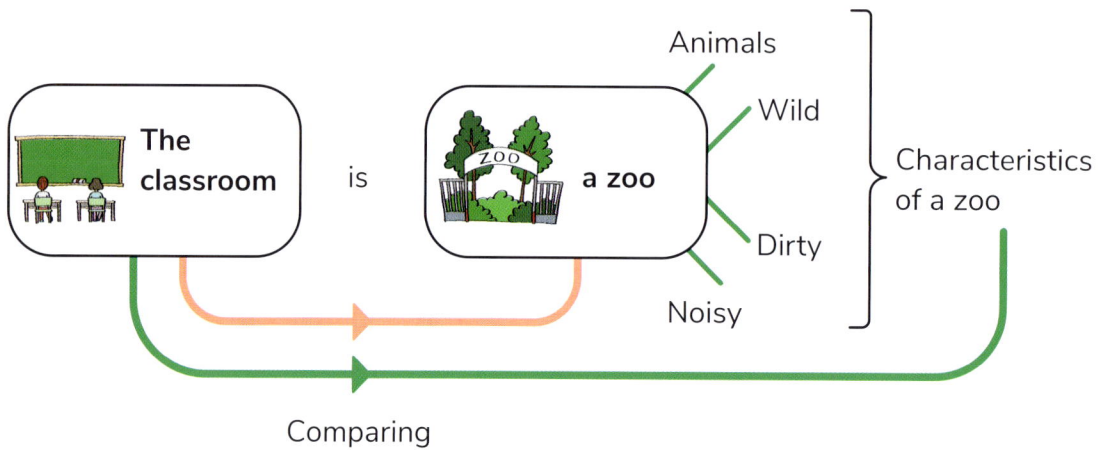

The classroom is a zoo

Animals
Wild
Dirty
Noisy

Characteristics of a zoo

Comparing

What is personification?

Personification is a language technique where non-human things are given human characteristics.

Etymology

The word 'personification' comes from Latin and means 'a mask' or 'false face'.

Examples

Lightning danced across the sky	The wind howled in the night	The car complained as the key was roughly turned in its ignition
Rita heard the last piece of pie calling her name	My alarm clock yells at me to get out of bed every morning	The avalanche devoured anything standing in its way

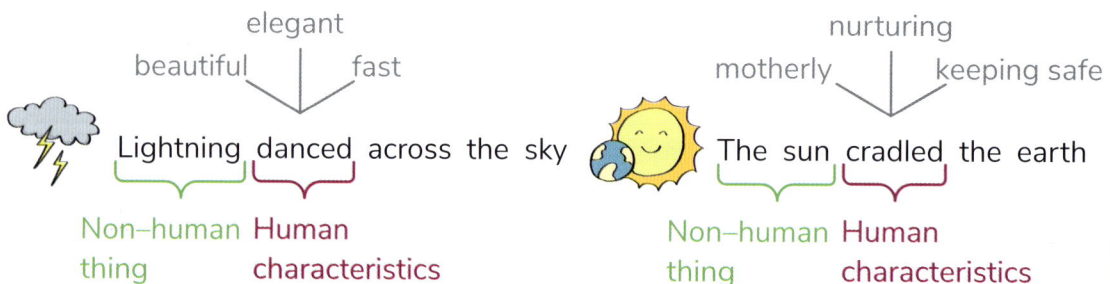

elegant
beautiful   fast

Lightning danced across the sky

Non–human thing   Human characteristics

nurturing
motherly   keeping safe

The sun cradled the earth

Non–human thing   Human characteristics

READING

ACTIVITY

Go to your activity book (see pages 38–39) to practise picking out examples of simile, metaphor and personification.

WRITING

ACTIVITY

Go to your activity book (see pages 40–41) and complete the tasks on using similes, metaphors and personification in your writing.

WRITING: WRITE A SIMILE POEM

Choose a subject to write about from the suggested topics below or feel free to invent your own.

trees	cars	bikes
food	the beach	mountains
horses	dogs	cats

Create a three-line simile poem by thinking about ways to compare your subject to something else.

Here is an example:

A Book Is Like

A book is like a longed for letter, when read again the friendship's better.
A book is like an unopened door, crying out for more, more, more.
A book is like a mysterious friend that keeps its secret to the end.

Writing Tips

- Before you start, write down your choice of topic in the middle of a spider diagram, like the example below, and then add everything you could compare that topic to.
- Then use the same sentence structure as in the example above to build your poem. For example: A .... is like a ....

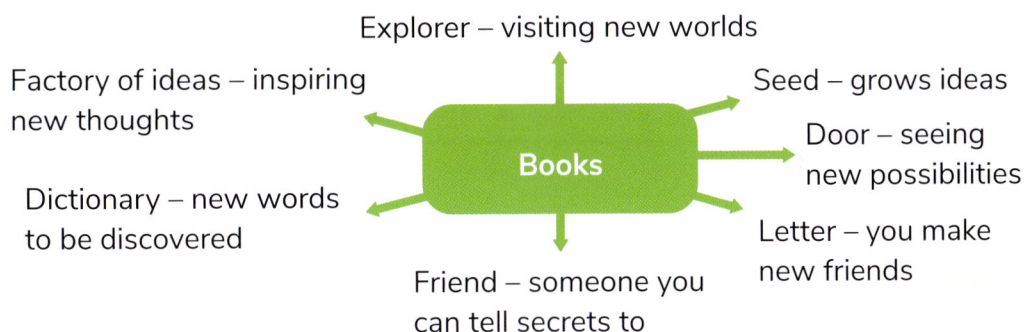

Explorer – visiting new worlds

Factory of ideas – inspiring new thoughts

Seed – grows ideas

Door – seeing new possibilities

Dictionary – new words to be discovered

Books

Letter – you make new friends

Friend – someone you can tell secrets to

WRITING: WRITE A METAPHOR POEM

Choose a subject to write about from the suggested topics below or feel free to invent your own.

a cloud	a cat	an apple	cheese
the ocean	an autumn leaf	the moon	a lake
a beach	a sunflower	chewing gum	fishing

Create a three-line metaphor poem by thinking of ways to compare your subject to something else, and so reveal their similarities.

Here is an example:

> ### The Sun
>
> The Sun is a menacing ball of fire
> A nurturing mother
> A glowing marble.

Writing Tips

- Before you start, write down your choice of topic in the middle of a spider diagram, like the one below, and then write everything you can think of about that topic, including things you could compare it to.
- Use the structure of the example to help you craft your poem.

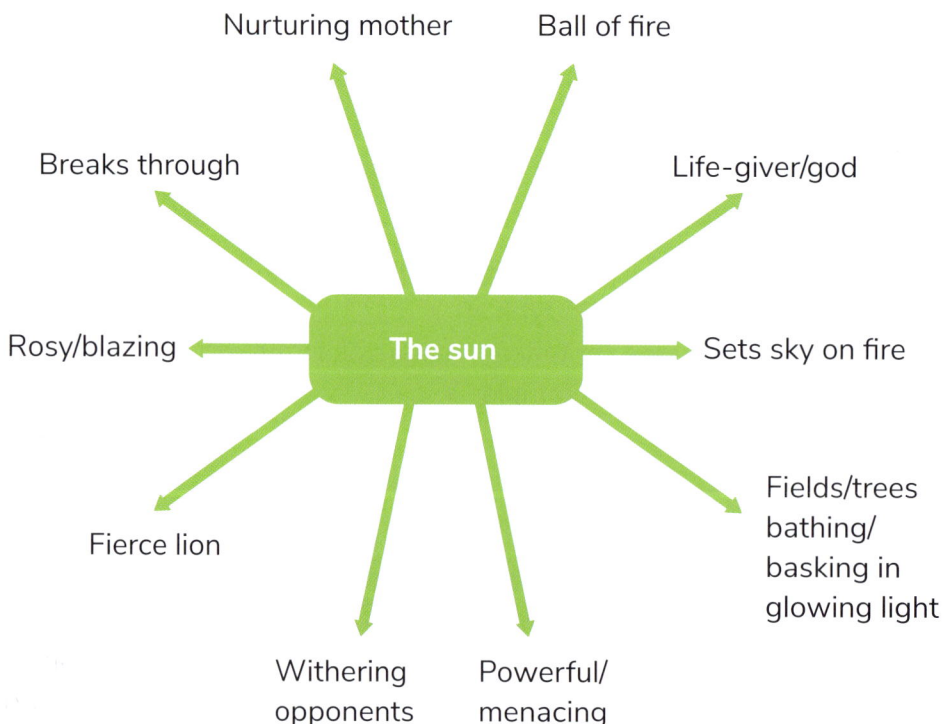

Nurturing mother   Ball of fire

Breaks through

Life-giver/god

Rosy/blazing   **The sun**   Sets sky on fire

Fields/trees bathing/ basking in glowing light

Fierce lion

Withering opponents   Powerful/ menacing

Inference

Video

Inference is not guessing, predicting or giving an opinion. It is finding exact clues from the text and using your own background knowledge to come up with an idea not stated obviously in the text. Making an inference is like assembling the pieces of a jigsaw puzzle. Once all of the pieces are together you can see the full picture.

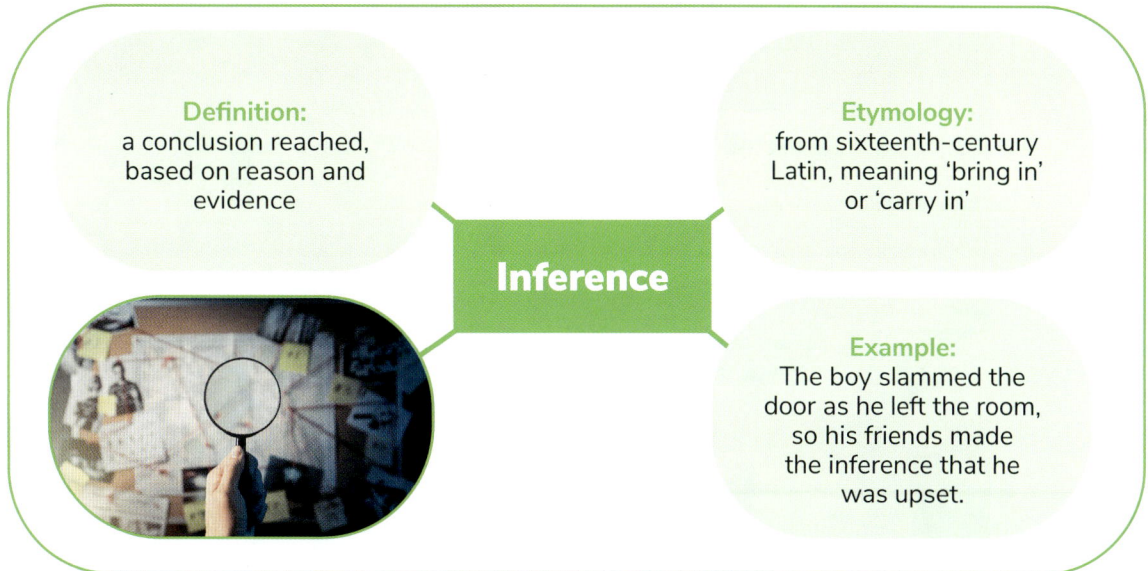

Definition:
a conclusion reached, based on reason and evidence

Etymology:
from sixteenth-century Latin, meaning 'bring in' or 'carry in'

Inference

Example:
The boy slammed the door as he left the room, so his friends made the inference that he was upset.

Why do we need inference skills?

As a student of English, one of your most important reading tasks will be making sense of poems, short stories, plays and novels. In order to figure out the deeper meaning of these texts, you will need to develop your inference skills.

The process is straightforward – first skim and scan the text to look for clues. Then connect these clues with your own background knowledge, before reaching a conclusion about what the text might be trying to say.

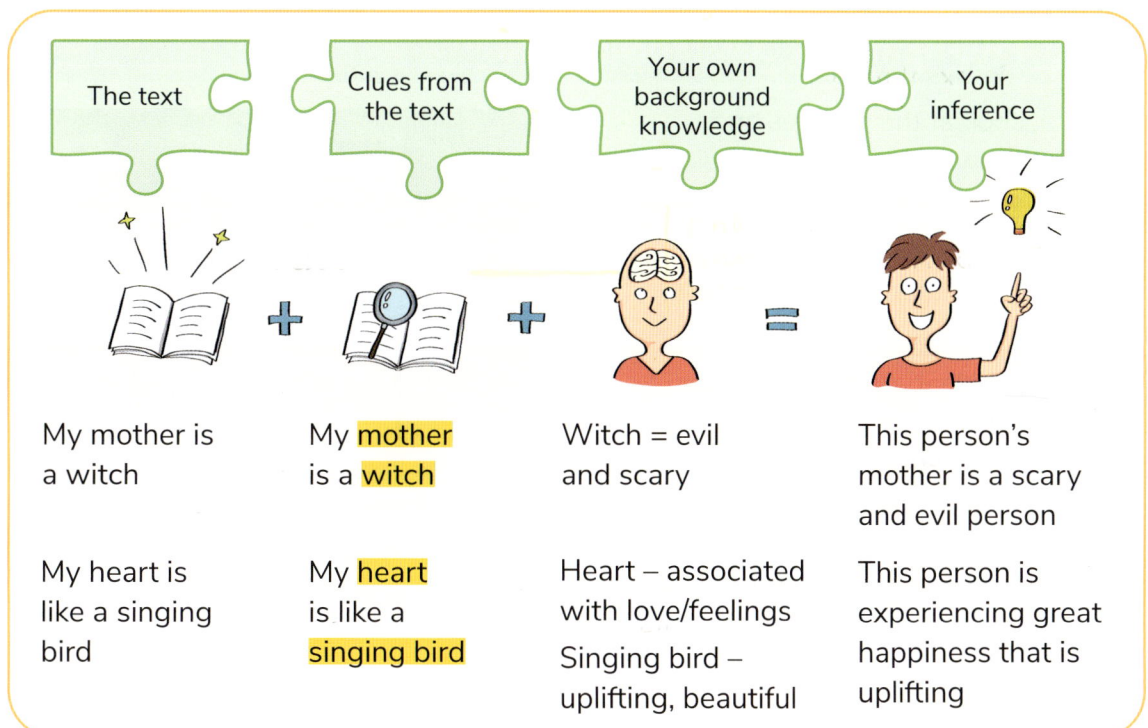

The text	Clues from the text	Your own background knowledge	Your inference
My mother is a witch	My **mother** is a **witch**	Witch = evil and scary	This person's mother is a scary and evil person
My heart is like a singing bird	My **heart** is like a **singing bird**	Heart – associated with love/feelings. Singing bird – uplifting, beautiful	This person is experiencing great happiness that is uplifting

READING

1 Look at the four pictures below and complete the picture inference jigsaw task in your activity book (see page 42).

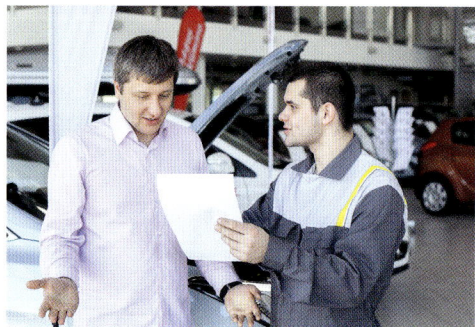

2 In a similar way to the picture activity you just completed, it is also possible to infer meaning from things people say in everyday speech, songs and poems. Complete the inference skills jigsaw tasks in your activity book (see pages 43–45).

'The door' by Miroslav Holub

PRE-READING: COMMUNICATING

Look at the pictures and answer the questions below.

1 What do you think of when you see an open door?

2 What do you think of when you see a closed door?

3 What are the similarities between the two doors?

4 What are the differences between the two doors?

5 Watch a short visual version of the poem: edco.ie/3qyx

Then complete the personal response quad in your activity book (see page 46). When you've jotted down your response, share your thoughts with your partner.

All about 'The door'

Miroslav Holub (1923–1998) was a Czech poet who also worked as a scientist. Holub wrote poetry while living in great poverty during a difficult time in his country's history, when it was under communist rule. His work was only published when communism fell. His poems were translated into thirty different languages and won praise around the world.

'The door' by Miroslav Holub

Go and open the door.
Maybe outside there's
a tree, or a wood,
a garden,
or a magic city.

Go and open the door.
Maybe a dog's rummaging.
Maybe you'll see a face,
or an eye,
or the picture
of a picture.

Go and open the door.
If there's a fog
it will clear.

Go and open the door.
Even if there's only
the darkness ticking,
even if there's only
the hollow wind,
even if
nothing
is there,
go and open the door.

At least
there'll be
a draught.

Translated by: Ian Melvin

READING

ACTIVITY

1 Complete the poem summary task in your activity book (see page 47).
2 Describe the speaker in this poem.
3 What is the subject of this poem?
4 Does this poem have any particular rhyme scheme or rhythm?
5 Complete the inference jigsaw task in your activity book (see page 48) and answer the question that follows.

READING

6 How did the poem make you feel at the end? Inspired? Motivated? Nervous? Explain your answer.

7 What technique is the poet using in his poem when he refers to the door: simile or metaphor or personification? Explain how you know this.

8 Change the adjectives and nouns in the stanzas of the poem below to make the opening of the door seem menacing and scary.

> Go and open the door.
> Maybe outside there's
> a tree, or a wood,
> a garden,
> or a magic city.
>
> Go and open the door.
> Even if there's only
> the darkness ticking,
> even if there's only
> the hollow wind…

WRITING

Create your own version of 'The door'. Your poem should also be about possibilities and taking chances on the unknown.

Writing Tips

- Think about what possibilities may await you in life if you take a chance and pursue them.
- Then think of what images might represent these choices. For example, if you want to pursue a career as an actor, you might use an image of a stage to represent this.
- Use the writing frame in your activity book (see page 49) to help you structure your writing.

ACTIVITY

'The Sky is low – the Clouds are mean' by Emily Dickinson

All about 'The Sky is low – the Clouds are mean'

Emily Dickinson (1830–1886) is one of America's most famous and important poets. She spent most of her life isolated at home and was considered an eccentric by locals. Only 8 of her 1800 poems were published during her lifetime.

PRE-READING: CHALLENGING VOCABULARY

Create two sentences using the word 'diadem' that show you understand what it means.

Definition:
a type of crown-like, ornamental headband, usually worn by royalty

Diadem

Synonyms:
crown, tiara, coronet

Example:
The royal guest wore a stunning diadem to the ceremony.

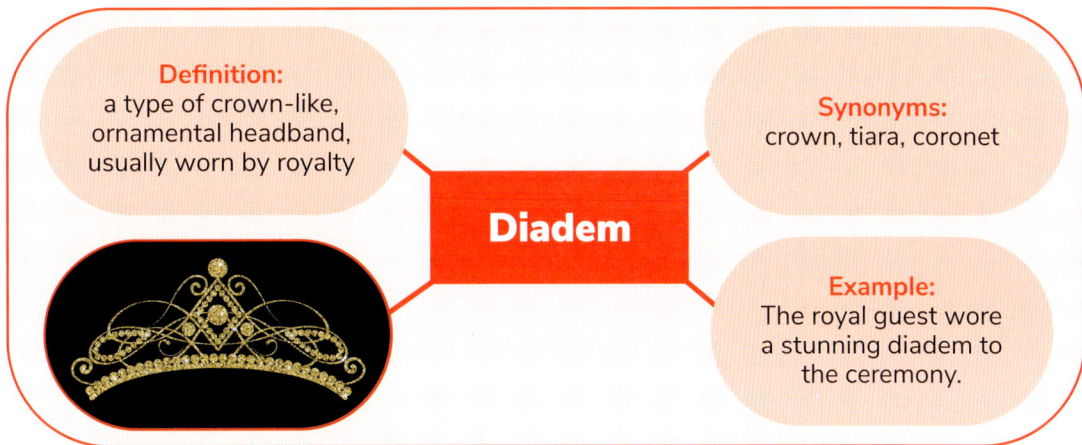

'The Sky is low – the Clouds are mean' by Emily Dickinson

The Sky is low – the Clouds are mean.
A Travelling Flake of Snow
Across a Barn or through a Rut
Debates if it will go –

A Narrow Wind complains all Day
How some one treated him
Nature, like Us, is sometimes caught
Without her Diadem.

READING

1 Describe the scene the poet is looking out at in one sentence.

2 Who is the speaker in the poem?

3 What is the subject of the poem?

4 Complete the inference jigsaw task in your activity book (see page 50).

5 Complete the personification task in your activity book (see page 51).

6 Can you remember a time when you experienced the same mood as in this poem?

7 Do you think the poet has used any words in the poem that are unnecessary? Which ones? Explain your choice.

8 The poet uses two commas in the lines below. What is the purpose of the commas placed where they are?

> Nature, like Us, is sometimes caught
> Without her Diadem.

9 Does this poem remind you of any other poem you have studied? In what way?

💬 COMMUNICATING

🌐 1 Listen to a reading of the poem: edco.ie/mm73
Complete the personal response grid in your activity book (see page 52).
Then divide into small groups and share your ideas.

✏️ 2 Create a dramatic performance of this poem. Think about which words
should be emphasised, what tone of voice you should speak in and what
kind of sound effects or backing music you might play in the background.

✏️ WRITING

Imagine you are looking out of your window and this picture is what you
see. Write a paragraph describing the weather in this picture.

Writing Tips

● Begin by listing all the
things you can see in
the picture.

● Try to think of any
adjectives you could use to
describe these things.

● Aim to use at least one
example of personification,
metaphor or simile to
describe what you see in
the picture.

'Daffodils' by William Wordsworth

💬 PRE-READING: COMMUNICATING

🌐 1 Watch these three versions of the poem:

edco.ie/ku7t   edco.ie/6c5z   edco.ie/b4yg

2 Then share your thoughts with your partner.

3 Which was your favourite poem reading and why?

All about 'Daffodils'

William Wordsworth (1770–1850) lived most of his early life in the natural paradise of the Lake District in England. His poetry expresses his deep love of nature and nature's healing effect on the soul. Wordsworth wrote this poem after taking a walk with his sister in the Lake District.

'Daffodils' by William Wordsworth

I wandered lonely as a cloud
That floats on high o'er vales and hills,
When all at once I saw a crowd,
A host, of golden daffodils;
Beside the lake, beneath the trees,
Fluttering and dancing in the breeze.

Continuous as the stars that shine
And twinkle on the milky way,
They stretched in never-ending line
Along the margin of a bay:
Ten thousand saw I at a glance,
Tossing their heads in sprightly dance.

The waves beside them danced; but they
Out-did the sparkling waves in glee:
A poet could not but be gay,
In such a jocund company:
I gazed—and gazed—but little thought
What wealth the show to me had brought:

For oft, when on my couch I lie
In vacant or in pensive mood,
They flash upon that inward eye
Which is the bliss of solitude;
And then my heart with pleasure fills,
And dances with the daffodils.

READING

ACTIVITY

1 Choose the two most important words from each stanza.

2 Describe the speaker in this poem.

3 Complete the mood task in your activity book (see page 53).

4 Complete the challenging vocabulary task in your activity book (see pages 54–55).

5 Complete the personification task in your activity book (see page 56) and answer the question that follows.

6 Complete the inference task in your activity book (see page 57) and answer the question that follows.

7 Did you like or dislike the poem? Explain why.

8 This poem was written in 1804, and some of the language used has gone out of fashion. List the words you feel are old-fashioned and suggest a modern version of each word that could be used instead.

9 Look at the line below.

> I gazed—and gazed—but little thought

Name the punctuation mark that is used here. What is the purpose of this punctuation mark? What effect does it have on the reader?

10 Does this poem remind you in any way of any other text you have studied?

WRITING

Which of these pictures of scenery do you like best and why? Can you remember a time when you were blown away by the beauty of nature?

Think back to a place of outstanding natural beauty that you have visited or choose one of the pictures above. Write a narrative paragraph that describes your actual or imaginary experience of that natural scenery.

Writing Tips

- Try using at least one example of a simile, a metaphor or personification.
- Aim to use some interesting descriptive adjectives.
- Add a variety of punctuation marks to add meaning to your paragraph. For example: –, ! and …

How A Poem Sounds

Hundreds of years ago, before people wrote down poems in books, they were recited or performed. Therefore, how a poem sounds has always been very important. There are a number of language techniques a poet can use to make their poem sound good, such as alliteration, assonance and onomatopoeia.

What is alliteration?

Alliteration is repeating the same letter or sound at the beginning of closely connected words.

Etymology

The word 'alliteration' comes from Latin and means 'to add on a letter'.

Examples

She sells sea shells on the sea shore	'From forth the fatal loins of these two foes…' (from *Romeo and Juliet* by William Shakespeare)	While I nodded, nearly napping, suddenly there came a tapping…' (from 'The Raven' by Edgar Allen Poe)

S

She **s**ells **s**ea **s**hells on the **s**ea **s**hore

F

From **f**orth the **f**atal loins of these two **f**oes…

N

While I **n**odded, **n**early **n**apping…

What is assonance?

Assonance is repeating similar vowel sounds in a series of words or phrases.

Etymology

The word 'assonance' comes from French and means 'to respond to sound'.

Examples

'The rain in Spain falls mainly on the plain' (from *My Fair Lady*)	Take the gun and have fun	Try as I might, the kite did not fly

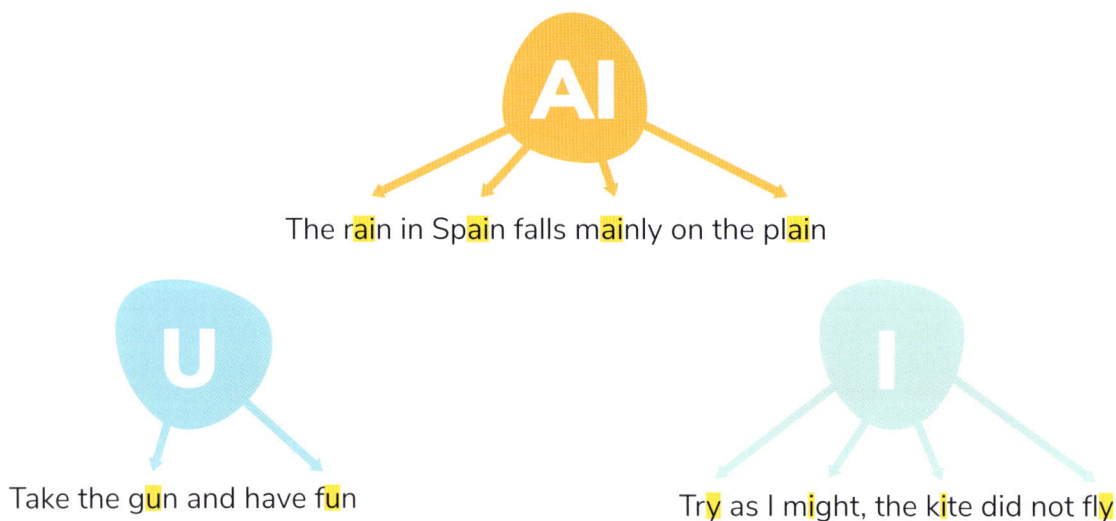

AI

The r**ai**n in Sp**ai**n falls m**ai**nly on the pl**ai**n

U

Take the g**u**n and have f**u**n

I

Tr**y** as I m**i**ght, the k**i**te did not fl**y**

What is onomatopoeia?

Onomatopoeia is when a word sounds like what it describes.

Etymology

The word 'onomatopoeia' comes from Greek and means 'name-making'.

Examples

'How they clang, and clash and roar!' (from 'The Bells' by Edgar Allen Poe)	'Small feet were pattering, wooden shoes clattering' (from 'The Pied Piper of Hamelin' by Robert Browning)	'Water plops into pond Splish-splash downhill' (from 'Running Water' by Lee Emmett)

How they **clang**, and **clash** and **roar**!

Small feet were **pattering**, wooden shoes **clattering**

Water **plops** into pond, **Splish-splash** downhill

READING

Look at the poem below, which makes good use of alliteration, assonance and onomatopoeia. Then answer the questions that follow.

'My Puppy Punched Me In the Eye' by Kenn Nesbitt

My puppy punched me in the eye.
My rabbit whacked my ear.
My ferret gave a frightful cry
and roundhouse kicked my rear.

My lizard flipped me upside down.
My kitten kicked my head.
My hamster slammed me to the ground
and left me nearly dead.

So my advice? Avoid regrets;
no matter what you do,
don't ever let your family pets
take lessons in kung fu.

1 Pick out and list all of the examples of alliteration in this poem.
2 Pick out and list all of the examples of assonance in this poem.
3 Pick out and list all of the examples of onomatopoeia in this poem.
4 Go to page 58 of your activity book and complete the task to increase your understanding of alliteration, assonance and onomatopoeia.

WRITING: ONOMATOPOEIA

Below is an extract from an onomatopoeia poem you may be familiar with from primary school. This poem appeals to a reader's sense of sound.

> ### From 'On the Ning Nang Nong' by Spike Milligan
>
> So it's Ning Nang Nong   Trees go ping!
> Cows go Bong!   Nong Ning Nang
> Nong Nang Ning   The mice go Clang!

Inspired by this poem, write your own five-line onomatopoeia poem that uses words that imitate sounds and that is a pleasure to read out loud.

Writing Tips

- Choose a topic for your poem (make sure the topic is rich in sound).
- List the sounds associated with your chosen topic and pick out the ones that are onomatopoeic.
- Here are some suggestions to help you:
  - Machine noises: honk, beep, vroom, clang, zap, boing
  - Animal names: cuckoo, whip-poor-will, whooping crane, chickadee
  - Impact sounds: boom, crash, whack, thump, bang
  - Voice sounds: giggle, growl, whine, murmur, blurt, whisper, hiss
  - Nature sounds: splash, drip, spray, whoosh, buzz, rustle.

WRITING: ALLITERATION

Write out the numbers one to five at the start of each line. Each word that follows in the line must begin with the same letter as the first letter of the number. Each number must be followed by an adjective, then a noun, then a verb, then a noun. Here is an example about animals:

> One over-anxious ox opening oranges
> Two timid tortoises taking torches
> Three thriving tarantulas tasting tea
> Four fierce fish fighting for freedom
> Five fearless flamingos following feathers

Below are some suggested topics, or you can choose your own.

| in the library | in the supermarket | under the floorboards |
| in the ocean | under my bed | in the haunted house |

Poetry Notes

Video

Making poetry notes is a reading strategy where you collect information on a topic and summarise the key points. Creating and organising your own notes can help you make sense of a poem and can also help you to remember and recall the details of the text.

Why create poetry notes?

One of the most effective ways of getting new information to stick in your head is by making and organising your own notes. Both the act of selecting what you will write and the act of writing down help you to process the new information, help your brain make sense of it as you absorb it and also help you remember it in the future. It is useful to revisit your own notes on a topic when you are studying for an exam.

Keep in mind the purpose of your poetry notes. You are making the notes to understand how a poet's writing choices impact the poem, which in turn impact the reader. Cut the information down to only the most essential elements: key words, key quotes and key techniques.

The layout of your notes should reflect your purpose. You could use the poetry organisers in your activity book (see pages 60, 64 and 66 for examples) to help you with the layout. Remember, a poet inputs their writing choices into a poem and the output is the impact on the reader.

Poet's writing choices
- Structure
- Speaker
- Rhythm
- Rhyme
- Personification
- Metaphor
- Simile
- Onomatopoeia
- Alliteration
- Assonance
- Tone

The poem
- The poet
- Summary

Effect on the reader
- Theme/message/lesson
- Connections to other texts
- Personal connection
- Mood

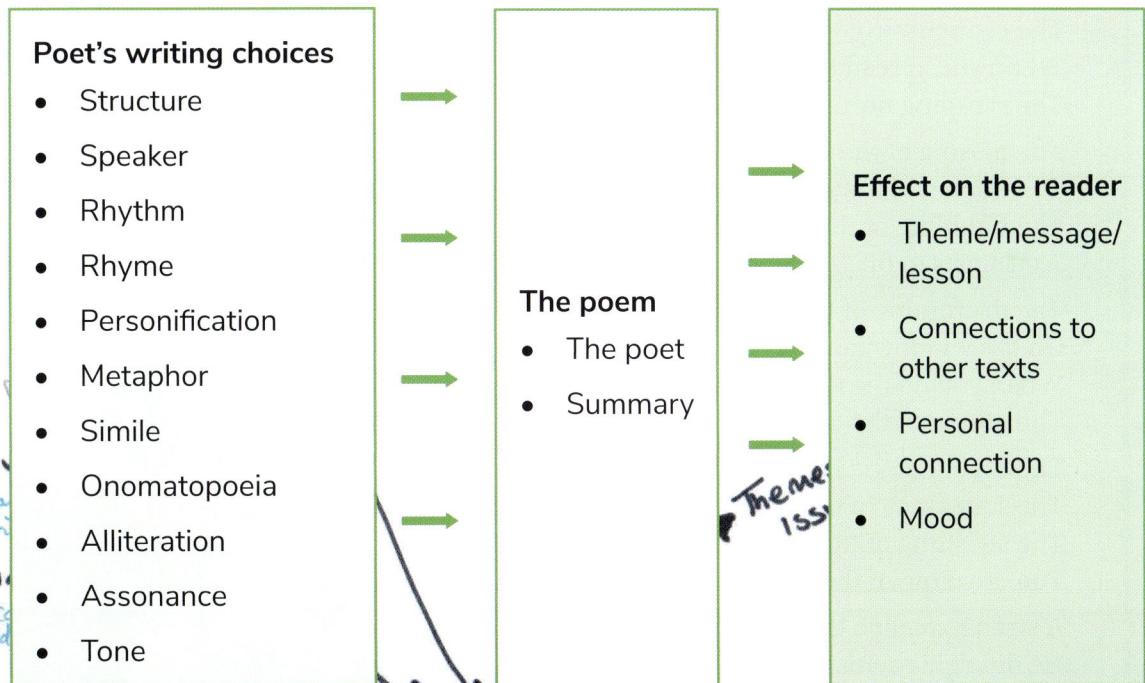

'The Sound Collector' by Roger McGough

All about 'The Sound Collector'

Roger McGough is a well-known and much-loved poet, playwright and author. He has written over fifty books of poetry. You may have come across his poems in primary school. This particular poem highlights the joy of everyday sounds around the house.

The Sound Collector

A stranger called this morning
Dressed all in black and grey
Put every sound into a bag
And carried them away

The whistling of the kettle
The turning of the lock
The purring of the kitten
The ticking of the clock

The popping of the toaster
The crunching of the flakes
When you spread the marmalade
The scraping noise it makes

The hissing of the frying pan
The ticking of the grill
The bubbling of the bathtub
As it starts to fill

The drumming of the raindrops
On the windowpane
When you do the washing-up
The gurgle of the drain

The crying of the baby
The squeaking of the chair
The swishing of the curtain
The creaking of the stair

A stranger called this morning
He didn't leave his name
Left us only silence
Life will never be the same

READING

1 Summarise the poem in the form of a short newspaper headline.

2 What time of the day did the sound collector call?

3 Why did the poet choose to dress the sound collector in black and grey?

4 Did you like the poem? Why? Why not?

5 List the onomatopoeic words in this poem. Which use of onomatopoeia is your favourite in the poem and why?

6 Why do you think the poet chose to have no punctuation in this poem?

7 Edit the poem by adding a descriptive adjective before the nouns at the end of each sentence in the lines below. The first one is completed as an example for you.

> The gurgle of the <u>hungry</u> drain
> The crying of the baby
> The squeaking of the chair
> The swishing of the curtain
> The creaking of the stair

8 Is this poem similar in any way to any other text you have studied?

9 Practise making poetry notes by creating a set of notes for this poem in your activity book (see page 60).

COMMUNICATING

1 If you had to be deprived of one of your senses for a week, which sense would you choose and why?

2 If you could have one super sense, what would it be and why?

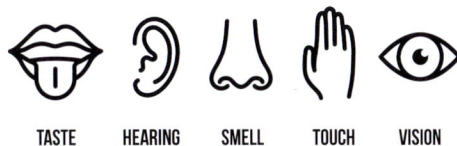

TASTE   HEARING   SMELL   TOUCH   VISION

3 Listen to a reading of this poem: edco.ie/ds2e

After listening, complete the response quad in your activity book (see page 61). Then share your thoughts with your partner.

4 Create and perform a dramatic version of this poem as a small group. You could use many different elements of performance, such as costume, lighting and props. However, the most important element of this poem's performance should be the sound. You could use instruments, household objects, a sound effects app or the voices of those in your group to create the sounds in the poem, for example: whistling, scraping and ticking.

WRITING

Write a poem entitled 'The Taste Collector', where a mysterious stranger calls to your house and collects and takes away all the tastes in your house.

Writing Tips

- Begin by brainstorming all of the possible things in your house that have a taste, for example: toothpaste, oranges, tea.
- You could start your poem with the same line as in 'The Sound Collector' and end your poem with the same line.

'Base Details' by Siegfried Sassoon

PRE-READING: DIARY EXTRACT

Read this first-hand account of a soldier fighting in the trenches during the First World War.

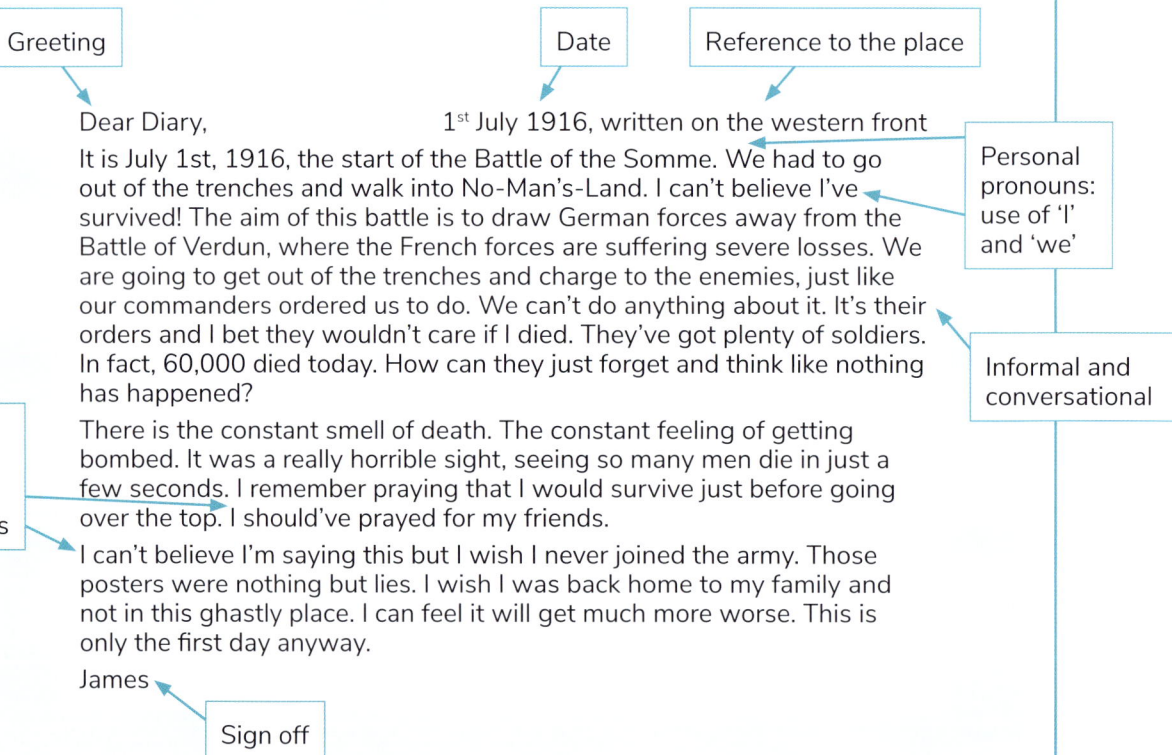

| Greeting | Date | Reference to the place |

Dear Diary,   1st July 1916, written on the western front

It is July 1st, 1916, the start of the Battle of the Somme. We had to go out of the trenches and walk into No-Man's-Land. I can't believe I've survived! The aim of this battle is to draw German forces away from the Battle of Verdun, where the French forces are suffering severe losses. We are going to get out of the trenches and charge to the enemies, just like our commanders ordered us to do. We can't do anything about it. It's their orders and I bet they wouldn't care if I died. They've got plenty of soldiers. In fact, 60,000 died today. How can they just forget and think like nothing has happened?

Personal pronouns: use of 'I' and 'we'

Informal and conversational

Expresses innermost thoughts and feelings

There is the constant smell of death. The constant feeling of getting bombed. It was a really horrible sight, seeing so many men die in just a few seconds. I remember praying that I would survive just before going over the top. I should've prayed for my friends.

I can't believe I'm saying this but I wish I never joined the army. Those posters were nothing but lies. I wish I was back home to my family and not in this ghastly place. I can feel it will get much more worse. This is only the first day anyway.

James

Sign off

1 How does the soldier feel about his commanders?
2 Why does the soldier feel powerless?
3 Does the soldier regret joining the army?
4 List three features of this piece of writing that lets you know it is a diary entry.

PRE-READING: CHALLENGING VOCABULARY

Write two sentences using the word 'petulant' that show you understand the word.

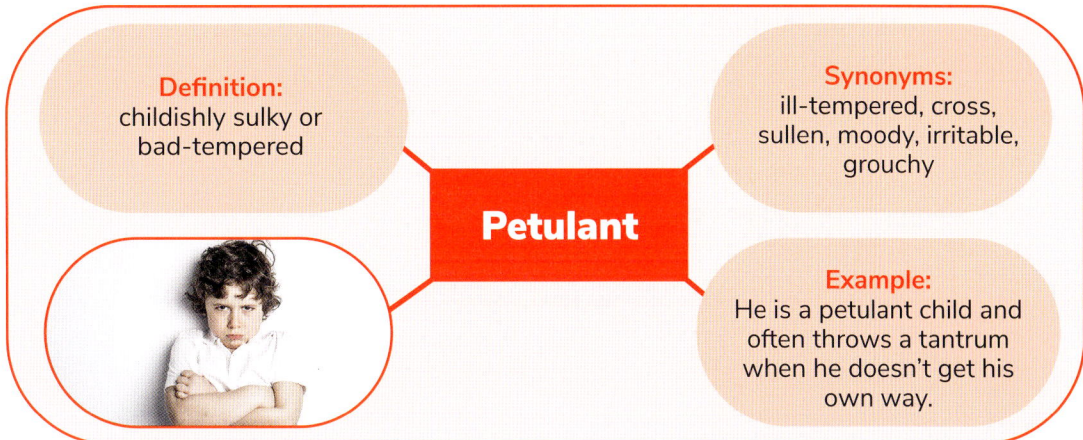

Definition:
childishly sulky or
bad-tempered

Petulant

Synonyms:
ill-tempered, cross,
sullen, moody, irritable,
grouchy

Example:
He is a petulant child and
often throws a tantrum
when he doesn't get his
own way.

PRE-READING: COMMUNICATING

1 Watch a reading of this poem: edco.ie/8er5
  Then watch it again.

2 When you have watched the performance twice, complete the personal
  response quad in your activity book (see page 61).

3 Then, share your thoughts and ideas with your partner.

4 Think about how you would make a video of this poem.

  • Who would you cast as the actor reading the poem?

  • How would you design the set?

  • What props would you use?

  • What sound effects would you use?

All about 'Base Details'

Siegfried Sassoon was an English gentleman and a poet. He served in the
English army during the First World War and saw first-hand the horrors and
grim realities of war. He was renowned for his bravery on the battlefield and
won a number of awards through his service. However, following a time of
recovery from illness back in England, Sassoon refused to return to the front and
was sent to a military hospital to recover from what the army referred to as his
mental-health difficulties.

'Base Details' by Siegfried Sassoon

If I were fierce, and bald, and short of breath
I'd live with scarlet Majors at the Base,
And speed glum heroes up the line to death.
You'd see me with my puffy petulant face,
Guzzling and gulping in the best hotel,
Reading the Roll of Honour. 'Poor young chap,'
I'd say – 'I used to know his father well;
Yes, we've lost heavily in this last scrap.'
And when the war is done and youth stone dead,
I'd toddle safely home and die – in bed.

READING

1   Who is the speaker in this poem?

2   List the adjectives used to describe the Majors and the ordinary soldiers. How do you think the poet feels about the Majors? And how does he feel about the soldiers?

3   List the uses of alliteration in the poem. Read them again out loud. What emotion, do you think, is the poet trying to get across to the reader through these uses of alliteration?

4   Complete the quote quest task in your activity book (see page 62) and answer the questions that follow.

5   Why did the poet choose the word 'petulant' to describe the Major?

6   How does the poet want the reader to feel by the end of the poem?

7   Speech marks are used within the poem to indicate when the Majors are speaking.

> …'Poor young chap,'
> I'd say – 'I used to know his father well;
> Yes, we've lost heavily in this last scrap.'

Why do you think the poet chose to do this? Is it an effective use of punctuation?

8   Does this poem link with any film, TV show or computer game you have seen?

9   Create a set of poetry notes on this poem in your activity book (see page 64).

WRITING

Write a diary entry from the perspective of a high-ranking commanding officer during the First World War. In the diary entry you should talk about your duties and the men under your command. You should adopt the same tone and attitude of the Major described in the poem.

Writing Tips

- Look at the example of a diary entry on page 98 to ensure you use all the correct features of a diary entry.
- Keeping in mind what you have learned from the poem, make sure your diary entry has the tone and displays the behaviour of the Major described in the poem.

'The Eagle' by Alfred, Lord Tennyson

PRE-READING: CHALLENGING VOCABULARY

Make a list of all of the things you can think of that are azure in colour.

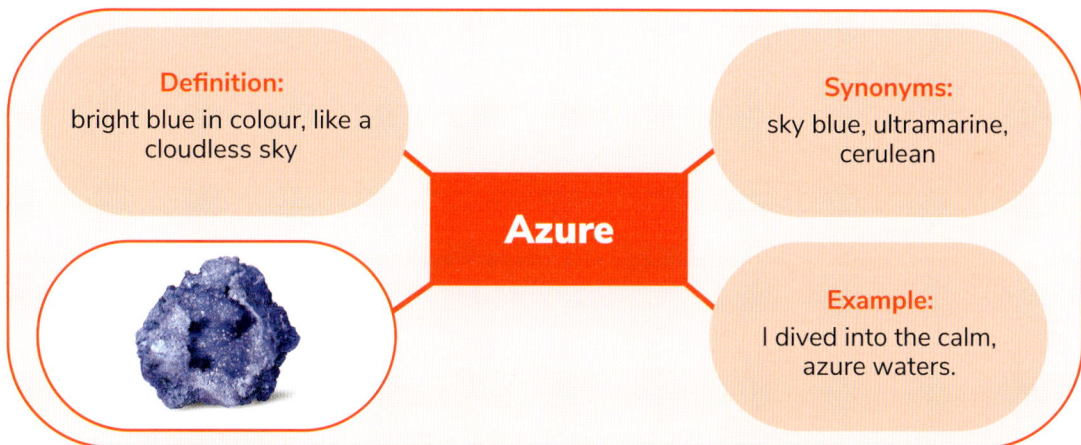

Definition:
bright blue in colour, like a cloudless sky

Synonyms:
sky blue, ultramarine, cerulean

Azure

Example:
I dived into the calm, azure waters.

All about 'The Eagle'

Alfred, Lord Tennyson was an English poet who lived in the nineteenth century. Tennyson was born into a middle-class family and was the first author to be honoured with a peerage, the title of Lord, for his writing abilities.

'The Eagle' by Alfred, Lord Tennyson

He clasps the crag with crooked hands;
Close to the sun in lonely lands,
Ring'd with the azure world, he stands.

The wrinkled sea beneath him crawls;
He watches from his mountain walls,
And like a thunderbolt he falls.

READING

1   Summarise the poem in six words. The words do not have to make a sentence.

2   What perspective is the poem written from? Explain how you know this.

3   Go to your activity book (see page 65) to practise annotating this poem.

4   Using your inference skills (see page 83), what do you think a crag is?

5   If you were to edit this poem and replace the word 'azure', what word would you replace it with and why?

6   The poet uses a semi-colon twice in the poem. What is a semi-colon? Explain why you think the poet chose to use this punctuation?

7   How do you think the poet wants you to feel about the eagle? How do you know this?

8   What does the poet compare the eagle to in the last line of the poem? Is it an effective comparison? Explain why.

9   Create a set of notes for this poem in your activity book (see page 66).

COMMUNICATING

1   Watch a performance of the poem: edco.ie/7xrt

2   An actor's performance can change based on the tone they use and the purpose of their performance. Prepare your own dramatic performance of this poem. Begin by choosing a purpose and then match that to a suitable tone. Then perform the poem. You could choose from the purposes below or select your own.

Purpose		
A voice-over for a...		
nature documentary	horror movie	superhero movie

You could choose from the tones below or select your own.

Tones		
amazed and in awe	unsettling and cold	extremely enthusiastic

WRITING

Walk on the Wild Side is a TV show that combines animal documentary and comedy. The show is comprised of short clips taken from animal documentaries with comedians doing voice-overs for the animals, thereby making the animals seem human, for comedic effect.

Write the voice-over script for a short scene for your own comedy nature documentary. Watch the humorous examples from *Walk on the Wild Side* for inspiration: edco.ie/n8y8

Writing Tips

- Find a short clip online of an animal doing something interesting and note down the animal's actions.

- Before you write the script of the voice-over, think about how you could make the animal's actions seem human. What are you reminded of?

PROJECT:
Perform A Rap

PROJECT BRIEF

Create your own group choral reading performance of the rap 'Alphabet Aerobics'.

To be successful in this piece of writing, you will need to:

- communicate clearly and confidently, and with fluency
- show clear awareness that the purpose of the performance is to entertain the audience
- sustain the performance throughout to a high standard
- make conscious choices about the staging and production of your performance.

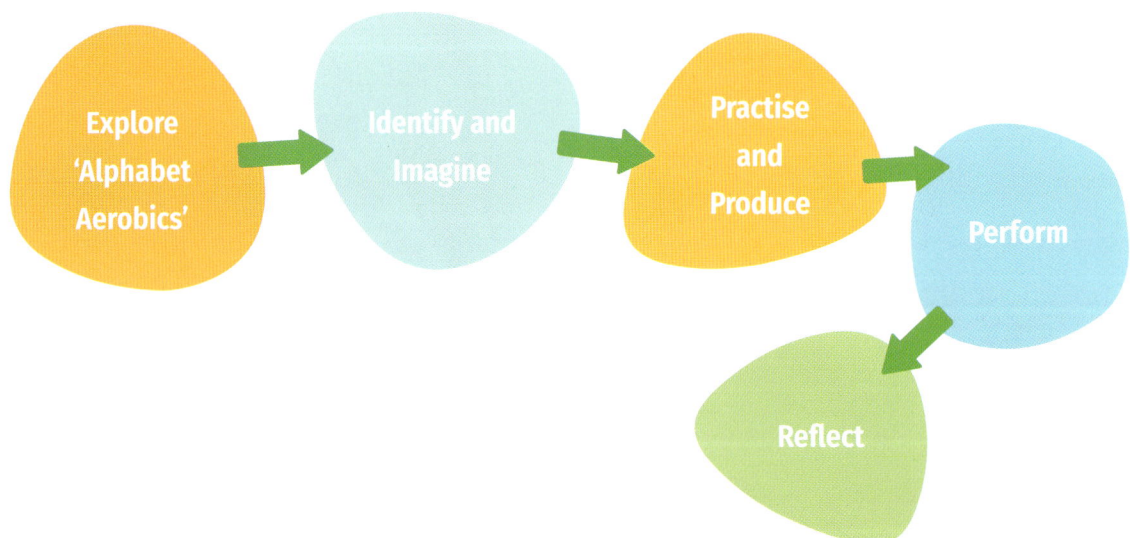

Explore 'Alphabet Aerobics' → Identify and Imagine → Practise and Produce → Perform → Reflect

COMMUNICATING: GROUP DISCUSSION

Watch Daniel Radcliffe perform 'Alphabet Aerobics' on America's *Tonight Show Starring Jimmy Fallon*: edco.ie/v4ah

Then discuss the questions below.

1 Did you like it? Why? Why not?
2 Is there anything surprising about this performance?
3 Do you think this is poetry? Why? Why not?
4 What's the message of the song?

'Alphabet Aerobics' by Blackalicious

Artificial amateurs aren't at all amazing
Analytically, I assault, animate things
Broken barriers bounded by the bomb beat
Buildings are broken, basically I'm bombarding
Casually create catastrophes, casualties
Cancelling cats got their canopies collapsing
Detonate a dime of dank daily doing dough
Demonstrations, Don Dada on the down low
Eating other editors with each and every energetic
Epileptic episode, elevated etiquette
Furious fat fabulous fantastic
Flurries of funk felt feeding the fanatics
Gift got great global goods gone glorious
Getting godly in his game with the goriest
Hit 'em high, hella hype, historical
Hey holocaust hints hear 'em holler at your homeboy
Imitators idolize, I intimidate
In an instant, I'll rise in an irate state
Juiced on my jams like Jheri curls jocking joints
Justly, it's just me, writing my journals
Kindly I'm kindling all kinds of ink on
Karate kick type Brits in my kingdom
Let me live a long life, lyrically lessons is
Learned lame louses just lose to my livery
My mind makes marvellous moves, masses
Marvel and move, many mock what I've mastered
Nickles nap knowing I'm nice naturally
Knack, never lack, make noise nationally
Operation, opposition, off not optional
Out of sight, out of mind, wide beaming opticals
Perfected poem, powerful punchlines
Pummelling petty powder puffs in my prime
Quite quaint quotes keep quiet it's Quantum
Quarrellers ain't got a quarter of what we got uh
Really raw raps, rising up rapidly
Riding the rushing radioactivity
Super scientific sound search sought
Silencing super fire saps that are soft
Tales ten times talented, too tough
Take that, challengers, get a tune up
Universal, unique untouched
Unadulterated, the raw uncut
Verb vice lord victorious valid
Violate vibes that are vain make 'em vanish
While I'm all well what a wise wordsmith just
Weaving up words, weeded up on my work shift
Xerox, my X-radiation holes extra large
X-height letters, and xylophone tones
Yellow-back, yak mouth, young ones' yaws
Yesterday's lawn yard sell our yawn
Zig-Zag zombies, zooming to the zenith
Zero in Zen thoughts, overzealous rhyme ZEALOTS!

Identify And Imagine

To develop a deeper understanding of the sense and the rhythm of 'Alphabet Aerobics', go to the writing frame in your activity book (see pages 67–68). As a group, discuss and collaborate to create your own alphabet rap, carefully choosing words and phrases for each letter to create lines that fit with the general beat of the original piece. Make sure you choose a good variety of verbs, nouns and adjectives to make your rap entertaining and interesting. Use a dictionary, thesaurus and rhyme dictionary to help you explore new and challenging vocabulary.

Practise And Produce

Use the performance planner in your activity book (see page 69) to help your group decide how you will perform 'Alphabet Aerobics'.

- This is a choral reading, which means that everyone must contribute in some way to the performance. Perhaps you will divide it up line by line, with everyone saying the last line together. Perhaps one person will say all the nouns and someone else all the verbs. Perhaps you will swap over every time it changes to another letter. It is up to you to make these choices.

- You do not have to perform all of the song; maybe you only want to do the first half or the last half. Remember, every choice you make will affect the overall performance in some way.

- Your main aim here is to stick with the rhythm of the song. Remember it gets faster and faster as the song goes on. If you like, play the karaoke version in the background of your performance to help you keep the rhythm: edco.ie/63tr

- Think about the visual aspect of your performance. Maybe you want to make letter signs and hold them up as you go through each letter, like in the video of Daniel Radcliffe that you watched. Maybe you want to place your group members on different sides of the room to give the impression you are playing tennis with your words.

- Practise, practise, practise. Rapping is hard – especially a song with such a quick rhythm. Knowing your lines really well will improve your performance.

Performance

- Take turns performing as a group.
- You can use the karaoke version of 'Alphabet Aerobics' as a backing track to keep the rhythm of the song: edco.ie/63tr
- Respect each other's performance by listening quietly.

REFLECTION

1 How did your group performance go?
2 Is there anything you would change about your group performance?
3 What were you impressed by in the other performances?
4 What did other groups do particularly well?

PROJECT:
The Poet's Toolbox

💡 PROJECT BRIEF

Create a visually appealing and informative booklet for aspiring teenage poets that outlines and explains a variety of poetic techniques, exploring the etymology (the history of a word or where the word comes from), morphology (the way a word is put together or structured) and definitions of simile, metaphor, personification, rhythm, rhyme, alliteration, assonance and onomatopoeia.

To be successful in this piece of writing, you will need to:

- be clear, informative and instructive in your explanation of the poetic techniques
- show awareness of your teenage audience through carefully chosen examples
- ensure your leaflet is visually appealing and clearly laid out.

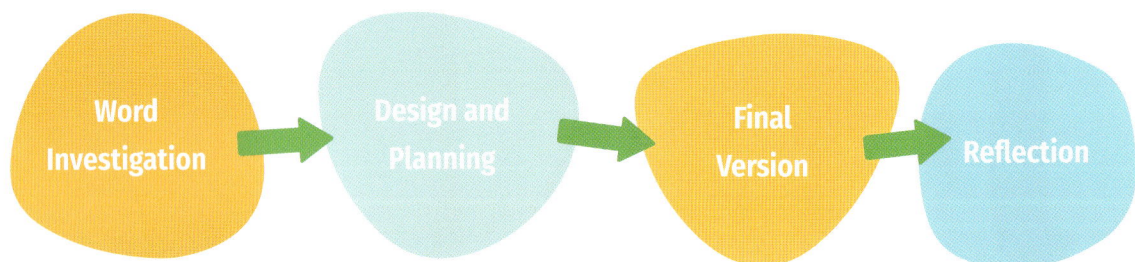

Word Investigation → **Design and Planning** → **Final Version** → **Reflection**

Word Investigation

In order to understand a new challenging word fully and to remember it, it is best to explore that word in a variety of different ways. This increases your chances of understanding it and recalling it down the road. Choose four ways to explore each word from the box opposite. There are a number of online resources you could use to help you:

- www.etymonline.com
- www.thesaurus.com
- www.dictionary.com

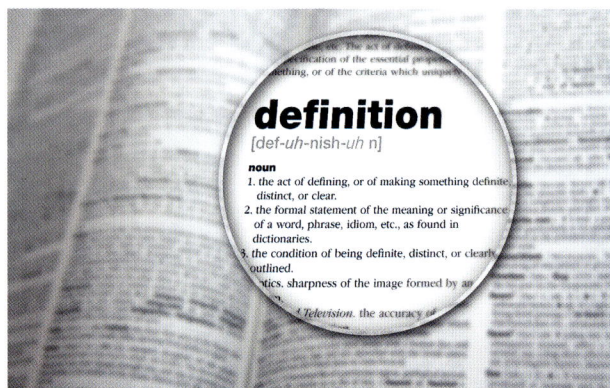

definition
[def-*uh*-nish-*uh* n]

noun
1. the act of defining, or of making something definite, distinct, or clear.
2. the formal statement of the meaning or significance of a word, phrase, idiom, etc., as found in dictionaries.
3. the condition of being definite, distinct, or clearly outlined.
   ...tics. sharpness of the image formed by an...
   Television. the accuracy of...

Word map: Does the word form part of any other words?

Definition: The meaning of the word in your own words.

Antonym: A word with the opposite meaning of the word.

Morphology: Each word can be broken down into parts – prefix, root and suffix.

Synonym: A word that means the same thing.

Draw it: Draw your understanding of the word.

Etymology: What is the history of the word? Where does it come from?

Sentence: Put the word in a sentence that shows you understand it.

Word class: Is it a noun, a verb, an adverb, an adjective?

You can use the word exploration grids in your activity book (see pages 70–71) to record your findings.

Design And Plan It

You need to plan how you will lay out your information, while keeping your teenage audience in mind. This should be an instructional text, which is a text that aims to teach its reader something.

- The language you use needs to be simple and clear.
- Your sentences should be short and simple, and each point should be summarised neatly.
- The layout must be clear and easy to understand, with headings and subheadings to help navigate the text.
- Only use images that will help your audience understand your instructional guide better.
- Remember your target audience here is teenagers, so the tone can be informal and humorous.

Final Version

Now it's time to create your booklet! You can do this on paper or on your computer. Word has a number of information leaflet templates that you might like or you can use PowerPoint and design the layout yourself. Visit thenounproject.com or flaticon.com to choose icons to help explain your poetic techniques. The most important thing to remember is that your layout should be clear and visually appealing.

REFLECTION

1 What three things did you learn from doing this project?
2 Do you think exploring a word in a variety of different ways has made it stick more easily in your memory?
3 Is there anything you feel you could add to improve your booklet?
4 Would you use this toolbox yourself when writing your own poetry?

PROJECT:
Spoken Word Poetry

What Is Spoken Word Poetry?

Spoken word poetry, or performance poetry, is poetry that is intended to be performed. It combines elements of traditional poetry, hip-hop, rap, storytelling and theatre. A live performance of one of these poems can stay with you long after it is over. Performance poetry usually deals with topics such as social issues, politics, class, race and community.

In Ireland, we have a proud tradition of poetry, from our ancient seanchaí to our present-day poets. We are respected around the world for our brilliant poets through the generations. We also now have a great tradition of spoken word poetry. In this project, you will watch and appreciate some of the stars of the Irish spoken-word scene and have a go at writing and performing some spoken word poetry yourself.

PROJECT BRIEF

Experience and appreciate the genre of spoken word poetry. Using the examples as a stimulus, create and perform some spoken word poetry about an issue or topic you are passionate about.

To be successful in this piece of writing, you will need to:

- show appreciation for spoken word poetry through thoughtful group discussion
- create a thought-provoking spoken word poem using a variety of poetic techniques
- perform your spoken word poem clearly, with confidence and fluency.

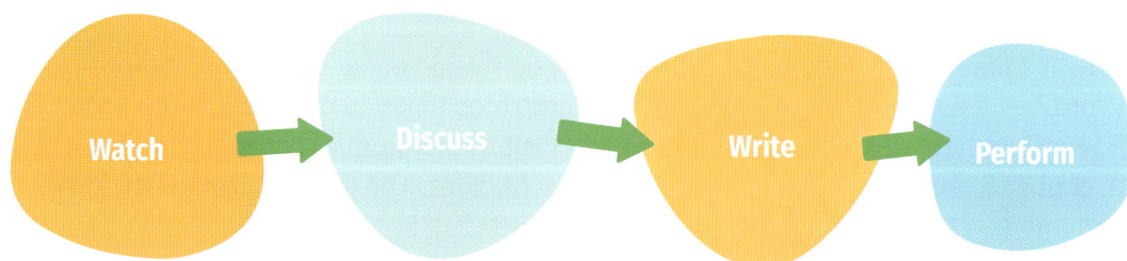

Watch → **Discuss** → **Write** → **Perform**

Watching Spoken Word Poetry

Watch the video performances of some spoken word poetry:

- 'Not Like Other Girls' by Natalya O'Flaherty edco.ie/p8y2
- 'My Ireland' by Stephen James Smith edco.ie/63qq
- 'Still' by Felispeaks aka Felicia Olusanya edco.ie/9mb4

1 What did you think were the messages behind each of these poems?
2 How did you feel after watching each of these performances? What mood were you left in?
3 Do you like the effect of combining the visual images and the spoken word poetry? Why? Why not?
4 Which was your favourite performance and why?

Writing Performance Poetry

1 **Choose a topic:** think of something you feel passionately about. This could be a social issue like homelessness, child poverty, climate change, social media or racism. It could also be something from your own life experience – maybe a person who influenced you growing up or something you've always been afraid of. If you like, you could use one of the poems you have watched as a source of inspiration – maybe you would like to write about your Ireland.

2 **Write the gateway line:** this is your poem's main idea. It lets the audience know what you're going to be talking about. While your first line prepares viewers for your subject matter, the rest of the poem should be spent reinforcing, supporting and expanding on that initial idea. Listen to the poems again to see how those poets develop their poems from their initial idea.

3 **Use repetition:** use your gateway line throughout the poem. Think of it as a chorus line in a song – something you keep returning to in order to emphasise the message of your poem.

4 **Paint with words:** try to use similes, metaphors and personification to paint a picture for your audience. These are good techniques to use to allow your audience to experience what you are experiencing.

5 **Sound:** think about the fact that a spoken word poem is supposed to be performed. That means that the sound of the poem is very important. You could try using alliteration, assonance or onomatopoeia to make your poem sound good.

6 **Free verse:** a spoken word poem does not need to stick to the strict structures or rhyme schemes of traditional poems. It should flow from one idea to the next as if you are telling a story.

Perform Your Poem

If you are feeling brave enough, you could perform your poem. You could do this in one of two ways: perform it live for your class or create a video of your performance, like the examples you have watched.

Test Your Knowledge

1 **The subject of the poem is ...**

a) The person who wrote the poem

b) The person, place, thing or feeling described in the poem

c) The class learning about the poem

d) The hidden meaning of the poem

2 **The tone of a poem is ...**

a) The emotion or feelings the poet puts across in their poem

b) The person who wrote the poem

c) How you feel after reading a poem

d) The way a poet uses language

3 **What is alliteration?**

a) Comparing one thing to another by using 'like' or 'as'

b) Comparing one thing to another

c) The repetition of the same vowel sound in closely connected words

d) Repeating the same letter or sound at the beginning of closely connected words

4 **'The trees whispered in the wind' is an example of which poetic technique?**

a) Metaphor

b) Personification

c) Alliteration

d) Assonance

5 **'The teapot sang as the water boiled' is an example of** ....

6 **The reader's** .... **is how the reader feels after reading the poem.**

7 **Match the poetic technique to the correct example.**

Poetic technique	Example
Alliteration	The rain in Spain falls mainly on the plain
Metaphor	Lightning danced across the sky
Personification	'Life is a broken-winged bird that cannot fly'
Assonance	'God with honour hang your head'

8 Match the poetic device to the correct definition.

Poetic device	Example
Theme	The beat of a poem
Rhythm	A comparison of one thing to another
Onomatopoeia	The idea or message behind the poem
Metaphor	A word that sounds like what it describes

9 What reading strategies might you use to understand a poem?

10 Explain a simile and give an example.

11 Explain a metaphor and give an example.

12 What is the difference between the subject of a poem and the theme of a poem?

13 Thinking back on all you have learned in this unit, try the personal dictionary task on pages 72–74 of your activity book.

Practise Your Writing Skills

1 You have been asked to choose a poem you have studied that would be good to read out loud on a radio programme. Write a short paragraph including each of the points below.

- Give the title of the poem and the name of the poet.

- Explain what your chosen poem is about.

- Why do you think your chosen poem would be good to read out loud on a radio programme? Explain your answer.

2 Choose a poem you have studied where the poet expresses a strong feeling about something they have experienced. Write a short paragraph including each of the points below.

- Give the title of the poem and the name of the poet.

- What was the poet feeling?

- Why, do you think, was the poet feeling that way?

- Do you think the poet chose a good title for their poem? Give a reason why.

- Do you like or dislike the poem you have chosen? Give a reason why.

Interactive website

Go to **www.edco.ie/touchstones1** for interactive activities based on this unit.

UNIT 3
FILM

FILM KNOWLEDGE ORGANISER

Things I need to know

- **Film genre:** a way of categorising films based on similarities of features. For example: horror, action, romantic comedy.

- **Mise-en-scène:** the arrangement of all the elements that appear on the screen to create the look of the film, including the costumes, the props, the set and the actors.

- **Colour palette:** the co-ordinated colour scheme used in costume, make-up, sets and lighting.

- **Camera angle:** the physical position of the camera when the shot is being taken.

- **Shot:** everything that goes on in a specific section of a script.

- **Film editing techniques:** what happens with the camera footage once the film has finished shooting.

- **Soundtrack:** the written music and songs that accompany a film to create a mood or atmosphere on screen.

- **Sound effects:** the sounds added during the editing process.

- **Voice-over:** when someone's voice narrates over a film.

Skills I will develop

- Understanding and using the language of film
- Understanding and appreciating the plot and characters in films
- Viewing and writing about film from a critical perspective
- Using viewing strategies to organise my ideas about films

Projects

- Film Critic: Commenting on and reviewing a movie for a film blog
- Sixty-Second Silent Movie: Planning, performing, filming and editing a silent film

What do I know?

What do you already know about film? What famous directors do you know? What is your favourite film? What is your favourite film genre?

Go to your activity book (see page 75) and complete the film knowledge download activity.

What Is Film?

PowerPoint

Film is the art of capturing stories on screen. It is an important art form, both as a source of popular entertainment, but also as a powerful medium for expressing ideas and educating people.

> I made some mistakes in drama. I thought the drama was when the actors cried. But drama is when the audience cries.
>
> **Frank Capra**

> If it's a good movie, the sound could go off and the audience would still have a pretty clear idea of what was going on.
>
> **Alfred Hitchcock**

> A film is never really good unless the camera is an eye in the head of a poet.
>
> **Khaled Hosseini**

> It's a writer's job not just to write about himself but to look at the rest of humanity and explore it – other people's way of talking, the phrases they use.
>
> **Quentin Tarantino**

Which of these quotes do you like best? Which quotes do you agree with? Are there any you disagree with?

COMMUNICATING: GROUP DISCUSSION

Divide into small groups and discuss the following questions.

1 What is your favourite film of all time?
2 Who is your favourite actor? Why?
3 What types of film do you like to watch? Why?
4 Do you enjoy going to the cinema? Why? Why not?
5 What types of film do you dislike? Why?

Introduction To Film-Making

In this chapter you will be looking at film-making techniques and exploring the film-making process, as well as learning how to view a film with a critical eye by writing a film review blog, how to appreciate a film and how to make your own film.

A film that you see in the cinema or at home on TV has gone through a long and arduous journey from the original idea to the finished film you see on the screen. The creative process of film-making moves back and forth between ideas, planning, scripting and editing in a similar way to writing a novel or poem or play.

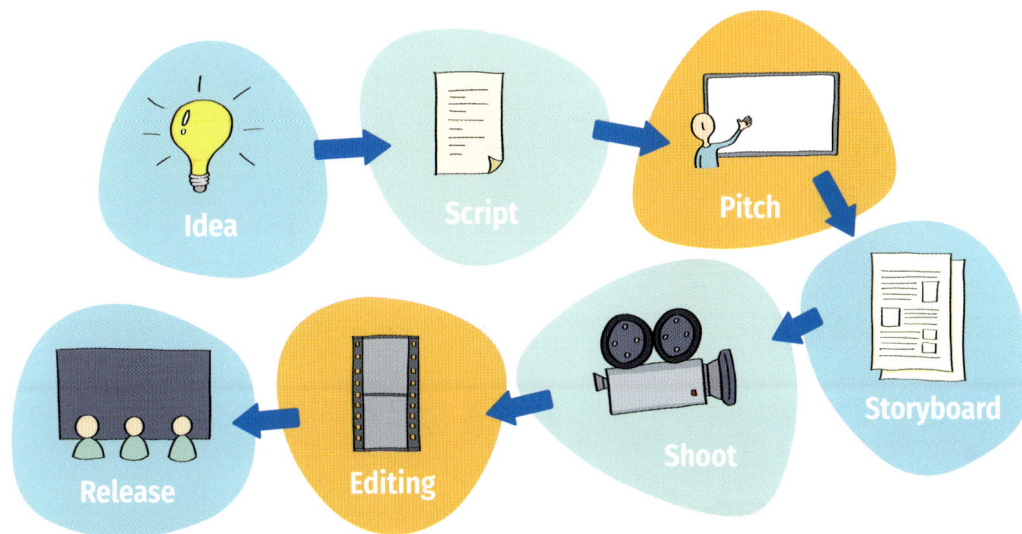

Depending on the size and budget of the film, there can be anything from 50 to 3,000 people working on a film. The record for the highest number of people working on a film is held by *Iron Man 3*, which had 3,310 people work on it throughout the creative process.

Some films also cost an extraordinary amount of money to make, with actors, special effects and crew costing millions of euros. Blockbusters such as the *Pirates of the Caribbean*, *Spider-man* and *Avengers* films can cost above 200 million euros each to make.

Film Genres

There are many different types of films, including action, comedy, romantic comedy, sci-fi, superhero, thriller, documentary and epic fantasy. These different types of films are called genres. Sometimes people have a favourite genre of film, such as horror or musical. This is similar to the way in which some people have a preference for a particular type of book, such as historical fiction or adventure.

Reading infographics

An infographic is a visual image used to represent data and information. Usually an infographic uses a minimal amount of words and a large variety of images, icons, charts and graphs to present information.

Since the beginning of cinema, there have been times when certain genres have been in and other times when they've been out of fashion. Look at the infographics on the following pages. The first three display the standard movie 'recipes' for three particular genres. The other infographic charts the rise and fall of several genres.

Spaghetti Western Movie Recipe:

Chick Flick Movie Recipe:

Alien Invasion Movie Recipe:

FILM GENRE POPULARITY 1910-2018

CLICK TO STANDARDIZE AXIS RANGE

BO MCCREADY 🐦 *@BOKNOWSDATA*

This graphic shows film genre popularity over time, represented as the percentage of all films released that year with the specified genre tagged on IMDB. Each genre has a different axis r...

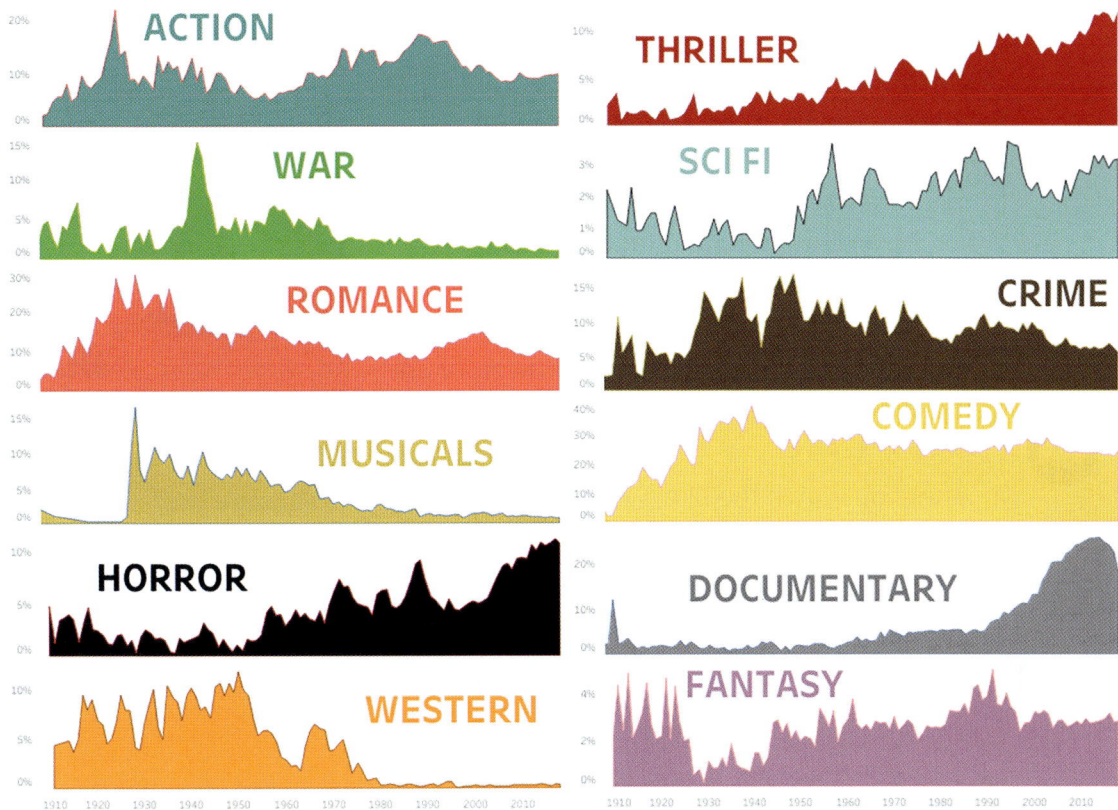

ACTION

THRILLER

WAR

SCI FI

ROMANCE

CRIME

MUSICALS

COMEDY

HORROR

DOCUMENTARY

WESTERN

FANTASY

READING

Look at the infographic above, then answer the questions below.

1 Which film genres have decreased in popularity over time?

2 Which film genres have increased in popularity over time?

3 Which film genres do you find yourself drawn to and why?

4 Are there any film genres that you dislike and would never consider watching? Why?

5 Some people watch film as a way to make sense of what's going on in their own lives. To what extent do you think this is true? Use the infographic as a source of evidence.

Look at the other infographics opposite, then answer the questions below.

6 From your own knowledge of these film genres, are there any corrections you would make to these infographics?

7 What do you notice about the punctation marks? Why are they included in the infographic?

8 In your activity book (see pages 75–76), create your own film genre infographics for a romantic comedy, a fantasy epic and an action movie. Include the four major ingredients of the genre – and don't forget the punctuation!

WRITING

New Boy is an Irish short film based on a short story by Irish writer Roddy Doyle. It was nominated for an Oscar for best short film in 2007. The film is about a young boy's experience as he moves from a rural town in Africa to Ireland. When he arrives in Ireland he has to cope with the experience of a completely different school system.

1 Watch the film to get the gist of the story and the characters:
   edco.ie/x2eu

2 After you watch the film, work with your partner or in a small group to come up with a one-line summary for the plot of the film and a sentence to describe the main character Joseph.

The Look Of A Film

Mise-en-scène

The **mise-en-scène** of a film is the arrangement of sets, props, costume, make-up and actors for a film shot – literally everything on the screen that makes up the overall look of the scene. It is important that everything within the mise-en-scène matches and complements the other elements. It would ruin the experience of watching a film if, for example, there was an iPhone in the middle of a scene from a film set in the 1800s. Film-makers use the mise-en-scène of a film to immerse an audience completely in the world of the film.

Definition:
the arrangement of all the elements that make up the look of a scene, such as costumes, make-up, props, scenery and lighting

Etymology:
from the French, meaning 'putting on stage'

Mise-en-scène

Example:
The MTV-style mise-en-scène of Baz Luhrmann's Romeo and Juliet is compelling.

Colour palette

Film-makers use a specific colour palette on the screen to help harness their storytelling capabilities. Different colours draw out different types of emotions from the audience. For example, joy and happiness could be represented by the colour yellow, and anger and rage by the colour red. The colour palette of a film signals to the audience the film-maker's intent to create an atmosphere or to send a message or to get an emotional response. This is achieved by matching costume, make-up, sets and lighting under one colour palette.

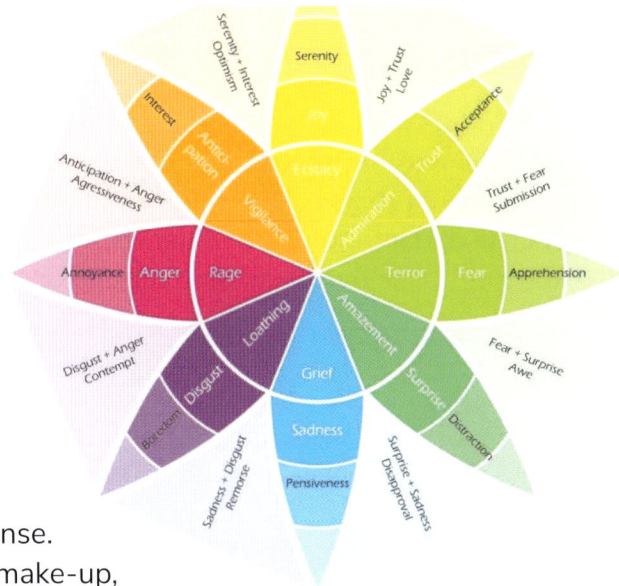

READING

A film still is a picture taken from a film. Below are three film stills from *Corpse Bride*, *Trolls* and *Marie Antoinette*.

- *Corpse Bride* is a stop-motion animated film about Victor, a groom who has to choose between two brides, one being a corpse who drags him to the underworld while his living bride is courted by another man.

- *Trolls* is a computer-animated children's film about Poppy, a joy-loving tiny troll on a quest to save her friends.

- *Marie Antoinette* is a historical drama about Queen Marie Antoinette in the lead up to the French revolution.

Each of these films has a very distinctive mise-en-scène and colour palette. Look at the film stills and complete the task in your activity book (see page 77).

Cinematography

The use of a camera is what makes a film different to a live acting experience on the stage. Cinematography is the art of camera work in film; good cinematography can add to the storytelling. The camera can be used by the director to create effects, build suspense and intrigue, and influence our emotions, making us feel for a character, scaring us, making us laugh and making us cry.

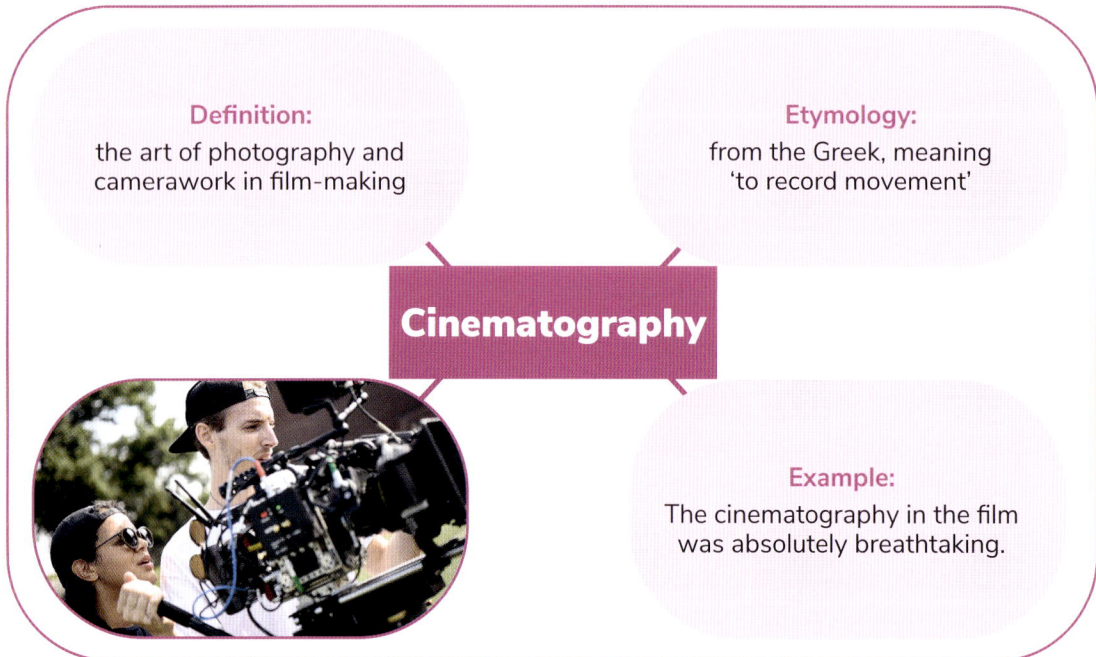

Definition:
the art of photography and camerawork in film-making

Etymology:
from the Greek, meaning 'to record movement'

Cinematography

Example:
The cinematography in the film was absolutely breathtaking.

Camera angles

A camera angle is the physical position of the camera when the shot is being taken. A specific camera angle can be used to position the audience so they feel that they are part of the action or to give them greater understanding of the relationships between characters. There are many different camera angles that directors use to add meaning to the story.

High angle	Eye-level angle	Low angle
Where the camera looks down on the subject. This can make the subject seem vulnerable or powerless.	Where the camera looks directly at the subject straight on. This puts the audience at the same level as the character.	Where the camera looks up at the subject. This can make the subject seem powerful and strong.

Shots

A shot is everything that goes on in a specific section of a script. It is like a page of a book or a stanza of a poem. A shot may include several different camera angles.

Close-up shot

Focused on the face, with the audience unable to see the rest of the scene. This type of shot can be used to establish a strong emotional connection with the audience, who are able to see intimate details and emotions on the subject's face.

Full shot

A wider shot, showing the character from head to toe, so the audience can clearly see what they're doing. This type of shot allows the audience to read emotions on a character's face while simultaneously seeing their physicality, body language and actions.

Establishing shot

An even wider shot, showing the surroundings and actions taking place in a wider setting. This type of shot establishes the geography, context or setting of the film, and informs the audience about where and when a scene is taking place.

READING

ACTIVITY

Look at the six film stills below. Each one is an example of the different camera angles and shot types you have just learned about. Complete the cinematography task in your activity book (see page 78).

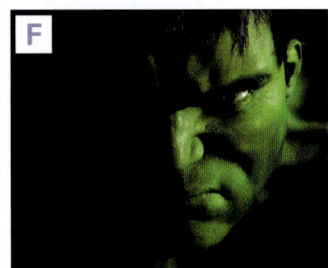

A

B

C

D

E

F

Editing Techniques

An editing technique is what happens with all the camera footage once the crew has finished shooting the film. Each individual shot is edited, then put together piece by piece like a jigsaw puzzle to make the final version of the film. It is at the editing stage that all the special effects and the sound are combined with the footage from the camera.

Montage	Cross-cutting	Bridging
Created by selecting, editing and piecing together parts of the footage, usually with background music. A montage is often used to show the passage of time.	An editing technique that takes two or more film sequences and cuts between them as the scene goes on. The audience can then see two or more storylines or pieces of action at once. Cross-cutting can be used to give the audience access to different perspectives or to build tension or suspense within a scene.	An editing technique used literally to bridge the gap between one scene and another, to explain a move in time or place. You may have seen a bridging shot in the form of pages flying off a calendar, leaves falling off trees or driving past a road sign of a new place.

READING

ACTIVITY

Complete the editing techniques activity in your activity book (see pages 78–79).

The Sound Of A Film

When you think of film, the first thing that pops into your head is probably something visual: a big cinema screen, a memorable scene you've never forgotten or the mise-en-scène of a film you've been totally immersed in. However, music and sound play an equally important part in telling the story of a film.

A film **soundtrack** is the written music and songs that accompany a film to create a mood or atmosphere on screen. A soundtrack, or **musical score**, helps convey meaning in a scene and can enhance our understanding of a character's point of view.

The accent of the characters' **dialogue** in a scene can sometimes give us a hint as to the setting of the film or the social class of each character.

A **voice-over** is when someone's voice narrates over a film. Sometimes a voice-over is only used at the start or end of a film, but at other times it can be used effectively throughout. The voice-over can be the voice of a character in the film or a character that does not appear in the film at all.

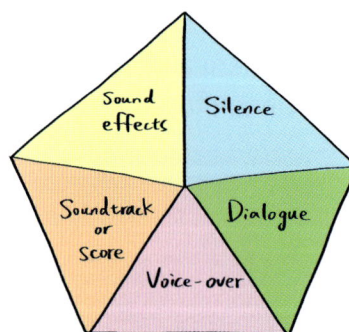

Sound effects are essential in creating a mood or atmosphere; imagine a horror film without creaking floorboards or an eerie breeze through trees.

Equally important in the sound of a film is the use of **silence**. Nothing creates tension and atmosphere better than when a character is creeping down a deserted corridor trying desperately not to make a sound. Silence can also be used to create an emotional response or a sense of isolation, or to heighten the awareness of the audience.

WRITING

Complete the Spotify soundtrack task and sound effects task in your activity book (see pages 81 and 82–83).

The Greatest Showman

The Greatest Showman is based on the life of P.T. Barnum, who was famous for running a museum of human curiosities and a travelling circus in the nineteenth century.

READING

Read more about the life and legacy of P.T. Barnum, then answer the questions that follow:

edco.ie/2ycv

edco.ie/bgyv

1 What was the most interesting thing you found out about P.T. Barnum?

2 From your research, do you think P.T. Barnum was a successful businessman?

3 What do you think people today would have thought of P.T. Barnum's show? Do you think people would think that he was exploiting his performers?

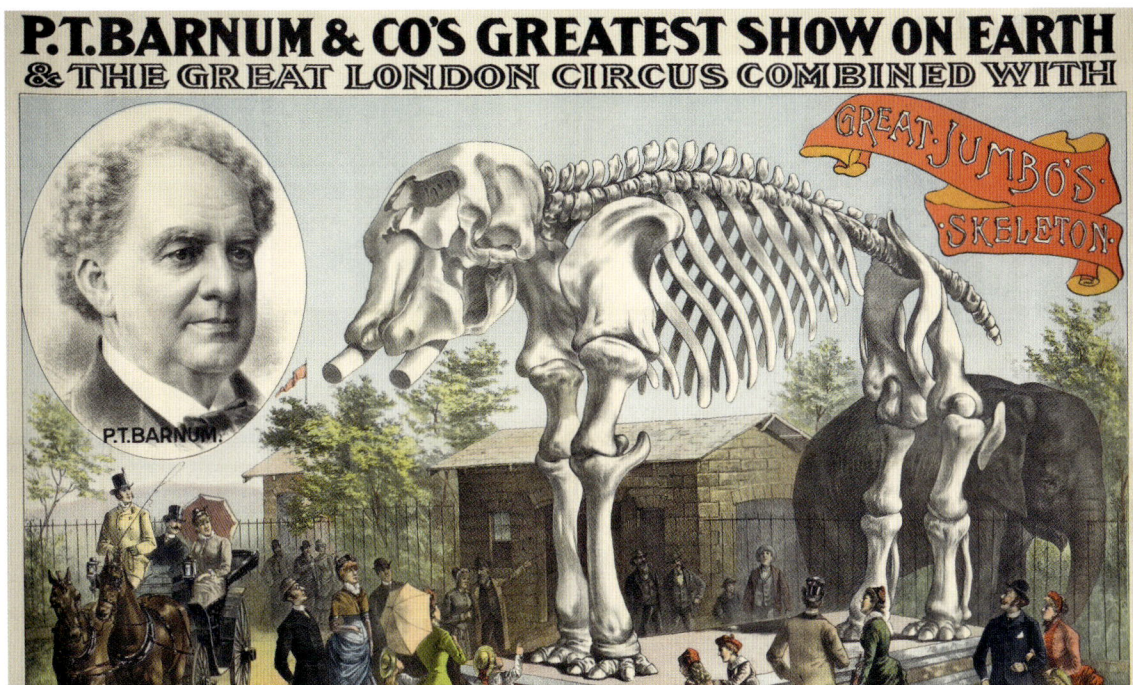

P.T. BARNUM & CO'S GREATEST SHOW ON EARTH & THE GREAT LONDON CIRCUS COMBINED WITH GREAT JUMBO'S SKELETON

P.T. BARNUM.

COMMUNICATING: GROUP DISCUSSION

What would you expect to see in the opening scene of a film? Why is the opening scene of a film important?

What would you expect to see in the end scene of a film? Why is the ending of a film important?

Watch the opening scene and the end scene of *The Greatest Showman*. Then, in small groups, discuss the questions below.

Opening scene

Watch the opening scene from *The Greatest Showman*:

edco.ie/6tpj

1 List any editing techniques you can spot in this scene.
2 Describe the mise-en-scène of this scene.
3 Describe the costumes in this scene.
4 Describe the use of sound in this scene. How does it affect the atmosphere?
5 Describe the lighting used in this scene.
6 List any camera angles used in this scene.
7 How are the opening credits used in this scene?
8 Do you want to keep watching? Explain why or why not.

End scene

Watch the end scene from *The Greatest Showman*:

edco.ie/pq5c

1 List any editing techniques you can spot in this scene.
2 Describe the mise-en-scène of this scene.
3 Describe the costumes in this scene.
4 Describe the use of sound in this scene.
5 Describe the lighting used in this scene.
6 List any camera angles used in this scene.

Comparing the two scenes

1 What was similar about the two scenes?
2 What did you notice that was different about the two scenes?

WRITING

Here is a film review of *The Greatest Showman*. It was written by a First Year English student. The teacher's feedback is below.

Look at each comment and think what improvements you would make to the text. Use the recommended resources indicated below to help you with your redrafting and editing.

A copy of the review is in your activity book (see page 84). Annotate the text with your changes, using the teacher's feedback to guide you.

The Greatest Showman – A Review ★★★★★★★★★★

RATING: 9.5/10
DIRECTOR: Michael Gracey
STORY BY: Jenny Bicks
SCREENPLAY: Jenny Bicks, Bill Condon
STARRING: Hugh Jackman, Zac Efron, Michelle Williams, Rebecca Ferguson, Zendaya

Hugh Jackman is one of my favourite actors and I was so excited about seeing *The Greatest Showman* mostly because it starred him and a bunch of good actors, I adore including michelle williams, zendaya and zac efron. *The Greatest Showman* is inspired by the true story of PT Barnum, how he created The Barnum & Bailey Circus and the lives of those involved. Hugh Jackman is such fun to watch and he did a good job as PT Barnum. Michelle Williams, Zac Efron, rebecca ferguson and zendaya all did great jobs with their roles and so did the supporting cast. Zendaya was the perfect actress for the role of Anne Wheeler . She looked so great and I couldn't get enough of her. It was filmed and directed so well and the music, which was choreographed so perfectly, made me happy.

The songs were very catchy .I couldn't stop listening to one song in my house and that song was 'This Is Me'. Musicals are not my favourite type of movie but when I saw *The Greatest Showman*, I was hooked. Yes, the plot may not match the true story but it was amazing nonetheless. I was gripped from beginning to the end. I loved the overall theme of acceptance, loving oneself and being content. It was a great film and I wouldn't mind seeing it again. If you want to go see a great movie, go and see *The Greatest Showman*.

Feedback	Resources to help you
There are several mistakes in the spelling and punctuation that you need to fix – in particular, some commas and capital letters are missing.	Go to page 272 to see the relevant advice on spelling, punctuation and grammar.
There is no variety in sentence types, which makes the writing repetitive and not as interesting as it could be.	Look at non-fiction sentence types on pages 215 and 241.
The descriptive adjectives need to be upgraded and varied.	Read up on adjectives on page 238.

A Single Life

A Single Life is a two-minute animated short film. It was created by a Dutch film-making company and was nominated for an Oscar in 2015. The film tells the story of someone's life through the use of flash-forward and flashbacks, backed by an interesting choice of music.

WRITING

Enjoy watching the short film: edco.ie/rk2t

Then watch it again and write your answers to the questions below.

1 Summarise the plot of the film in one sentence.
2 Write a short paragraph to describe the setting of the film.
3 Write a short paragraph to describe the mise-en-scène and colour palette used in this film.

COMMUNICATING: GROUP DISCUSSION

Now watch *A Single Life* for a third time and discuss the questions below with your partner or with your class.

A

B

C

D

E

F

1 One of the most interesting things about this film is how it plays around with narrative structure. The record skips and Pia's life flashes forwards and backwards. Put the still pictures in the order that they appear in the film.
2 Now reorder the stills using a linear narrative structure from childhood to old age. Which do you think is more effective and why?
3 What elements of sound are used in this film and what elements of sound are not used?
4 Did you think the director's choices around sound were a good idea or not? Why? Why not?
5 What, do you think, is the message of this short film?
6 Did you enjoy watching this film? Why? Why not?

Film blog

The film review below was published on a film blog. The features of a film review blog are annotated. The features are the things you would expect to find in this type of text.

Short film review: A Single Life (2015) ← Title

Concept:	10
Story-telling:	10 ← Rating
Music:	10
Director:	Marieke Blaauw, Joris Oprins, Job Roggeveen ← Film details

This Oscar-nominated animation is a magical time-travelling ditty that's well worth a spin. ← Tagline: sell or pan the film in one sentence

You'd be surprised at just how much you can squeeze into a couple of minutes. But what if those couple of minutes were able to fit in the whole of time? ← Conversational

That's what happens in Marieke Blaauw, Joris Oprins and Job Roggeveen's short film, *A Single Life*, in which a young woman discovers a vinyl record that has the ability to travel back and forth in time.

It's a gloriously elegant premise, and it's one that the film communicated without saying a single word – a remarkable feat in itself, given the mumbo-jumbo exposition ← Humorous you'd usually expect to find in a timey-wimey sci-fi feature. Instead, they explain it to us visually, using that universal household object: a slice of pizza. Go forward in time? The slice is gone. Go back? You can eat it all over again. In less than 30 seconds, we understand exactly what's going on. And probably want some pizza to boot.

The woman, Pia, is naturally excited by the potential the disc opens up, rewinding back into her childhood and zipping along into the future to see what's in store. Adulthood. A job. A baby. Old age. There's no end to the possibility of what she can see – and, accompanied by Happy Camper's soundtrack (available on Spotify), there's a beautiful synchronicity between the precisely metered out music and the haphazard flurry of chronological silliness. Pizza gives way to zimmer frames with laugh-out-loud wit, before it raises a poignant question: if minutes of our existence fly past every time we close our eyes and listen to a song, what happens when the needle jumps and skips a few bars? The result is a quietly deep reminder of the importance of not rushing to the final bar of the piece – a lesson wrapped up in a 120-second track that's endlessly surprising and guaranteed to leave a smile on your face.

Nominated for an Oscar in 2015, it was one of the shortest contenders that year – and, although it lost out to Disney, it was also the best. Squeezing decades of time into a couple of minutes? *A Single Life* is a magical piece of art that's well worth a spin.

READING

1 List the adjectives the reviewer uses to describe the film. Are there any adjectives used that could be upgraded?

2 Complete the challenging vocabulary task in your activity book (see page 85).

3 Why is the short film described as poignant by the reviewer?

4 Do you think the synchronicity of the music and the action creates an interesting effect on the audience? What is the effect?

5 Do you think the film deserved to be Oscar-nominated? Why? Why not?

PROJECT:
Film Critic

PROJECT BRIEF

Read through the summaries of the four short films below. Choose one you would like to watch and, when you've seen it, write a film review on it. The film review is to appear on a film blog with a teenage audience.

To be successful in this project, you should:

- use the features of a blog creatively
- comment positively or negatively on the storytelling elements of the film
- comment on how the film-making techniques affect the audience
- appeal to your audience by making the review humorous and conversational.

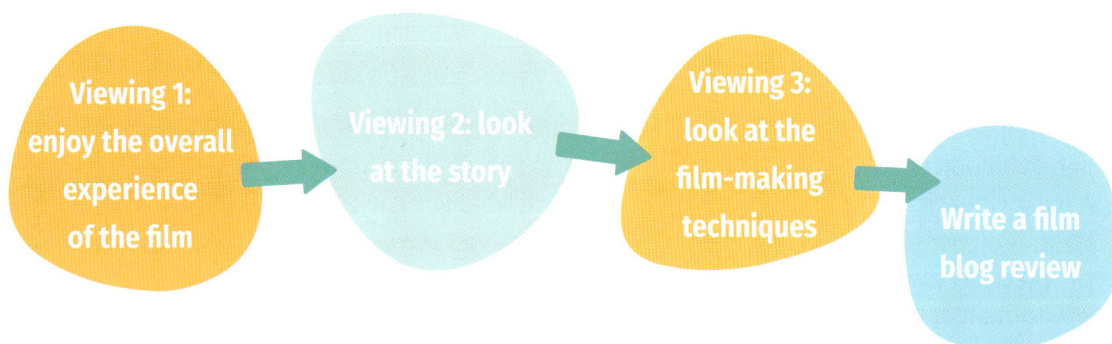

Viewing 1: enjoy the overall experience of the film → **Viewing 2:** look at the story → **Viewing 3:** look at the film-making techniques → **Write a film blog review**

Choose Your Film

Yu Ming is Ainm Dom

Is there a place in the world for Yu Ming? He's a clerk at a convenience store in China, bored with his life. At a library, he spins a globe and stops it with his finger, which turns out to be touching Ireland. He reads about the country and teaches himself Irish, flies to Dublin and finds to his chagrin that no one understands him. He assumes that his Irish is at fault, until he walks into a bar looking for work. edco.ie/ey87

Badly Drawn Roy

Meet Roy, Ireland's only living animated character, born into an ordinary 'live action' family. Roy is intelligent but unfortunately for him he is badly drawn. His failure to gain steady employment finally leads him to Hollywood in search of fame, fortune and cosmetic corrective surgery. edco.ie/mt8w

The Crush

Eight-year-old Ardal develops a crush on his teacher Miss Purdy and decides that her loutish boyfriend is not good enough for her, so he challenges him to a duel. The duelists meet but, unlike his rival, Ardal has a real gun, stolen from his Garda father. edco.ie/6ure

The Wonderful Story of Kelvin Kind

Meet Kelvin Kind, a wonderful loser with a heart of gold. Spending his time fixing toasters and watching cable TV, he is blissfully unaware of his own loneliness. But when a beautiful girl moves into the apartment across the hall, Kelvin's solitary world is turned upside down. edco.ie/764e

1 **Viewing 1:** Choose one film and enjoy watching it.

2 **Viewing 2:** When you watch the film for the second time, focus on the story. In your activity book there is a graphic organiser (see page 86) to help you record your thoughts during your second viewing.

3 **Viewing 3:** The third and final time you watch the film, focus on the film-making techniques, such as mise-en-scène, sound, colour palette, editing techniques, shots and camera angles. Record your thoughts on your third viewing in the graphic organiser in your activity book (see page 87).

Write Your Review

There are a number of supports listed below that you can use to help you write an excellent film review.

- Use both the graphic organisers in your activity book to help you write your review. These are your notes that should help you comment on both the story and the film-making techniques.

- You can also use the film-review writing frame in your activity book (see pages 88–89) to help you structure your review in the format of a blog.

- Remember your style of writing should be humorous and conversational.

PROJECT:
Sixty-Second Silent Movie

💡 PROJECT BRIEF

Create a sixty-second silent movie with a basic plot. A silent movie has no dialogue, but you can use music, sound effects and silence to add impact to your film. You should show your understanding of the technical aspects of film and of how your choices as a director might impact the audience.

To be successful in this project, you will need to:

- use camera angles, film shots and editing techniques creatively to tell a story
- use mise-en-scène, colour and sound to add to the story
- create a clear narrative structure
- engage imaginatively in the film-making process from pitch to editing.

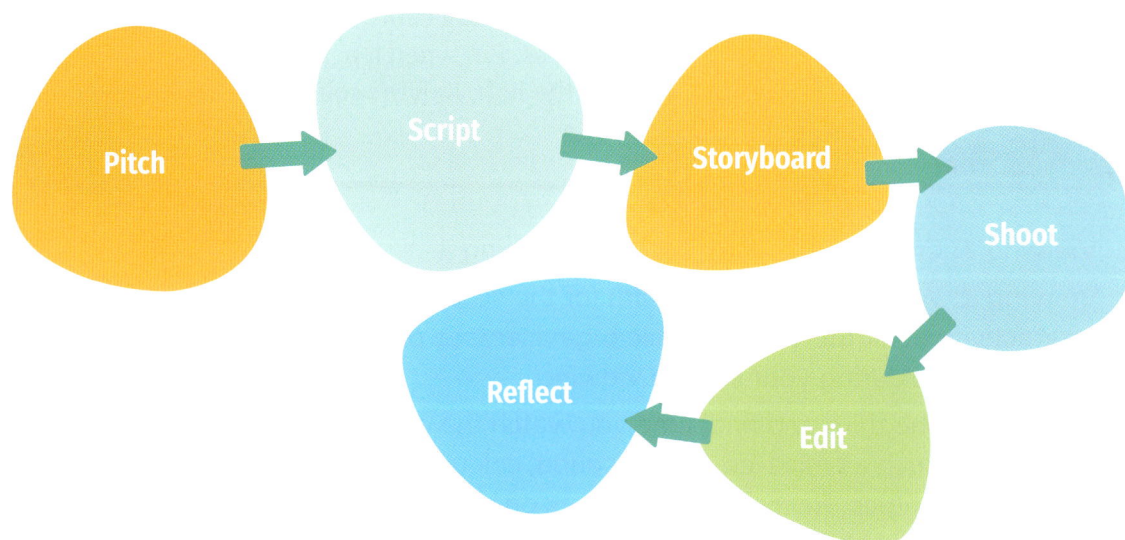

Pitch → Script → Storyboard → Shoot → Edit → Reflect

Watch these three examples of short silent films for inspiration:

- Seen edco.ie/32sw
- Days edco.ie/vdpj
- Life edco.ie/5zvf

There are also excellent examples of short films on the TikTok app:

- Vacation @Sallydarrgriffin
- How black and white movies used to be made @zachking

Plan It

1 **Brainstorm:** Keep it very simple. Your film only needs to be sixty seconds long, so a very basic plot is vital. Bear in mind where you are going to be shooting your film – will it be at school, outside or at home? This will have an impact on your film.

2 **Casting:** Keep your characters to one or two maximum. You may choose to use yourself as the actor, or someone else in your house, or classmates at school. You may also choose to use a household object as your subject (for example: a cup, a spoon or a teddy bear) or even the family pet.

3 **Pitch your film:** Pitching means summarising and selling your film idea in sixty to ninety seconds. It is sometimes called an 'elevator pitch', as a journey in an elevator (or lift) is the amount of time you usually have to persuade a studio executive to buy your film. The pitch should showcase all the main selling points of your film.

Below is the pitch written by The Duffer Brothers who created *Stranger Things*. It summarises and sells their idea to the film-making studio.

INTRODUCTION

Montauk is an eight-hour sci-fi horror epic.

Set in Long Island in 1980 and inspired by the supernatural classics of that era, we explore the crossroads where the ordinary meets the extraordinary.

The feeling of fear and wonder as Elliot approaches a fog-drenched shed in *E.T.*... the helpless dread that consumes Chief Brody as he watches a boy and his raft dragged under the water by an unseen monster in *Jaws*... the crackling television in *Poltergeist*... the horror of a cackling clown in *It*... the friendship and adventure of *Stand By Me*...

Emotional, cinematic, and rooted in character, Montauk is a love letter to the golden age of Steven Spielberg and Stephen King – a marriage of human drama and supernatural fear.

STORY

We begin at Camp Hero in the fall of 1980, a few months before the base will be shut down by the U.S. government. A mysterious experiment has gone horribly awry. And something has gotten out.

On this very night, a young, boy, WILL BYERS, vanishes into thin air. His disappearance has a potent effect on the small town community, particularly on his best friend, MIKE WHEELER, his brother, JONATHAN, his mother, JOYCE, and the reluctant Chief of Police, JIM 'HOP' HOPPER. We will follow each of these characters as they grapple with and investigate Will's disappearance.

As they peel back the layers of this mystery, they will all arrive at the same shocking conclusion: Will was abducted by supernatural entities which were inadvertently released during an experiment. These entities exist between dimensions and have begun to feed on life from our world – Will's disappearance is only the beginning...

Over the course of the series, the 'tear' or 'rip' that separates their world from ours will begin to spread across Montauk like a supernatural cancer. This cancer will manifest itself in increasingly bizarre paranormal ways. Electrical fields will be disrupted. Strange fungi will grow on structures and people. A heavy fog will drift in from the Atlantic. The temperature will plummet. Food will rot. Gravity will fluctuate. People will glimpse bizarre entities in their homes and businesses. There will be an escalating number of 'vanishings'. The entire town will become 'haunted' – and in grave danger. If people can disappear... can an entire town?

Create your own movie pitch using the movie pitch worksheet in your activity book (see page 89).

Script It

A film script does much more than contain the dialogue for the film. It is basically the instruction manual for the director and producers for the mise-en-scène, the dialogue, the sound and the camera angles.

Look at the script below of the opening scenes from the very first episode of *Stranger Things*. There is no spoken dialogue, but the story begins to take shape without it, through the use of the other elements of film-making.

Stranger Things: Pilot Episode

Fade in:

TITLES OVER BLACK:

1942. WORLD WAR II. THE UNITED STATES BUILDS A MILITARY BASE AT THE EASTERN-MOST POINT OF MONTAUK, NEW YORK. IT SPANS 278 ACRES. IT IS CALLED CAMP HERO.

1972. THE COLD WAR. AN ALLEGED SERIES OF TOP-SECRET EXPERIMENTS BEGIN TO TAKE PLACE AT CAMP HERO.

DECEMBER, 1980. CAMP HERO IS SHUT DOWN FOR UNDISCLOSED REASONS.

TO THIS DAY, ITS RECORDS REMAIN CLASSIFIED.

1. EXTERNAL SHOT – Mountain SKY – NIGHT

We FADE UP on the night sky. Dark clouds swallow the stars.

We hear a LOW-END RUMBLE. It sounds almost like thunder, only it is somehow more alive. Like the growl of an unseen beast.

We TILT DOWN to find CAMP HERO MILITARY BASE.

It is an imposing cement building in a dense forest. A LONG-RANGE SEARCH RADAR DISH rotates atop its roof. Around and around.

Superimpose titles:

CAMP HERO. MONTAUK, NEW YORK.

OCTOBER 5. 1980.

TWO MONTHS BEFORE THE SHUTDOWN.

2. INTERNAL – CAMP HERO – TUNNEL SYSTEM – NIGHT

We move down a long windowless corridor.

There is a STEEL DOOR at the end.

We draw closer to this door–

And closer–

And–

WHOOM! THE DOOR SUDDENLY EXPLODES OPEN. THE HINGES SHRIEK.

A SCIENTIST staggers out into the corridor. He is gasping for breath. A hazmat suit melts off his body. We can see some skin beneath; it is burned, shredded, bloody. His entire left arm is missing.

He collapses to the floor. Twitches. Stills. Dead.

His eyes remain open. Frozen in a look of sheer terror.

We continue past him–

Moving into–

A LABORATORY.

A DOZEN MORE SCIENTISTS lie dead on the ground.

They too are burned; many also missing limbs. Some, heads.

We survey the lab around them. There are BULKY COMPUTERS, MYSTERIOUS ANALOG EQUIPMENT and most striking of all:

An ISOLATION TANK, an upright metal cylinder filled with water. A tangle of electrical wires connect this tank to–

A METAL DOOR FRAME. The door leads nowhere; there is just empty white space behind it. The base of the door is on fire.

We watch as this fire begins to spread across the lab.

The flames grow hotter–

And hotter–

And–

HISS! FIRE SPRINKLERS kick on.

Write the script for your sixty-second silent movie, using the example above as a guide. Remember this is a silent film, so your script, like the *Stranger Things* script above, will have to use descriptions of sets and setting, instructions for what you want your actors to do and details of any elements of sound you will use.

Storyboard It

Before you go ahead and shoot your movie, you will need to think like a film director and storyboard your film outline. Each frame or shot you're going to create needs to be planned out in detail. Look below at the storyboard for the scene of the Battle of the Department of Mysteries from *Harry Potter and The Order of the Phoenix*.

The purpose of the storyboard is to provide a clear and detailed plan for each shot. The camera angles, shot types and the actions of each scene are planned in advance, as each choice has a purpose. For example: The bird's-eye angle of the first shot shows the audience how small and insignificant Harry and his friends are, which creates a sense of fear that they are walking into a battle against a more powerful enemy that they may not win.

You should consider each shot carefully. Think about what impact you are trying to make on your audience through your choice of shot, camera angles and sound. Draw in the action that you want to happen in each shot.

Create your storyboard using the storyboard worksheet in your activity book (see page 90) and using your script as a guide.

Shoot It

Below you'll find some tips for shooting your film.

- Use your phone as your camera. Make sure your phone is fully charged so you don't run out of power halfway through a scene and that you have a video-editing app downloaded and available.
- You should have your storyboard and your script with you as a guide.
- You should also have any costumes, props and actors you need to create your film.
- If you have an iPhone, iMovie is an excellent video editor that is already on your iPhone.
- If you have an Android, Videoshow or FilmoraGo are both free apps that you can download to your phone.
- TikTok is another excellent video-making app.
- Set up your shots one by one, using your storyboard to guide you on angles and shots. Tick off each shot on your storyboard once you've got it.

Edit It

Once you've got all your shots, you need to edit your movie together. This is where you need to consider using a variety of editing techniques, for example: bridging shots, montage, cross-cutting, fade in/out, etc.

This is also the point where you need to work on the sound of your movie. As it is a silent movie, you will not have any dialogue, but you can create a soundscape through the use of music, sound effects and silence. Don't forget to add in the movie credits at the end!

Once your movie is complete, check the success criteria in the project brief box again (see page 132) to make sure you've shown a good understanding of the techniques of film-making and their impact on the audience.

Now you can upload the movie to the sharing platform suggested by your teacher.

REFLECTION

1 What did you find challenging about this project? Why?

2 What did you find enjoyable about this project? Why?

3 Did you think the pitch and storyboard helped you to shoot and edit your film? Why? Why not?

4 What connections can you now make between choices a director makes and their intended impact on an audience? Give one example from your film.

5 Rank, in order of importance, the aspects of making a film:

mise-en-scène	colour palette	camera shots
camera angles	sound	editing techniques

6 Explain how completing this film has changed/not changed your understanding of the film-making process.

Test Your Knowledge

1 **What is a high camera angle?**

   a) When the camera looks up at the subject

   b) When the camera looks directly at the subject straight on

   c) When the camera looks down on the subject

   d) The matching colour scheme used in costume, make-up, sets and lighting

2 **An establishing shot...**

   a) Sets up the context or setting of the scene

   b) Contains a full shot of the character and what they are doing

   c) Focuses on a character's face, with the audience unable to see the rest of the scene

   d) Is an editing technique used to explain a move in time or place

3 **A montage is...**

   a) Created by selecting, editing and piecing together bits of footage, usually with background music

   b) An editing technique that takes two or more film sequences and cuts between them as the scene goes on

   c) An editing technique used to explain a move in time or place, e.g. pages flying off a calendar, leaves falling off trees or a road sign of a new place

   d) The physical position of the camera when the shot is being taken

4 **What is a soundtrack?**

   a) The written songs that accompany a film to create a mood or atmosphere on screen

   b) When someone's voice narrates over a film

   c) The matching colour scheme used in costume, make-up, sets and lighting

   d) An editing technique that takes two or more film sequences and cuts between them as the scene goes on

5 **The colour** .... **a director uses, is the matching colour scheme used in costume, make-up, sets and lighting.**

6 **Some films share features in common, which allows them to be categorised into** .... **, such as drama, comedy and** .... **.**

7 Match the camera angles with their explanations.

Camera angle	Explanation
High angle	Camera looks up at the subject
Eye-level angle	Camera looks down on the subject
Low angle	Camera looks directly at the subject straight on

8 Match the shot types with their explanations.

Shot type	Explanation
Close-up shot	Contains a shot of the character from head to toe so the audience can clearly see what they are doing
Establishing shot	Sets up the context or setting of the scene
Full shot	Focused on the face, with the audience unable to see the rest of the scene

9 List five examples of different film genres.

10 What does the mise-en-scène of a film include?

11 What are sound effects? Give three examples.

12 Explain what a voice-over might be used for in a film.

13 Thinking back on all you have learned in this unit, try the personal dictionary task on pages 91–92 of your activity book.

Practise Your Writing Skills

You have been given the job of directing a film version of a book or short story you have read. Write a short paragraph on each of the points below.

- Name your chosen book or short story and explain why you picked it.
- Explain the setting of the story and choose a real location that would match. Explain your choice.
- Name the main characters from the story and choose an actor to play each one. Explain your choices.
- Give three pieces of advice to the actor playing the main character about how they should portray the character.
- Explain the costume and make-up you would choose for your main character.

Interactive website

Go to **www.edco.ie/touchstones1** for interactive activities based on this unit.

UNIT 4
DRAMA

DRAMA KNOWLEDGE ORGANISER

Things I need to know

- **Stage:** The place where a drama or play is performed.

- **Theatre-in-the-round stage:** Has a central performance area enclosed by the audience on all sides.

- **Flexible stage:** Stage and seating are not fixed and can be altered to suit the needs of the play or the whim of the director.

- **Three-sided or thrust stage:** Juts out into the audience, with the audience sitting on all three sides.

- **Proscenium arch stage:** Framed by an arch – like a window that frames the action happening on stage.

- **Set design:** All the scenery, furniture and props the audience sees at a production of a play.

- **Props:** The objects that appear on stage or that characters use in a play.

- **Costumes:** The clothes that an actor wears during the performance of a play.

- **Sound:** Includes actors' voices speaking dialogue, sound effects and music.

- **Lighting:** Includes floor lights, spotlights and floodlights that a lighting director might use to create an effect or atmosphere on stage.

- **Stage directions:** The playwright's instructions to the actors as to what to do on stage.

- **Acting:** How an actor chooses to portray their character using their voice, facial expressions, gestures and movement.

Skills I will develop

- Understanding and using the language of drama
- Participating actively in group performance activities
- Collaborating to deliver short oral texts
- Reading and engaging with play scripts and performances

Project

- From Page To Stage: Planning, writing, producing, performing and directing a one-scene play

What do I know?

What do you already know about drama? Have you ever seen a play? Have you got a favourite musical? Have you been to a pantomime?

Go to your activity book (see page 93) and complete the drama knowledge download activity.

What Is Drama?

PowerPoint

We come across drama in every aspect of our lives: an argument between two friends in the yard, a conflict between a customer and a bus driver on the way to town, the nightly soap opera on TV, a student challenging a teacher in the classroom. The study of drama looks at these types of events through a performance on stage. A play can cover real-life events or totally fictional events, or a mixture of both.

> All the world's a stage,
> And all the men and women merely players;
> They have their exits and their entrances
> And one man in his time plays many parts...
> **William Shakespeare, As You Like It**

> I regard the theatre as the greatest of all art forms, the most immediate way in which a human being can share with another the sense of what it is to be a human being.
> **Oscar Wilde**

> Theatre is a mirror, a sharp reflection of society.
> **Yasmina Reza**

> Drama is life with the dull bits cut out.
> **Alfred Hitchcock**

Which of these quotes do you like best? Which quotes do you agree with? Are there any you disagree with?

People have always loved both performing and watching drama. The very first theatres were in Greece around 350BC. The word drama comes from Greek and means 'to do or to perform'. There are many different genres of drama, including comedy, tragedy, history and musical. You may be familiar with some of these genres already.

The purpose of a play depends on the playwright and could include bringing joy and entertainment, celebrating someone's life and work or giving the audience insight into the life of a particular person and the historic context of the times they lived in. The building blocks of a play are **acts** (like chapters in a novel), which are further broken down into **scenes**.

The unique thing about a play or dramatic performance is that it takes place in front of a live audience and can't be edited or changed.

COMMUNICATING: GROUP DISCUSSION

In pairs, look at the difference in layout between a novel and a play script in the examples below from *Holes* by Louis Sachar.

What do you notice that is different and what do you notice that is similar?

Make a list of your findings.

Novel	Play script
The bus was slowing down. The guard grunted as he stretched his arms. 'Welcome to Camp Green Lake,' said the driver. Stanley looked out of the dirty window. He couldn't see a lake. And hardly anything was green. Stanley felt somewhat dazed as the guard unlocked his handcuffs and led him off the bus. He'd been on the bus for over eight hours. 'Be careful,' the bus driver said as Stanley walked down the steps.	*The bus. Arriving at Camp Green Lake.* **Bus driver:** Welcome to Camp Green Lake. *Stanley looks out of window. He gets off the bus, dazed, after 8-hour journey.* **Bus driver:** Be careful. *Stanley walks down the steps.*

Staging A Play

Getting a play from an idea to a script and then to a performance is a long creative process. This can include numerous people with different jobs and responsibilities collaborating to produce the final performance.

	Scriptwriting	Staging	Performance
People involved	Playwright	Theatre manager Director Sound engineer Set designer Lighting director Costume designer Set designer	Actors or cast
Things to think about	Plot Dialogue Stage directions Setting Characters	Stage type Props Sets Costumes Lighting Sound	Voice Gestures Movement Facial expressions

Types of stage

Choosing which stage type they need is one of the first and most important decisions a director must make. Their choice will depend on a variety of factors, but it is vital that the stage type suits the needs of the production. There are many different types of stages – below are those that are most commonly used.

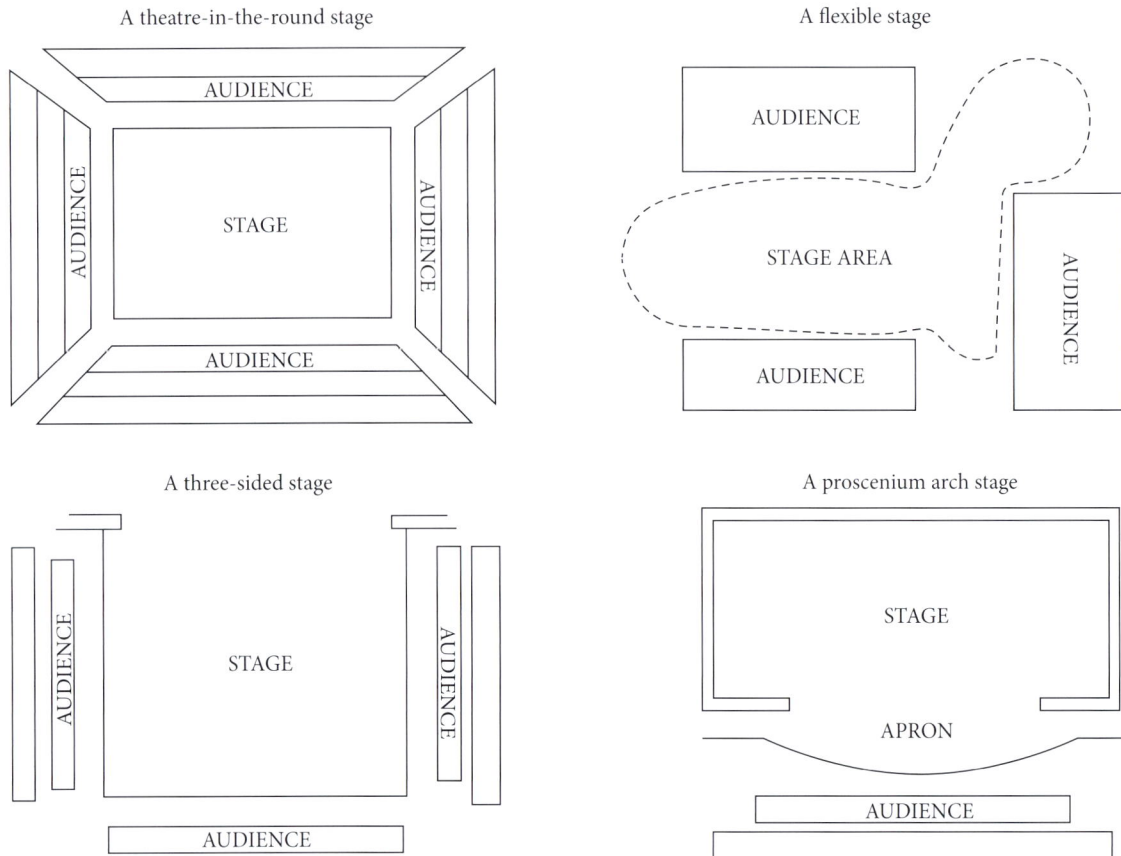

A theatre-in-the-round stage

AUDIENCE

AUDIENCE | STAGE | AUDIENCE

AUDIENCE

A flexible stage

AUDIENCE

STAGE AREA

AUDIENCE | AUDIENCE

A three-sided stage

AUDIENCE | STAGE | AUDIENCE

AUDIENCE

A proscenium arch stage

STAGE

APRON

AUDIENCE

A **theatre-in-the-round stage** has a central performance area enclosed by the audience on all sides. The arrangement is rarely 'round'; more usually the seating is in a square around the space where the actors perform. The actors enter this space via aisles and scenery is minimal and carefully positioned to ensure it does not get in the way of the audience's view.

A **flexible stage** is exactly as its name suggests. Stage and seating are not fixed. Instead, each can be altered to suit the needs of the play or the whim of the director. This type of stage is used to create a unique experience for the audience.

A **three-sided stage** or **thrust stage** juts out into the audience, with the audience sitting on all three sides. Sometimes the thrust stage area is square but it can also be semi-circular. This type of stage is often used to increase intimacy between the actors and the audience.

A **proscenium arch stage** is a stage framed by an arch, just as the name suggests. It is like a window that frames the action happening on stage. The stage reaches far back and sometimes is gently sloped, rising away from the front, to allow the audience to see the actors at the back of the stage. Sometimes the front of the stage extends past the proscenium arch into the audience area – this is known as the **apron**.

Upstage right	Upstage	Upstage left
Stage right	Centre stage	Stage left
Downstage right	Downstage	Downstage left

AUDIENCE

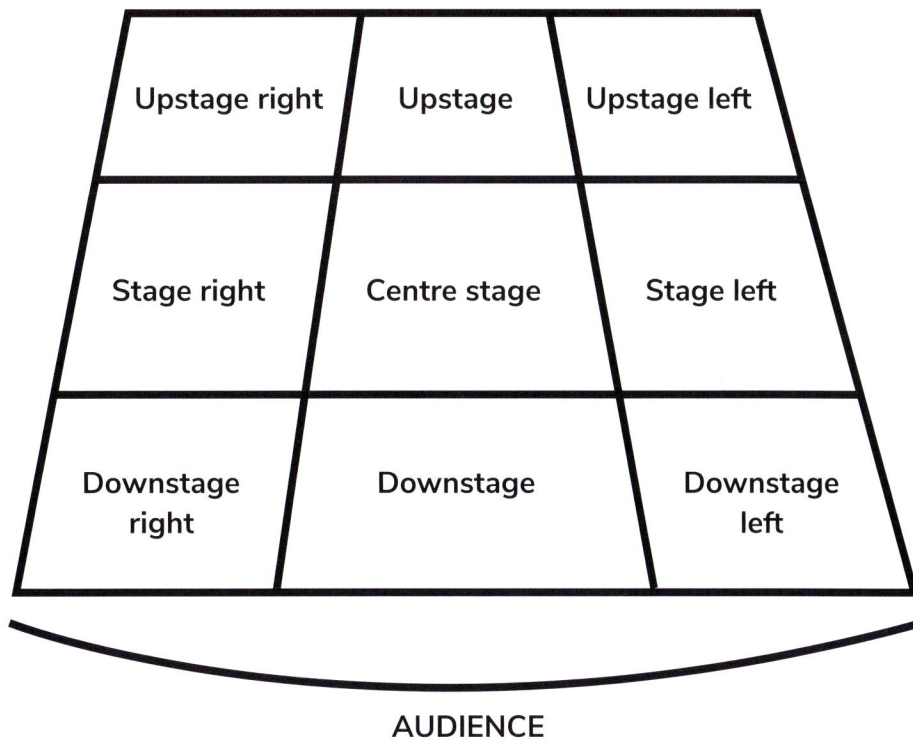

Areas of the stage

An actor needs to know whereabouts on the stage to enter for a scene and they need to know where to move on stage. A stage is divided up into nine sections and each has its own name to help an actor navigate where they are supposed to be. These stage directions are always given from the actor's perspective.

Upstage is the part of the stage furthest away from the audience. **Downstage** is the part of the stage nearest the audience. The reason behind these names is interesting. During the Renaissance (between the fourteenth and seventeenth centuries), when theatres weren't quite as sophisticated as they are now, some audience members would have had to stand for the entire play, their heads level with the stage. This would have made it ridiculously hard to see a performance if the stage was flat. To solve this problem, stages were tilted so that the back was higher than the front, allowing the entire audience to see all the actors at all times. This meant that an actor walking away from the audience would literally be walking up the stage, while an actor coming down towards the audience would be going down the stage. That is how we get the words 'upstage' and 'downstage'.

COMMUNICATING: GROUP DISCUSSION

Divide into pairs or small groups. Discuss what type of stage you would use for the following shows if you were the director, and why.

| A one-man show about exploring the Arctic | A show-stopping musical with a large cast |
| A two-man show, a tragedy about doomed lovers | A comedy about the highs and lows of secondary school, with a cast of ten |

PERFORMING

This game of Simon Says will improve your knowledge of stage directions. It works best in an open space.

- Your chosen area is the pretend stage.
- Your teacher will point out the different sections of the space and name them using the stage directions in the picture on page 145.
- Your teacher will call out stage directions, such as 'Downstage right!' or 'Centre stage!'
- But... students should only move to that area of the space if the teacher uses the phrase 'Simon says' in front of the direction. For example, if the teacher says, 'Simon says centre stage!', the students should quickly move to centre stage.
- Any students who move without the teacher saying 'Simon says' are eliminated. For example, if the teacher says 'Centre stage!', anyone who does move should be eliminated.
- The aim of the game is to be the last person standing.

Set Design And Props

All the scenery, furniture and props the audience sees at a production of a play make up the **set design**. **Props** are all of the objects that appear on stage. The set designer's job is to design and create the look of the physical space in which the action will take place, ensuring everything matches and fits with the director's intention and the requirements of the play script. It is the overall look of the set that gives the audience information about the setting and world of the text.

The picture below left is a set designer's sketch of the set for a staging of *Romeo and Juliet*. The picture below right is a photograph of how the actual set looked on stage.

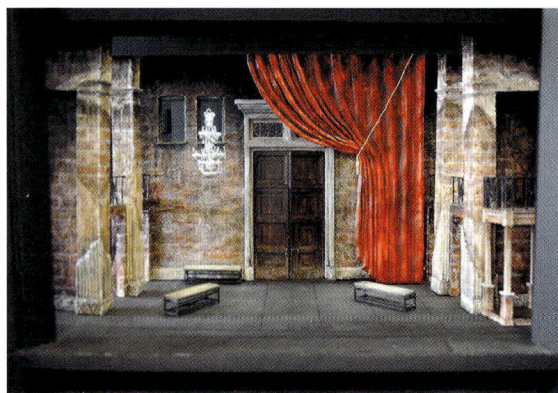

COMMUNICATING: GROUP DISCUSSION

You can usually tell a lot about the world of the play by looking at the set design and the props the actors use. Divide into small groups, then take a look at the four sets below. What can you figure out about the world of these plays just from looking at the sets? Where and when might the plays take place? How do you know?

WRITING TASK

Imagine you have been given a job as a set designer for a theatre company. Design the stage set for one of the following plays:

Twelve Angry Men by Reginald Rose	The Girl from the North Country by Conor McPherson	The Shadow of a Gunman by Sean O'Casey
This is a 1957 New York courtroom drama, where the fate of a young Puerto Rican teenager is being decided by twelve jurors.	This is a musical set in a boarding house in Minnesota, USA, during the Great Depression of 1929.	This play is set in 1920's Dublin during the time of the Irish War of Independence, with the action taking place in a Dublin tenement building.

Writing Tips

- Research the setting of each play. Look through pictures online to get a sense of how things looked at the time.
- Make a list of the things you would expect to see in this setting.
- Sketch out your set design in your activity book (see page 93).
- Finally, write a paragraph explaining the choices you have made.

ACTIVITY

Costume

A costume is the clothes that an actor wears during the performance of a play. Directors use costumes as a way of communicating things about the characters on stage. For example, a director may want to present a character as dangerous or dark or evil, so may use the colour red or black, or something sharp, in the costume of that character, to give the audience a hint. The costumes each character wears can tell the audience a lot about the setting of the play as well, in particular the country and period of history in which the action is set.

COMMUNICATING: GROUP DISCUSSION

Look at the pictures below of characters from different plays. Study the costumes and discuss what you can figure out about the characters on stage by looking at what they are wearing. Do the costumes reveal something about the characters' personalities or background or the era they live in?

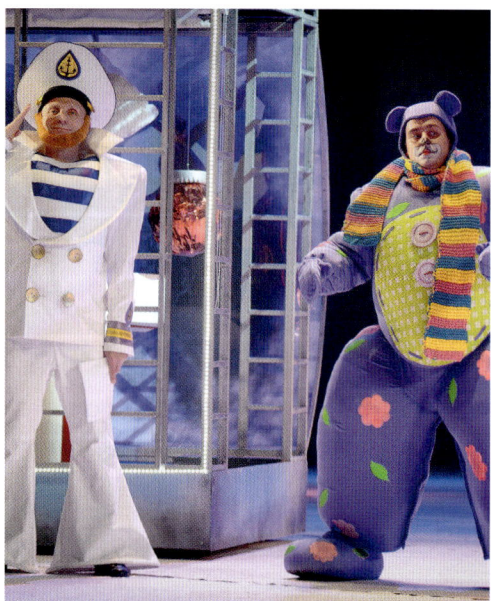

READING

This is a short extract from the play script of the musical *Annie*. It is 1930's New York and this scene is set in an orphanage run by the mean and abusive Miss Hannigan. She is very strict and makes the children work hard all the time to keep the orphanage clean. Read the extract and complete the reading activity below.

(ANNIE sneaks across the stage. As she reaches to open the door, MISS HANNIGAN flings open the door.)

MISS HANNIGAN: Aha! Caught you! (ANNIE falls backward.) Get up. Get up!

ANNIE (standing up): Yes, Miss Hannigan.

MISS HANNIGAN: Rotten orphan.

ANNIE: I'm not an orphan. My mother and father left a note saying they loved me and they were coming back for me.

MISS HANNIGAN: That was 1922; this is 1933. (Blows her whistle.) Get up! All of you. Now, for this one's shenanigans, you'll all get down on your knobby little knees and clean this dump until it shines like the top of the Chrysler Building.

(The ORPHANS all get out of bed.)

TESSIE: But it's four o'clock in the morning.

MISS HANNIGAN: Get to work!!

ANNIE, ORPHANS: Yes, Miss Hannigan.

MISS HANNIGAN: Why any kid would want to be an orphan, I'll never know.

1 Look at the extract for clues about how to design the characters' costumes. Does the text mention anything at all that could give you ideas for costumes?

2 Sketch and label the costumes for Annie and Miss Hannigan in your activity book (see page 94).

PERFORMING

Create and stage a performance of the short extract above in small groups.

- You will need five actors for the scene: Miss Hannigan, Annie, Tessie and two other orphans (non-speaking parts).
- Think about how you might portray the character you are playing. Think about your voice, your gestures, your facial expressions and your movement around the stage.
- Consider how you will use your classroom to create a stage and how you could use the existing furniture and classroom objects for the set and as props and costumes.

Sound

Sound is one of the most important aspects of theatre. Along with actors' voices speaking dialogue, a performance can also include sound effects and music. Sound can create atmosphere and emotion for the audience and can also play a part in the plot. A sound engineer is usually in charge of this aspect of each performance in the theatre.

COMMUNICATING: GROUP DISCUSSION

In small groups, discuss what elements of sound you would choose for the following scenes to add to the audience's experience of the performance in the theatre, and why.

Scene 1	Scene 2
Two men talking on the deck of a famine ship on the way to America in 1847	A flustered receptionist in a doctor's surgery with a waiting room full of patients
Scene 3	**Scene 4**
A mother and baby yoga class gone horribly wrong	A group of old men watching a game of rugby from the stands

PERFORMING

Divide into small groups to create a soundscape for one of the scenes below. A soundscape is a group of all the different sounds and noises that help create a sense of place.

a busy city	a storm	a supermarket checkout
the jungle	the seaside	a hair salon

- You can create sounds by using your own voice or by using the objects around you.
- One person in your group should be the conductor or director of the soundscape and should give everyone their cues to start making their individual noises and sounds.
- The conductor should also be in charge of controlling the noise level, raising a hand to increase the volume and lowering a hand to decrease the volume.
- To practise, you could try recording your soundscape and playing it back to see where you need to make improvements.

Lighting

Lighting in the theatre is controlled by the lighting director, who plans all the different types of lighting for each scene in a play. Lighting in a play contributes to the atmosphere and mood that an audience feels. It can also be used to indicate what time of day it is and even what the weather is like. The lighting director may decide to create dark, moody lighting for a murder scene or bright, colourful lighting for a wedding scene. Floor lights, spotlights and floodlights are some of the types of lights that a lighting director might use to create an effect or atmosphere on stage.

COMMUNICATING: GROUP DISCUSSION

Look at the examples below of interesting lighting effects used by lighting directors in performances. Divide into small groups and discuss what you can tell about the mood of each of these shows just by examining the lighting.

WRITING

If you were the lighting director of a show, how would you light the scenes described below? Write a paragraph to explain your choices for each scene.

Scene 1	Scene 2	Scene 3
A romantic scene between two people sitting on a car bonnet watching the stars	A tense scene where a soldier is trying to make it across no-man's land under heavy fire from the enemy in the trenches on the other side	A gripping scene with an old man on stage on his own, recounting stories from his youth

PERFORMING

Look at the three pictures below of performances of famous plays. The lighting in each of these photos is telling you something about what might happen next in the play. The lighting is helping to tell the story.

Divide into small groups and discuss what you think happens next in each play. Then create a freeze-frame of the action of the next scene.

A **freeze-frame** is like pressing pause on a remote control. You use your bodies to create a scene but then stop all movement.

Stage Directions

Stage directions are the playwright's instructions to the actors as to what to do on stage. Some playwrights give detailed instructions and some give very basic ones. They are different to the dialogue, which tells an actor what to say on stage. Look at page 145 and at the examples below to see how stage directions and dialogue are laid out in a play script.

CHORUS: School. Billy dreaded school. Although there were some things he liked. The teachers were nice, more or less. And the other kids, were mostly okay. Except for one. And that one was there to meet him as he walked through the gate.

Setting ⟶ *[Bridget strides on to the stage area. She has hair in long plaits that stick out from the sides of her head. She advances aggressively towards Billy.]*

BRIDGET: Hello, Billy? What's for lunch? Open your bag.

CHORUS: Her name was Bridget the Bruiser. The school bully. Billy quaked as she walked towards him. Everybody quaked when the burly Bridget approached.

[Bridget snatches Billy's bag and roughly unzips it. She takes out his ⟵ Stage directions *sandwiches and empties the rest of the bag onto the ground.]*

Characters ⟶ BRIDGET: You should be more careful, Billy. One day you'll lose something.

[Bridget next unwraps Billy's sandwiches and throws the paper on the ground. She then peels the slices of bread away to look at the filling inside.]

Not peanut butter again! Can't your Mother make anything else? Hey, what's this?

[Bridget dips her finger into the peanut butter and digs out a gooey, brown lump.]

Err, what is it? It looks like...what's that word Mrs Jennings uses whenever a dog's been in the school yard?

MRS JENNINGS: *[prompting from the side]* Droppings! ⟵ Dialogue

BRIDGET: Yeah, 'droppings'.

READING

Here are two short scenes from a play about school. The dialogue is exactly the same in both scenes, but the stage directions are different. Read both scenes through carefully.

> **Cast of characters**
> SEAN, a student
> SARAH, a student
> BRID, another classmate
> JOEY, another classmate
> MR MYLOD, the Geography teacher
>
> **Setting**
> A modern Irish secondary school

SCENE A

SEAN and SARAH are sitting next to one another in their classroom, slouched on their chairs. BRID sits beside JOEY. JOEY is asleep on his desk. MR MYLOD is standing in front of the class. On the whiteboard behind MR MYLOD is written: 'Rocks Test on Wednesday'.

MR MYLOD: Okay, students. Your test will take the full class tomorrow. Are there any questions?

(The room is silent. No one raises a hand. SEAN and SARAH glance at one another and roll their eyes.)

MR MYLOD: (with enthusiasm, waving a small piece of paper in front of the class) I have a special incentive for you. The student with the highest score will receive this ticket, enabling him or her to skip the next test. So go and study hard, everybody!

(The bell rings. Students stand and begin to file out of the classroom quietly.)

SCENE B

SEAN and SARAH are sitting next to one another in their classroom. BRID sits beside JOEY. All students have their copybooks and textbooks open. MR MYLOD is standing in front of the class. On the whiteboard behind MR MYLOD is written: 'Rocks Test on Wednesday'.

MR MYLOD: Okay, students. Your test will take the full class tomorrow. Are there any questions?

(The room bursts into conversation. Everyone raises their hand. BRID and JOEY can't wait to ask their questions, so they start talking before they're called on.)

MR MYLOD: (frustrated, holding a small paper in his hand) I have a special incentive for you. The student with the highest score will receive this ticket, enabling him or her to skip the next test. So go and study hard, everybody!

(The bell rings. Students gather to try to see the ticket that MR MYLOD is holding.)

Think about what the stage directions are aiming to tell you about the characters and complete the table in your activity book (see page 95).

WRITING

ACTIVITY

In your activity book (see page 96), write another version of the stage directions for the scene on page 153 to change the audience's perception of the characters. For example, you could make one of the characters a difficult student, or you could make the teacher angry or too nice.

PERFORMING

Create and stage a performance of either Scene A or Scene B from the previous page in a small group.

- Remember that there are five actors needed for the scene. Others in the group could be the lighting director or the sound engineer.
- Think about how you will use your classroom to create a stage.
- Consider how you could use the existing furniture and classroom objects for the set and as props and costumes.

Acting

Acting in a play requires a lot of careful thought on the part of the actor. First, they need to consider any clues in the script about the character they are playing. Then they need to think about where the scene appears in the plot of the play. They also need to be conscious of their character's relationships with other characters. Once all these things are considered, an actor can begin to think about how they will portray their character using their voice, facial expressions, gestures and movement.

An actor's voice is their most important tool. Speaking well and pronouncing words clearly allows the audience to follow the plot of the play properly and it also gives an insight into the characters and their motives.

Facial expressions tell the audience what the character is thinking and feeling. Actors also use gestures and movement to portray their character on the stage. This could be something subtle, such as a slight hand gesture, or something dramatic, like marching across the stage.

Sometimes during a performance, an actor has to use their improvisation skills. Improvising means to invent and create a performance on the spot without any prior rehearsal.

PERFORMING

An actor has to consider a lot of things during their performance. Practise your acting skills by performing this improvisation activity. This activity is best done in pairs.

- Each of you should choose a character to play from the list below.
- Then each of you should pick an emotion for your chosen character to portray.
- Finally, choose a scenario together.
- Now you need to improvise a short interaction between your partner using your chosen characters, emotions and scenario. For example, you may select: the cowboy (cheerful) and the ballerina (anxious) on a beautiful countryside cycle.
- Think about what you could do with your voice, facial expressions and gestures, and how you might move around your performance space.
- Each pair should perform for the rest of the class. At the end of each performance, the audience should try to figure out what characters, emotions and scenario were being acted out.

Character	Emotion	Scenario
A cowboy with an imaginary friend	Angry	A wedding where the groom doesn't show up
A ballerina who believes in vampires	Happy	A commentary box at a GAA match
A playschool teacher who is easily addicted to things	Bored	Trying to cheat in an exam
A supermodel who is obsessed with things being clean	Amused	At a ceilidh that's getting out of hand
A used-car salesman who is terrible at selling	Aggressive	On a beautiful countryside cycle
A gloomy office worker who thinks aliens will soon invade and destroy the earth	Anxious	Doing the grocery shopping
A scientist who is the most boring person alive	Fascinated	Putting out the bins
	Friendly	Stowing away on a ship
	Cheerful	Cleaning up after a kid's birthday party
	Confident	Learning how to fly a plane
	Hopeless	Getting caught shoplifting
	Disappointed	
	Nervous	
	Tormented	
	Outraged	
	Panicked	

A Christmas Carol

This is the opening scene of Act One, in which Scrooge and his nephew discuss Christmas. Scrooge is a mean and wealthy businessman with no family of his own. The play is set in London during Victorian times, when poverty was widespread.

Cast of Characters

Narrator

Scrooge (a grumpy old man)

Nephew (a cheerful young man)

NARRATOR: Once upon a time, upon a Christmas Eve, old Scrooge sat busy in his counting-house.

NEPHEW: A Merry Christmas, uncle!

NARRATOR: It was the voice of Scrooge's nephew.

SCROOGE: Bah!…Humbug!

NEPHEW: Christmas a humbug, uncle! You don't mean that, I am sure?

SCROOGE: I do. Out upon merry Christmas! If I had my will, every idiot who goes about with 'Merry Christmas' on his lips should be boiled with his own pudding. He should!

NEPHEW: Uncle!

SCROOGE: Nephew, keep Christmas in your own way, and let me keep it in mine.

NEPHEW: Keep it! But you don't keep it.

SCROOGE: Let me leave it alone, then. Much good may it do you! Much good it has ever done you!

NEPHEW: I have always thought of Christmas time as a good time; a kind, forgiving, charitable, pleasant time. And therefore uncle, though it has never put a scrap of gold or silver in my pocket, I believe that it has done me good, and will do me good; and I say, God bless it!

SCROOGE: Good afternoon.

NEPHEW: I'll keep my Christmas humour to the last. So a Merry Christmas, uncle!

WRITING

Create a comic strip version of this short scene from A *Christmas Carol*. A comic strip uses a variety of ways of communicating a story:

- a caption in which the narrator tells the story
- speech bubbles containing the dialogue
- thought bubbles showing the thoughts of the characters
- images or drawings depicting the action of the story.

Writing Tips

- Use the comic strip panels in your activity book (see page 97) to help you.
- In each box, summarise the action of the story in the captions.
- Think about how you might draw the action of each panel.
- Decide what your characters should say to each other in each panel and put their words into speech bubbles.
- Consider what the characters might be thinking and put their thoughts into thought bubbles.

PERFORMING

Create a performance of this short extract from A *Christmas Carol*.

- Divide up into groups of four, with three people as actors and one person in the role of director.
- The director's job is to plan out how to play the scene. They should consider staging, costume and props.
- The actors' job is to portray their characters on the stage. They should think about their voice, their accent, their gestures and their movement across the stage.
- Use the graphic organiser in your activity book (see page 98) to plan out how you would direct the scene or act your part.

Alone It Stands by John Breen

This play is set on 31 October 1978, in Thomond Park, Limerick. The mighty New Zealand All Blacks, the most feared rugby team on the planet, are on an Irish tour. They are in Limerick to take on the Munster Rugby team – and, to everyone's surprise, they lose 12–0. In this play, there are a total of sixty-two characters, but both teams, plus fans, children, relatives and even a dog, are portrayed by a cast of six, with no props, no set and only a half-time change of shirt. None of the actors ever leaves the stage and when they are not part of the scene they freeze at the side of the stage. The physical performance of the actors is particularly important as they are portraying a rugby match on stage.

Act 1: Scene 19

We see the scrum head on. Three players form the front row – from right to left, McLoughlin, Knight and Robertson – and we see the faces of the second row – Canniffe and Tucker – as their heads come between the thighs of the front row. The scrum half (the Ward actor with a New Zealand accent) stands to one side.

MCLOUGHLIN: Feet dig in, claw at earth.

ROBERTSON: Shoulder on buttock.

CANNIFFE: Cheek on thigh.

TUCKER: Arms under.

KNIGHT: Arms over.

SEAMUS: Steam rising.

WARD: Breath foaming.

MCLOUGHLIN: Shoulders twisting, voices cursing.

KNIGHT: Hooker watching.

SEAMUS: Props crushing.

TUCKER: Necks aching.

WARD: Deep heat burning.

CANNIFFE: Vaseline cooling.

MCLOUGHLIN: Tempers fraying.

SEAMUS: Fists flying.

WARD: Scrum half's waiting.

CANNIFFE: Flankers farting.

KNIGHT: Throats burning, eyes streaming.

MCLOUGHLIN: Scrum turning.

WARD: Ref whistling.

SEAMUS: Prop's rising.

TUCKER: Ref talking.

WARD (in a Welsh accent): No more biting, gouging, punching or swearing, you.

ROBERTSON: Right Ref, down we go.

MCLOUGHLIN: Feet dig in. Claw at earth.

CANNIFFE: Shoulder on buttock.

TUCKER: Cheek on thigh.

KNIGHT: Props crushing, hooker watching, arm tapping, hooker sweeping.

CANNIFFE: Scrum half spinning.

WARD (now as himself): Ward taking, looking. Drop goal on.

The lights return to the cold exterior setting.

Robertson breaks from the scrum and moves downstage centre. The other actors run backwards in slow motion.

ROBERTSON: Running, arms outstretched, anticipate flight path of ball.

WARD: Head up, head down, drop, and strike spinningly.

ROBERTSON: Arcingly, arcingly between the posts.

WARD: Whistle.

ROBERTSON: Three points.

All freeze apart from Ward.

WARD: Yesss. Inside pleasure explodes in my brain. Wohoooooooooo! Outside, turn and grimace. Rugby demands modest, humble celebrations of joy. Extravagant celebrations by scoring players are considered from the spirit of rugby. Emotion is best turned inward. To stroke the fire in the belly. One or two players punch me in the small of the back or on the top of the head.

The others do so, the blows getting more ridiculous and harder as they go on.

It is manly acknowledgement of my skill. It hurts like hell but they mean well.

Seamus kicks Ward in the backside.

SEAMUS: Good man, Wardy.

READING

1 Summarise what has happened in this scene in one sentence.

2 What do you learn about rugby from this scene?

3 What is humorous about this scene?

4 In this scene, the actors narrate the action as well as physically displaying the action, like individual sports commentators. What do you think of this? Is it necessary? Does it add to the humour of the scene?

5 The same six actors play a cast of sixty-two characters. What do you think the actors do to ensure the audience knows when an actor has changed character?

6 What type of stage would you use if you were directing this play and why? (See page 144.)

7 If you could add three sound effects to this scene, what would you add and why?

8 Why are there so many colons in a play script? What is their purpose? (See page 274.)

9 Does this text remind you of any sporting occasion you have been to?

WRITING

Sports commentators use language to create a sense of narrative, drama and suspense when they are covering a sports event. Part of that excitement is created on the field of play itself, but sports commentary also has an impact on the audience watching live sport on TV or listening on the radio. Watch well-known sports commentator Andrew Cotter reporting on the daily lives of his dogs Mabel and Olive. He creates a sense of drama, suspense and story through his witty use of the language usually used in sports commentary:

edco.ie/rhg3

Using the same style, write your own sports commentary transcript to narrate over a nature video clip, with the sound switched off.

- Start by choosing a short nature video clip from YouTube. Make sure to pick a clip where there is plenty of action.
- Watch the clip twice, then jot down the actions in the clip.
- Think about what sport you could compare the actions in the clip to.
- Think about what sport-specific language you could use.
- Decide how to build the story and how to add suspense around the narrative to make it dramatic.
- Write the commentary transcript.
- Record or perform your animal commentary and play it for your class.

PERFORMING

Divide into small groups, then pick one of the machines from the list in the box below. As a group, you will have to come up with a way of performing as this machine.

dishwasher	microwave	tractor	popcorn-making machine
bulldozer	sewing machine	toaster	speedboat
drill	treadmill	lawnmower	vacuum cleaner

- Think about how you might use your bodies to create the shape or action of the machine.
- Consider the use of a soundscape. Are there any sound effects or noises you could create to bring your machine to life?
- Perform as your chosen machine to your classmates.
- At the end of your machine performance, the audience should try to guess what type of machine you were performing as.

Blood Brothers by Willy Russell

Blood Brothers is set in 1970's Liverpool, when unemployment and poverty were widespread. Mickey is one of Mrs Johnstone's many children. At the start of the play he's only seven years old and living in poverty. Growing up with no father figure, he idolizes his older brother Sammy.

In the play, the seven-year-old Mickey is played by an adult, adding to the humour of this scene, which is delivered as a **monologue**. This is a technique in drama where an actor communicates their character's innermost thoughts and feelings directly to the audience.

MICKEY:

I wish I was our Sammy,
Our Sammy's nearly ten.
He's got two worms and a catapult
An' he's built an underground den.
But I'm not allowed to go in there,
I have to stay near the gate,
'Cos me Mam says I'm only seven,
But I'm not, I'm nearly eight!
I sometimes hate our Sammy,
He robbed me toy car y'know,
Now the wheels are missin' an' the top's broke off,
An' the bleedin' thing won't go.
An' he said when he took it, it was just like that,
But it wasn't, it went dead straight,
But y'can't say nott'n when they think y' seven,
An' y' not, y' nearly eight!
I wish I was our Sammy,
Y' wanna see him spit,
Straight in y' eye from twenty yards
An' every time a hit.
He's allowed to play with matches,
And he goes to bed dead late,
And I have to go at seven,
Even though I'm nearly eight!
Y'know our Sammy
He draws nudey women,
Without arms, or legs, or even heads
In the baths, when he goes swimmin'.
But I'm not allowed to go to the baths,
Me Mam says I have to wait,
'Cos I might get drowned, 'cos I'm only seven,
But I'm not, I'm nearly eight!

Y' know our Sammy,

Y'know what he sometimes does?

He wees straight through the letter box

Of the house next door to us.

I tried to do it one night,

But I had to stand on a crate,

'Cos I couldn't reach the letter box,

But I will by the time I'm eight!

READING

1 List all the cool things that Sammy owns that Mickey is envious of.

2 List all the cool things that Sammy does that Mickey idolizes him for.

3 Why do you think Mickey looks up to Sammy so much?

4 What can you tell about Mickey's upbringing from the way that he talks? Think about the use of the apostrophe to join words together and the accent he is speaking in.

5 Complete the stage directions editing task in your activity book (see pages 99–100).

6 Complete the performance task in your activity book (see page 101).

7 When you were a small child, who did you idolize and why?

COMMUNICATING: GROUP DISCUSSION

Watch the performance of 'I wish I was our Sammy'. Then discuss the questions below:

edco.ie/5qe6

1 What do you think the audience learns about Mickey from the performance of this scene?

2 What did you notice about the staging of the scene: lighting, sound, props, set design?

3 What was enjoyable about this performance?

4 Were there any similarities to how you planned to perform this scene?

WRITING

Can you remember anything that you really wanted to do as a small child but were told you could not do because you were too small? Write a dialogue between your seven-year-old self and the person who told you that you couldn't do something because of your age.

PERFORMING

Get into groups of four. For this performance task, one of you is going to be a teacher and the other three are going to be seven-year-old children.

In this scenario, the class goldfish bowl was smashed at breaktime. The teacher has narrowed the culprits down to three children in her class. She investigates by talking to these students outside the classroom. Two of the children are the bowl smashers and the other child is completely innocent.

Pick up the scene from here and improvise what you think might happen next.

Frankenstein, adapted by Philip Pullman

This play is based on the novel *Frankenstein* by Mary Shelley. Philip Pullman adapted it for the stage. *Frankenstein* is the famous story of a young man who thinks he can change the world by making better human beings. Instead, he creates a living monster with a mind of its own, with disastrous and murderous consequences. This scene is known as the creation scene, where the monster is brought to life. Clerval is Frankenstein's friend and is about to try to stop him from creating the monster.

FRANKENSTEIN: Must it finish, then? So close…so nearly ready!

He holds his head in his hands.

After a moment there comes a tremendous clap of Thunder – deafening – as if right overhead. Frankenstein sits up at once and stares at the form on the bench. It is quite still. He jumps up and runs to the window, through which we can hear the start of heavy rainfall. He looks out and upwards, and is outlined in a flash of lightning. He looks around again, checking the wire, but still the figure lies unmoving. Then comes more thunder – longer and even louder than before.

Feverishly he runs to the bench, checks the wire, and folds back the sheet a little way so that he can see the Monster's face.

FRANKENSTEIN: It must be tonight – it must be!

A frantic knocking on the door.

CLERVAL: [Off] Frankenstein! Open up! Open up!

FRANKENSTEIN: No! Go away Clerval! I can't be disturbed!

CLERVAL: Frankenstein I must talk to you—

FRANKENSTEIN: Impossible! Go away man!

More furious hammering on the door.

CLERVAL: You must let me in – I know what you're doing, Frankenstein—

Frankenstein runs to the door.

FRANKENSTEIN: Clerval, I beg you – leave me alone – you don't know how dangerous this could be—

But the door bursts open. Frankenstein is flung aside as Clerval runs in, looks around and runs to where the Monster is lying. He tears off the sheet and flings it to the floor as Frankenstein recovers and runs across to tear him away.

FRANKENSTEIN: Don't! Don't touch it! The lightning could strike at any moment—

They struggle in front of the window, illuminated by another great flash of lightning; and almost at once comes the thunder. They freeze, both looking in apprehension at the bench. Then comes another flash, lighting up the whole room, accompanied by showers of sparks and wreaths of smoke – and on the bench the Monster tenses convulsively.

CLERVAL: No!

FRANKENSTEIN: Leave it – leave it—

Another flash, more Thunder – and this time the Monster really comes alive, thrashing from side to side as if trying to sit up. Clerval breaks away from Frankenstein and stares at it in horror.

CLERVAL: Frankenstein – what have you created?

FRANKENSTEIN: I told you not to come in!

CLERVAL: This is pure evil, Frankenstein—

He starts forward as if to destroy it, but Frankenstein, seeing his intention, seizes a chair and strikes him with it from behind. The chair breaks – Clerval falls stunned.

FRANKENSTEIN: Oh, my friend – you don't know how important it is…

He runs to the Monster's side and tears off the wires, and then helps it to sit up. The storm is still raging outside, and there are flashes of lightning. The Monster is enormously tall and powerfully built. His open eyes are hideous, red rimmed and glaring in a waxy yellow face. His lips are black, scars crisscross his cheeks and his face is framed with matted black hair. He is naked to the waist. He wears nothing but simple breeches.

The Monster stands there swaying as Frankenstein moves back to get a better look at his creation. Then the Monster raises a hand and Frankenstein reaches up to touch it.

My creature! And living! Let me see you – let me look at you – ah…

He runs his hands over the Monster's limbs, checking their soundness, helping him balance upright. The Monster's eyes follow him as if confused.

Then Frankenstein stands back, and a first realisation of what he has made passes over him. He shudders.

But you're not what I thought you'd be… I thought I was making an angel! D'you know that? I thought I was making something better than human! Something so precious and beautiful that everyone would love it – and look at you. Look at what I've done.

The Monster takes a lurching step towards him. Frankenstein backs away nervously.

No! This isn't what I wanted. Oh, dear God, what have I done? Is it alive after all?

The Monster makes a strange noise.

No! I didn't mean this! I didn't want this at all—

He turns away, and with a cry of fear and horror, runs out of the room.

No – no!

The Monster stumbles forward and falls over the body of Clerval lying in his way. He recovers and kneels up, and runs his hands wonderingly over Clerval's face – and then, as wonderingly, over his own. He looks up and around, seeing everything for the first time. Then, with heavy grace, he gets to his feet and moves towards the open door. He stops there – looks back once at Clerval – then goes out as Clerval stirs and groans.

CLERVAL: Frankenstein – where are you…

Clerval pushes himself up and looks around. Seeing the empty bench, he staggers up, finds the trailing wire and looks at the open door.

It's gone! It's gone! Frankenstein… in God's name what have you done?

He runs out. A final flash of lightning fills the window, the Thunder crashes out and dies away as darkness falls.

READING

1 Summarise the action in this scene in one sentence.

2 At what exact point do you think Frankenstein regrets what he has done?

3 Frankenstein dug up dead bodies to experiment with, in order to create his monster. Do you think this makes him a monster or not?

4 Who do you think is a more frightening character – Frankenstein or the monster? Why?

5 If you had the power to create and bring a human being to life, would you?

6 How do you think things will go for Frankenstein and his monster in the future?

7 List all the sound effects you would need to use if you were staging this scene. What impact do you think using sound effects would have on the atmosphere of the scene?

8 Complete the staging a scene task in your activity book (see page 102).

9 The script includes the use of a lot of exclamation marks. What does this tell an actor reading this script? (See page 272).

10 Does this scene remind you of any other text you have studied this year? In what way is it similar?

COMMUNICATING: GROUP DISCUSSION

There have been many films made about Frankenstein. Watch this clip of the monster coming to life from the 1931 film and then discuss the questions below:

edco.ie/6k39

1 How do you think the director intended you to feel after watching that scene?

2 How *did* you feel after watching that scene?

3 Compare the film scene to the drama extract you have read. Which, do you think, would be more appealing to an audience of teenagers and why?

WRITING

Sometimes the most terrifying thing in a story is a character who initially looks very normal but slowly reveals themselves to be a monster. For example, a character might betray themselves to be a vampire by showing their fangs or a werewolf when the full moon comes out. Write a paragraph describing a transformation of a character from man to monster.

Writing Tips

- First choose the type of monster you want your character to transform into.

- Think about how the character looked before, what triggered their transformation and what they looked like afterwards.

- You should use the senses to describe the monster: what they looked like, sounded like, smelled like and felt like.

PERFORMING

Create a monster character for a group performance. Choose attributes for your monster from the lists below. Select an unusual physical characteristic, a supernatural power and a bizarre sound that they make.

Unusual physical characteristic	Supernatural power	Bizarre sound
Flippers for feet	Can see through walls	A car beeping
Seventeen eyes	Invisibility	Teeth grinding
Eight legs	Self-cloning	A sheep bleating
Covered in slime	Fire-breathing	Growling
Shark head	Super strength	Buzzing like a bee
Giant body	360-degree vision	Singing like a bird
Covered in armour	Mind control	Hissing like a snake
Headless	Melting and reforming	Tick-tock of a clock

Divide into groups of three. Pick a scenario from the list below. Then perform an improvisation sketch to your classmates, with each of you in your monster character.

Competing at a table quiz	Dancing to hip-hop music	Running a marathon
Heading into battle during a war	On a reality TV dating show	Taking part in a cookery competition

PROJECT:
From Page To Stage

PROJECT BRIEF

Write, produce and perform your own one-scene comedy play. The play should be loosely linked to your experience of secondary school – although it can be purely fictional – and the intended audience is teenagers.

To be successful in this project, you will need to:

- bring an imaginative and creative idea from page to stage
- write an engaging and humorous short play script
- make consistently imaginative choices in staging the play
- perform convincingly, speaking clearly with sustained engagement with the audience.

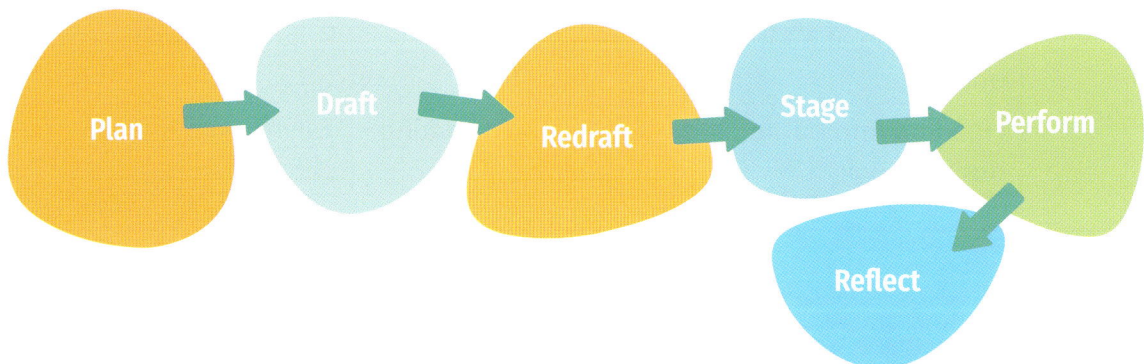

Plan → Draft → Redraft → Stage → Perform → Reflect

Plan It

The basic theme or idea for the script could develop from absolutely anything to do with school. Here are some ideas to get you started:

Someone has left their PE gear at home – again	Someone is late for school – again	Someone suspicious is in the school building
Someone has been threatened by an older student and ordered to bring in some money or 'there will be trouble'	Someone is in trouble for something they haven't done	Someone has lost something 'borrowed' without permission

1 Brainstorm a list of potential ideas: think about funny or dramatic things you've seen so far this year or maybe funny stories you've heard about school.

2 Once you have chosen your basic idea, you must now try to develop the plot. Complete the plot development exercise in your activity book (see pages 103–104).

3 Now complete the planning the plot exercise in your activity book (see page 104).

4   Next, you should develop the characters in your play by giving them a backstory. How did they become who they are the day the audience meets them onstage? Write a short paragraph detailing each character's backstory. For example:

> Jane is twelve. She was happy at primary school but finds secondary school rather large and unfriendly. Her best friend from primary school has moved away. She has just found a new friend, Sally, who is fun to be with, but sometimes skips school and is often in trouble. Jane used to get on well with her mum, but recently there have been lots of arguments…

Draft It

Create your first draft of your play. Remember to use a play script layout (see page 152). Don't forget stage directions are what you want your characters to do and dialogue is what you want your characters to say.

Redraft It

Organise a read through of your play. Ask your friends to read the different parts and listen to how the dialogue flows.

- Change anything that sounds like a narrative story into dialogue.
- Have you left out any punctuation? Was that line a statement or a question? Your actors will need to know how to deliver their lines.
- Have you left out any stage directions?
- Have you laid out the play script properly? Look back at the annotated example on page 152 to check your punctuation and layout.

Stage It

In your activity book (see page 105), use the staging a scene graphic organiser to plan how you will stage your play. Then complete the justifying your choices worksheet (see pages 106–107), which helps you explore why you made the decisions you have for your play.

Perform It

In your activity book (see page 108), complete the preparing a performance graphic organiser to ensure you're ready for your performance.

Decide whether you will perform each play in turn or choose one play script you would all like to perform. You also need to decide who will direct the play and who will play each part.

Then it's time to perform your one-scene play with the rest of your class as your audience!

> ## REFLECTION
>
> 1   Which element of this project did you enjoy the most? Why?
> 2   Which element did you find most difficult? Why?
> 3   If you had to do it all again, what would you change?

Test Your Knowledge

1 **What is a theatre-in-the-round stage?**

a) A stage framed by an arch, which is like a window that frames the action

b) A central performance area enclosed by the audience on all sides

c) A stage that juts out into the audience, with the audience sitting on three sides

d) When the stage and seating is not fixed and can be altered to suit the needs of the play or the whim of the director

2 **What are props?**

a) The clothes that an actor wears in the performance of a play

b) The objects that characters use in a play

c) All the scenery, backdrops and furniture the audience sees at a production of a play

d) The places where a drama or play is performed

3 **What is a playwright?**

a) The person who designs the lighting

b) The person who designs the costumes

c) The person who writes the play

d) The person who acts in the play

4 **What are stage directions?**

a) The people who direct a play

b) The sounds used in a play

c) The places where the props and sets should go

d) The playwright's instructions to the actors as to what to do on stage

5 A .... stage juts out into the audience with the audience sitting on three sides.

6 A .... stage is framed by an arch, which is like a window that frames the action happening on stage.

7 **Match the theatre job with the job description.**

Theatre job	Job description
Director	The person who writes the script for the play
Costume designer	The person who designs the lighting for the stage
Playwright	The person who interprets the script and tells the actors how to perform
Lighting director	The person who chooses the clothes and make-up for the actors

8 **Match the element of stagecraft with the explanation.**

Element of stagecraft	Explanation
Props	The clothes that an actor wears in the performance of a play
Costume	All the scenery, backdrops and furniture the audience sees at a production of a play
Lighting	The objects that characters use in a play
Sets	The floor lights, spotlights and floodlights that a lighting director might use to create an effect or atmosphere

9 **What might be important to know if you were designing a set for a play?**

10 **What are the three things that make up the sound of a play in the theatre?**

11 **How might a director use costume to tell the audience something?**

12 **What things must an actor consider before playing a part?**

13 **Thinking back on all you have learned in this unit, try the personal dictionary task on pages 109–110 of your activity book.**

Practise Your Writing Skills

1 **Write a short scene using one of these prompts.**

- A thief caught red-handed tries to convince a Garda that they are innocent.
- Two people have the exact same strange dream and tell each other about it.
- A singer is judged after her terrible performance on a TV talent show.
- A tiger has escaped from his cage at the zoo and people are panicking.
- A two-year-old has run away and his babysitter is frantically looking for him.

2 **You have now been given the job of producing your one-scene play. Write a short paragraph on each of the points below.**

- Explain what type of stage you would choose and why.
- Explain what props you would need and why.
- Explain how you would design the set and why.
- Describe the costumes you would choose for your characters and explain your choices.

Interactive website

Go to **www.edco.ie/touchstones1** for interactive activities based on this unit.

UNIT 5
SHAKESPEARE

SHAKESPEARE KNOWLEDGE ORGANISER

Things I need to know

- **Performance:** Shakespeare's plays were written to be performed. Theatre in Shakespeare's time was different – there was no lighting, no roof and some people had to stand to watch a performance.

- **Punctuation:** When you are reading a Shakespeare play, you need to get into the habit of looking at the punctuation, not the line breaks, to figure out when a sentence ends.

- **Inventions:** Shakespeare invented over 400 words by joining two words together, adding prefixes or suffixes, changing nouns into verbs and coining totally new words.

- **Insults:** Shakespeare used impressive insults to keep his audience entertained and amused.

- **Retired words:** Some words that Shakespeare used will look unfamiliar as they have completely fallen out of use or been replaced by more modern words.

- **Pronouns:** A pronoun is a part of speech that replaces a noun in a sentence. When Shakespeare was writing his plays, there were more pronouns in speech than we have today.

- **Contractions:** Shakespeare often cut out syllables and replaced them with an apostrophe to make the rhythm of a line fit better.

- **Inversions:** Sometimes Shakespeare changed the order of words in his lines to fit a particular rhythm or to make a rhyme.

Skills I will develop

- Engaging and participating in dramatic oral communication exercises
- Delivering short oral texts using appropriate language
- Identifying and understanding the grammatical features of Shakespeare's English
- Reading and understanding a Shakespearean text

Project

- Who Was William Shakespeare?: Researching and writing about the life and times of William Shakespeare

What do I know?

What do you already know about William Shakespeare? Do you know any of his plays or poems? Do you know where he is from? Do you know why he is famous?

Go to your activity book (see page 111) and complete the Shakespeare knowledge download activity.

Who Is Shakespeare?

PowerPoint

William Shakespeare is often regarded as the best writer in the English language. He was born in Stratford-upon-Avon in England in 1564. He wrote 38 plays and about 160 poems. Shakespeare's plays have been adapted and performed thousands of times, all around the world. Both his plays and his poems remain popular to this day.

To find out more about William Shakespeare, complete the Who Was William Shakespeare? project on page 194.

> He was not of an age, but for all time!
> **Ben Jonson**

> Shakespeare has united the powers of exciting laughter and sorrow not only in one mind, but in one composition.
> **Samuel Johnson, Preface to Shakespeare**

> He was naturally learned; he needed not the spectacles of books to read nature; he looked inwards, and found her there.
> **John Dryden, 'Essay of Dramatic Poesy'**

> When I read Shakespeare I am struck with wonder That such trivial people should muse and thunder In such lovely language.
> **D.H. Lawrence**

Which of these quotes do you like best? Which quotes do you agree with? Are there any you disagree with?

Performances

One of the most important things to bear in mind when navigating your way through the works of Shakespeare is that his plays were not written to be read out of a book, but to be performed on stage. The theatre was one of the most popular forms of entertainment in Shakespeare's time – our modern-day equivalent would be the cinema.

Inside Shakespeare's theatre – the Globe Theatre in London – there were two pillars on the stage that supported a roof over the actors' heads. This was called the 'Heavens' and was painted with stars, a sun and a moon – it had a trapdoor in it, from which actors could be lowered on a rope or a wire. At the back of the stage was the musicians' gallery. Musicians with trumpets, drums and other instruments played songs and made sound effects. Shakespeare had to include a lot of descriptive detail when describing the setting of his plays and he had to make sure to let the audience know if day changed to night as there was no lighting.

The audience would have included many different types of people. At the top of the building there were galleries where the middle-class audience sat. There were 'Gentlemen's Rooms', or boxes, for the rich and famous people, and these cost a lot of money. The lower-class citizens, the servants and apprentices, had to stand in the 'pit' in front of the stage and were known as 'groundlings'. They didn't have to pay much to get in, but they did have to stand for the whole performance. The audience would have made a lot of noise during performances – more like fans at football match than an audience in a modern-day theatre – cheering, hissing, clapping, booing and crying.

All this had a big impact on how Shakespeare wrote his plays; sometimes a play could go on for three hours and he had to keep his audience entertained and engaged. Shakespeare had to make sure there was plenty of conflict and tension in each act to keep the audience interested. He also included moments of comedy and romance, as well as sword fights and the throwing of vicious insults to keep the audience on their toes.

The actors were professionals and they had to learn up to 800 words a day. Women were not allowed to act on stage, as it was seen as improper. So young men had to play the female parts in plays; perhaps this is why Shakespeare went into such detail when describing his leading ladies. The actors also had to do all of the other jobs that go along with running a theatre, such as design the sets, produce the special effects, sell the tickets and refreshments, and prompt the other actors on stage.

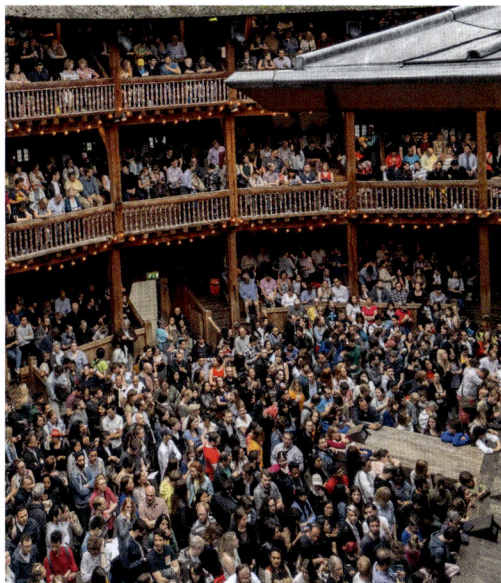

READING

ACTIVITY

In your activity book, complete the then and now sorting activity (see page 112) to learn about the differences between theatre today and in Shakespeare's time.

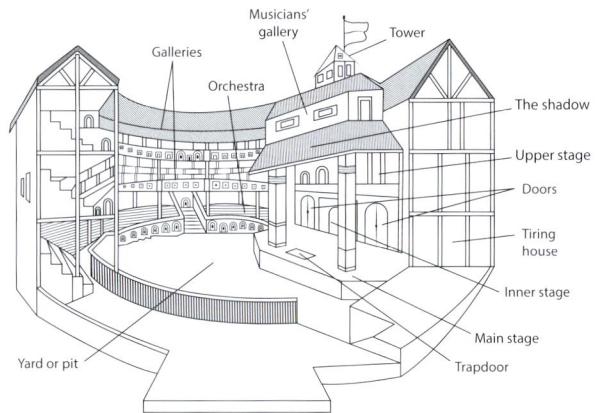

Galleries

Musicians' gallery

Tower

Orchestra

The shadow

Upper stage

Doors

Tiring house

Inner stage

Main stage

Yard or pit

Trapdoor

WRITING

Imagine you have the power to time travel. You have just returned to the present day after a trip to 1592, where you visited the Globe Theatre to see one of Shakespeare's plays being performed. Write a diary entry where you describe what you saw and compare it to your experience of a theatre in the present day.

PERFORMING

Divide up into groups of three to create an improvised performance. Each of you should choose a character from the list below.

Imagine you are all walking to an opening night performance at Shakespeare's Globe Theatre in the 1500s. The characters should walk up and down the performance space as if they are walking through the streets of London and should chat about the things they are seeing.

Character 1	Character 2	Character 3
Shakespeare, worried about how his new play will be received	An actor in Shakespeare's theatre company	Another actor in Shakespeare's theatre company

Shakespeare's Punctuation

Shakespeare wrote his plays using prose, blank verse and rhymed verse. Therefore, the script of a Shakespearean play looks quite like a poem in places and very different to a modern play script. When you are reading a Shakespeare play, you need to get into the habit of looking at the punctuation, not the line break (where the sentence jumps down onto the next line). Just because a line finishes and the text moves to the next line, this does not mean that the sentence has ended.

How lines look in the script ⟶

> How if, when I am laid into the tomb,
> I wake before the time that Romeo
> Come to redeem me?

How lines should be read

> How if, when I am laid into the tomb, I wake before the time that Romeo come to redeem me?

PERFORMING

Go to your activity book and complete the oral language tasks on reading Shakespeare's punctuation (see pages 113–114).

Shakespeare's Words

Inventions

If Shakespeare could not find the exact word he was looking for, he often invented words himself. In fact, Shakespeare was the most productive inventor of words for the English language in the history of the world, ever. There are 422 words in the Oxford English Dictionary that Shakespeare invented.

So, how did he do this? Turn the page to find descriptions of the different techniques Shakespeare used to invent words.

Joining two words together			
Modern examples	crowdfunding staycation		
Shakespearean example 1	arch-villain	By joining these two words, Shakespeare made the description more extreme than just 'villain'.	'You that way and you this, but two in company; / Each man apart, all single and alone, / Yet an arch-villain keeps him company.' – Timon *Timon of Athens*, Act V, Scene I
Shakespearean example 2	cold-blooded	By joining the words 'cold' and 'blooded' together, Shakespeare created an image of a person that is cruel and unfeeling.	'Thou cold-blooded slave, hast thou not spoke like thunder on my side, been sworn my soldier, bidding me depend upon thy stars, thy fortune and thy strength?' – Constance *King John*, Act III, Scene I

Adding prefixes or suffixes			
Modern examples	hyperlink preteen		
Shakespearean example 1	uncomfortable	By adding the prefix 'un' to the word 'comfortable', Shakespeare created an opposite.	'Uncomfortable time, why camest thou now / To murder, murder our solemnity?' – Capulet *Romeo and Juliet*, Act IV, Scene V
Shakespearean example 2	fashionable	By adding the suffix 'able' to the word 'fashion', Shakespeare created a useful adjective for everything that is popular or approved of in today's world.	'For time is like a fashionable host that slightly shakes his parting guest by the hand, and with his arms outstretch'd, as he would fly, grasps the comer: welcome ever smiles, and farewell goes out sighing.' – Ulysses *Troilus and Cressida*, Act III, Scene III

Changing nouns into verbs			
Modern examples	google troll		
Shakespearean example 1	elbow	By changing the noun 'elbow' into a verb, Shakespeare created a new way to hurt someone.	'A sovereign shame so elbows him...' – Kent *King Lear*, Act IV, Scene IV
Shakespearean example 2	champion	By changing the noun 'champion' to a verb, Shakespeare created a new way to express that you supported or defended a person or a cause.	'Rather than so, come fate into the list. / And champion me to the utterance!' – Macbeth *Macbeth*, Act III, Scene I

Coining a new word			
Modern examples	totes noob		
Shakespearean example 1	swaggered	Swaggered comes from the word 'swag', meaning 'to sway from side to side'.	'An't please your Majesty, a rascal that swaggered with me last night...' – Williams *Henry V*, Act IV, Scene VII
Shakespearean example 2	manager	The root of the word – the Latin 'manus' – means 'hand'. So to be a manager is to have a hand in something, or to control something.	'Where is our usual manager of mirth?' – Theseus *A Midsummer Night's Dream*, Act V, Scene I

READING

Go to your activity book and complete the invented words task (see page 115).

WRITING

1 Find out three other words that Shakespeare invented. Look for the line and play they appeared in. Can you figure out what technique Shakespeare used to invent the word?

2 New words or invented words are added to the Oxford English Dictionary every year. Research three words that were added to the dictionary last year and try to work out how or why they were made up: oxfordlearnersdictionaries.com

3 Invent your own words! Try using one of Shakespeare's word invention techniques to create new words for the following things:

An abnormally large fruit or vegetable	An older person incapable of using any form of technology	A person addicted to using their phone
A breed of hairless rabbit	A car that uses rubbish as fuel	A naughty toddler who is always running off

PERFORMING

Get into a group of four and act out an interview improvisation scenario. The interview is for a job as a teacher in a secondary school. There is a board of interviewers and an interviewee. The interviewee tries to sound smart by inventing words in the middle of the interview and the interviewers react.

Take some time to think about your character before you begin. If you are the interviewee, what words might you make up to impress the board? If you are on the interview board, are you the principal? The deputy principal? A subject teacher? Do you ask difficult questions or easy questions? Do you appear cold and frosty or warm and kind?

Insults

Shakespeare was a master of writing insults. His put-downs are legendary and an Elizabethan theatre audience would have thoroughly enjoyed their appearance in a play.

COMMUNICATING: GROUP DISCUSSION

Take a look at the examples of Shakespearean insults in the box below. Discuss what you think the character is trying to say about the person they are insulting.

'I am sick when I do look on thee.'	A Midsummer Night's Dream (Act II, Scene I)
'Away, you three-inch fool!'	The Taming of the Shrew (Act IV, Scene I)
'More of your conversation would infect my brain'	Coriolanus (Act II, Scene I)
'Thou lump of foul deformity'	Richard III (Act I, Scene II)

PERFORMING

Go to your activity book to complete the tasks on Shakespearean insults (see pages 115–117).

Retired words

There are hundreds of words in Shakespeare's plays that will look unfamiliar to you, but you may be able to figure them out by using clues in the text around the word. There are also hundreds of words in Shakespeare's plays that you will never have come across before, words that have completely fallen out of use or, in some cases, been replaced by more modern words.

Examples of words you may be able to figure out	Examples of words that have fallen out of use
visage – face	capon – chicken
prithee – I beg you	choler – cranky
methinks – I think	cozen – cheat
naught – nothing	jakes – toilet
yore – a long time ago	parley – talk
yonder – over there	quaff – drink

READING

ACTIVITY Go to your activity book to complete the retired words matching task (see page 118).

PERFORMING

Divide into pairs and try this improvisation task. In this scenario, one person is trying to order a meal at a fast-food restaurant. The customer is speaking in Shakespearean English and the person working at the cash register cannot understand what they are trying to order.

If you are playing the customer, think about what retired Shakespearean words might be good to use, as well as any other words or phrases you've learned so far. The fast-food worker should try to remain calm but will become increasingly frustrated.

Shakespeare's Grammar

Pronouns

A **pronoun** is a part of speech that replaces a noun in a sentence (see page 276 for more on pronouns). When Shakespeare was writing his plays, there were more pronouns in speech than we have today – for example, he regularly uses 'thy', 'thine', 'thee' and 'thou'. There are different types of pronouns, depending on what part of a sentence they appear in.

	Pronoun = subject of the sentence	Pronoun = object of the sentence	Pronoun = possessive determiner	Pronoun = possessive
Modern English	**You**	**You**	**Your**	**Yours**
	You are a potato.	Potato likes **you**.	**Your** potato is mouldy.	It is not my potato, it's **yours**.
Shakespeare's English	**Thou**	**Thee**	**Thy**	**Thine**
	Thou art a potato.	Potato liketh **thee**.	**Thy** potato is mouldy.	It's not my potato, it's **thine**.

READING

ACTIVITY Go to your activity book to complete the tasks on pronouns (see pages 118–119).

PERFORMING

In the theatre, the word **corpsing** is used to describe when an actor breaks character while in the middle of performing onstage, usually in the form of laughing. The word 'corpse' is used because when you break character, your character is essentially dead.

For this activity, sit in a circle with your group. Each person should pick a character type from the list in the box below.

a vain hero	a terrifying villain	a strict teacher
a bold student	a grumpy grandparent	a sad clown

Now, as a group, choose one of the short Shakespearean phrases from the list in the box below to be passed from person to person around the circle.

To be, or not to be, that is the question.	Is this a dagger which I see before me?	Get thee to a nunnery!
A horse! A horse! My kingdom for a horse!	Off with his head!	A plague o' both your houses!
A rose by any other name would smell as sweet.	Now is the winter of our discontent.	I must be cruel, only to be kind.

Each person should say the phrase as the character that they have chosen, passing the phrase around the circle. The aim of the game is to stay in character and not break character or corpse as the game progresses. When someone corpses they are out. Keep going until only one person is left.

Contractions

A **contraction** is when you make a word smaller by taking out a letter and replacing it with an apostrophe (see page 273). Shakespeare often cut out syllables and replaced them with an apostrophe to make the rhythm of a line fit better.

Over ⟶ O'er

Them ⟶ 'em

Taken ⟶ Ta'en

It is ⟶ 'tis

Never ⟶ Ne'er

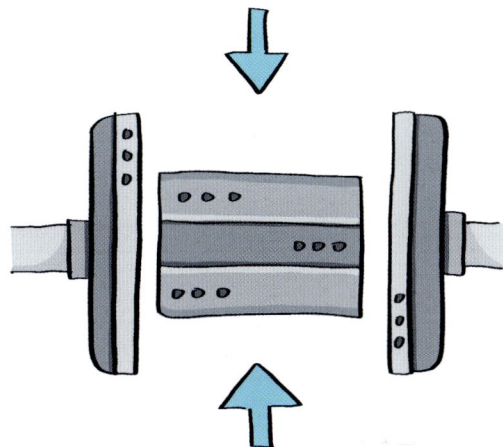

READING

Turn to your activity book to complete the tasks on contractions (see pages 119–120).

Inversions

Sometimes Shakespeare changed the order of words in his lines to fit a particular rhythm or to make a rhyme.

Normal order ⟶ I went to Dublin

Inverted order ⟶ To Dublin went I

Inverted order	Normal order
'Of honourable reckoning are you both' ⟶	You are both of honourable reckoning
'Never was seen so black a day as this' ⟶	A day as black as this was never seen

READING

Turn to your activity book to complete the word inversion task (see page 121).

PERFORMING

In pairs, create a performance where one person speaks in inversions and the other person speaks normally. The person speaking normally should get increasingly more and more frustrated with the person speaking in inversions. Pick from the list of scenarios in the box below.

Ordering a pizza on the phone	A talk-show host interviewing a guest	An awkward first date
A lawyer convincing a judge to dismiss a case	Two people fighting about a seat on the bus	Trying to return a faulty item of clothing to a shop

Translating Shakespeare

Below is the prologue (the beginning) of Shakespeare's play, *Romeo and Juliet*. Alongside it is the modern translation or version.

Shakespeare's original text	No Fear version
Two households, both alike in dignity, In fair Verona, where we lay our scene, From ancient grudge break to new mutiny, Where civil blood makes civil hands unclean. From forth the fatal loins of these two foes A pair of star-cross'd lovers take their life; Whose misadventured piteous overthrows Do with their death bury their parents' strife. The fearful passage of their death-mark'd love, And the continuance of their parents' rage, Which, but their children's end, nought could remove, Is now the two hours' traffic of our stage; The which if you with patient ears attend, What here shall miss, our toil shall strive to mend.	In the beautiful city of Verona, where our story takes place, a long-standing hatred between two families erupts into new violence, and citizens stain their hands with the blood of their fellow citizens. Two unlucky children of these enemy families become lovers and commit suicide. Their unfortunate deaths put an end to their parents' feud. For the next two hours, we will watch the story of their doomed love and their parents' anger, which nothing but the children's deaths could stop. If you listen to us patiently, we'll make up for everything we've left out in this prologue onstage.

COMMUNICATING: GROUP DISCUSSION

Divide into small groups to discuss the main differences between the two versions of the prologue in the box above.

READING

Turn to your activity book to complete the translation task (see pages 121–222).

WRITING

Write a short scene for a play using Shakespearean language. Use all of the knowledge and skills you have gathered so far in this unit to help you with your writing. Remember that this is a scene for a play, so it should involve stage directions for the action and dialogue for the speech.

Choose from the scene ideas in the box below.

Two brave knights have fallen in love with the same woman	A young man is visited by the ghost of his father and told to avenge his death	A king decides to divide up his kingdom between his three daughters, based on who loves and adores him the most

Romeo and Juliet

Romeo and Juliet is the tragic story of two young lovers from rival families. This extract from Act II Scene II, known as the balcony scene, is one of Shakespeare's most well-known scenes. At this point in the play, Romeo and Juliet have met at Juliet's father's party and fallen in love at first sight. Soon after, they learn they are from rival families. Romeo leaves the party with his friends, but runs back to the Capulet mansion.

A **soliloquy** is a private speech or monologue that a character makes when they are alone, giving the audience an insight into what the character is thinking and feeling.

Romeo and Juliet Extract from Act II, Scene II	
Shakespeare's original text	**No Fear version**
ROMEO He jests at scars that never felt a wound. *Enter Juliet above.* But, soft, what light through yonder window breaks? It is the east, and Juliet is the sun. Arise, fair sun, and kill the envious moon, Who is already sick and pale with grief, That thou her maid art far more fair than she: Be not her maid, since she is envious: Her vestal livery is but sick and green And none but fools do wear it, cast it off. It is my lady, O, it is my love! O, that she knew she were! She speaks, yet she says nothing: what of that? Her eye discourses: I will answer it. I am too bold, 'tis not to me she speaks: Two of the fairest stars in all the heaven, Having some business, do entreat her eyes To twinkle in their spheres till they return. What if her eyes were there, they in her head? The brightness of her cheek would shame those stars, As daylight doth a lamp; her eye in heaven Would through the airy region stream so bright That birds would sing and think it were not night. See how she leans her cheek upon her hand! O, that I were a glove upon that hand, That I might touch that cheek! **JULIET** Ay me!	**ROMEO** It's easy for someone to joke about scars if they've never been cut. *Juliet enters on the balcony.* But wait, what's that light in the window over there? It is the east, and Juliet is the sun. Rise up, beautiful sun, and kill the jealous moon. The moon is already sick and pale with grief because you, Juliet, her maid, are more beautiful than she. Don't be her maid, because she is jealous. Virginity makes her look sick and green. Only fools hold on to their virginity. Let it go. Oh, there's my lady! Oh, it is my love. Oh, I wish she knew how much I love her. She's talking, but she's not saying anything. So what? Her eyes are saying something. I will answer them. I am too bold. She's not talking to me. Two of the brightest stars in the whole sky had to go away on business, and they're asking her eyes to twinkle in their places until they return. What if her eyes were in the sky and the stars were in her head? – The brightness of her cheeks would outshine the stars the way the sun outshines a lamp. If her eyes were in the night sky, they would shine so brightly through space that birds would start singing, thinking her light was the light of day. Look how she leans her hand on her cheek. Oh, I wish I was the glove on that hand so that I could touch that cheek. **JULIET** O my!

ROMEO
She speaks:
O, speak again, bright angel, for thou art
As glorious to this night, being o'er my head
As is a wingèd messenger of heaven
Unto the white-upturnèd wond'ring eyes
Of mortals that fall back to gaze on him
When he bestrides the lazy puffing clouds,
And sails upon the bosom of the air.

JULIET
O Romeo, Romeo, wherefore art thou Romeo?
Deny thy father and refuse thy name,
Or if thou wilt not, be but sworn my love,
And I'll no longer be a Capulet.

ROMEO
(aside) Shall I hear more, or shall I speak at this?

JULIET
'Tis but thy name that is my enemy;
Thou art thyself, though not a Montague.
What's Montague? It is nor hand, nor foot,
Nor arm, nor face, nor any other part

Belonging to a man. O, be some other name.
What's in a name? that which we call a rose
By any other word would smell as sweet,
So Romeo would, were he not Romeo called,
Retain that dear perfection which he owes
Without that title. Romeo, doff thy name,
And for that name, which is no part of thee,
Take all myself.

ROMEO
I take thee at thy word:
Call me but love, and I'll be new baptized;
Henceforth I never will be Romeo.

JULIET
What man art thou that thus bescreened in night
So stumblest on my counsel?

ROMEO
By a name
I know not how to tell thee who I am:
My name, dear saint, is hateful to myself,
Because it is an enemy to thee.
Had I it written, I would tear the word.

ROMEO
(to himself) She speaks. Oh, speak again, bright angel. You are as glorious as an angel tonight. You shine above me, like a winged messenger from heaven who makes mortal men fall on their backs to look up at the sky, watching the angel walking on the clouds and sailing on the air.

JULIET
(not knowing ROMEO hears her) Oh, Romeo, Romeo, why do you have to be Romeo? Forget about your father and change your name. Or else, if you won't change your name, just swear you love me and I'll stop being a Capulet.

ROMEO
(to himself) Should I listen for more, or should I speak now?

JULIET
(still not knowing ROMEO hears her) It's only your name that's my enemy. You'd still be yourself even if you stopped being a Montague. What's a Montague anyway? It isn't a hand, a foot, an arm, a face, or any other part of a man. Oh, be some other name! What does a name mean? The thing we call a rose would smell just as sweet if we called it by any other name. Romeo would be just as perfect even if he wasn't called Romeo. Romeo, lose your name. Trade in your name – which really has nothing to do with you – and take all of me in exchange.

ROMEO
(to JULIET) I trust your words. Just call me your love, and I will take a new name. From now on I will never be Romeo again.

JULIET
Who are you? Why do you hide in the darkness and listen to my private thoughts?

ROMEO
I don't know how to tell you who I am by telling you a name. I hate my name, dear saint, because my name is your enemy. If I had it written down, I would tear up the paper.

JULIET	JULIET
My ears have yet not drunk a hundred words Of thy tongue's uttering, yet I know the sound: Art thou not Romeo and a Montague?	I haven't heard you say a hundred words yet, but I recognize the sound of your voice. Aren't you Romeo? And aren't you a Montague?
ROMEO	**ROMEO**
Neither, fair maid, if either thee dislike.	I am neither of those things if you dislike them.

COMMUNICATING

Directors make choices when creating a play or a film version of a Shakespearean play. They make choices about the setting of the play, the costumes that the actors wear and what lighting to use to create a certain type of atmosphere.

Watch these three different performances of this scene, then complete the task in your activity book (see pages 123–124):

Franco Zeffirelli 1968 edco.ie/d8rg

Baz Luhrmann 1996 edco.ie/6m82

Royal Shakespeare Company 2018 edco.ie/9z4e

READING

1 Summarise the action in this scene in one sentence.

2 Romeo pays Juliet a number of compliments in this scene. He does this by comparing her beauty to other things. Complete the compliment task in your activity book (see page 124).

3 What is Juliet's problem with Romeo's name?

4 What is Romeo prepared to do to be with Juliet?

5 What pronouns do Romeo and Juliet use when they are speaking to each other? What does their use of pronouns reveal about their relationship?

6 List four words from this text that you think are retired words. Find out what these words mean.

7 Can you pick out an example of a line inversion from this extract?

8 Can you pick out an example of a contraction from this extract? What is the full word being contracted?

WRITING

At the beginning of this scene, Romeo watches Juliet on her balcony and speaks about her beauty. He compares her to the sun, to the stars and to an angel. Love song lyrics often do something similar. Try creating a modern version of Romeo's speech about Juliet by finding and using modern song lyrics.

First use the internet to research and pick out some suitable love song lyrics.

Then create your own version of Romeo's speech, using the writing frame in your activity book (see page 125).

ROMEO AND JULIET: Act 2, Scene 1 (part 2)

©2017 Mya Lixian Gosling   www.goodticklebrain.com

PERFORMING

Create a group freeze tag performance of Romeo's monologue.

- Get into groups of five and divide the lines of the monologue between you.
- Line up in the order in which you are saying the lines.
- One person should act out their line or lines at a time. Your voice, facial expressions, hand gestures and movements should all help communicate the line or lines you are saying.
- All the other members of the group should stay frozen until it is their turn.
- To 'unfreeze' the next performer and hand the performance over to them, choose a dramatic handover exchange to wake them up. This could be a relay baton handover, a secret handshake or an attack with a pretend sword.

A Midsummer Night's Dream

This is an extract from Act III Scene II of this famous Shakespearean comedy. Hermia and Helena have been close friends since they were young, but recently their friendship has come under strain due to jealousy. As the play begins, Hermia and Lysander are in a loving relationship, and Helena loves Demetrius. The four lovers set out into the forest on a midsummer's night. Everything changes, however, when Demetrius turns his gaze from Helena in order to pursue Hermia. Suddenly, Hermia has two suitors, and Helena has none. Helena is left feeling cast aside and unappealing. But mischief is afoot, in the form of a magic plant used by the fairies of the forest that causes the mortals to fall in love with the first person they see when they wake up. Lysander wakes up in love with Helena and chaos ensues...

A Midsummer Night's Dream Extract from Act III, Scene II	
Shakespeare's original text	**No Fear version**
LYSANDER Ay, by my life. And never did desire to see thee more. Therefore be out of hope, of question, of doubt. Be certain, nothing truer. 'Tis no jest That I do hate thee and love Helena.	**LYSANDER** I certainly did, and I never wanted to see you again. So stop hoping and wondering what I mean. I've spelled it out for you clearly. It's no joke. I hate you and love Helena.
HERMIA O me! (*to* HELENA) You juggler, you cankerblossom! You thief of love! What, have you come by night And stol'n my love's heart from him?	**HERMIA** Oh, no! (*to* HELENA) You trickster, you snake! You thief! What, did you sneak in at night and steal my love's heart from him?
HELENA Fine, i' faith! Have you no modesty, no maiden shame, No touch of bashfulness? What, will you tear Impatient answers from my gentle tongue? Fie, fie! You counterfeit, you puppet, you!	**HELENA** Oh, that's very nice! You ought to be ashamed of yourself! You're going to make me mad enough to answer you? Damn you, you faker, you puppet!

HERMIA

'Puppet'? Why so? – Ay, that way goes the game.
Now I perceive that she hath made compare
Between our statures. She hath urged her height.
And with her personage, her tall personage,
Her height, forsooth, she hath prevailed with him. –
And are you grown so high in his esteem
Because I am so dwarfish and so low?
How low am I, thou painted maypole? Speak.
How low am I? I am not yet so low
But that my nails can reach unto thine eyes.

HELENA

(to LYSANDER and DEMETRIUS)
I pray you, though you mock me, gentlemen,
Let her not hurt me. I was never cursed.
I have no gift at all in shrewishness.
I am a right maid for my cowardice.
Let her not strike me. You perhaps may think,
Because she is something lower than myself,
That I can match her.

HERMIA

'Lower'? Hark, again!

HELENA

Good Hermia, do not be so bitter with me.
I evermore did love you, Hermia,
Did ever keep your counsels, never wronged you –
Save that, in love unto Demetrius,
I told him of your stealth unto this wood.
He followed you. For love I followed him.
But he hath chid me hence and threatened me
To strike me, spurn me – nay, to kill me too.
And now, so you will let me quiet go,
To Athens will I bear my folly back
And follow you no further. Let me go.
You see how simple and how fond I am.

HERMIA

Why, get you gone! Who is't that hinders you?

HELENA

A foolish heart, that I leave here behind.

HERMIA

What, with Lysander?

HELENA

With Demetrius.

LYSANDER

Be not afraid. She shall not harm thee, Helena.

DEMETRIUS

(to LYSANDER) No, sir, she shall not, though you take her part.

HERMIA

'Puppet'? Why 'puppet'? – Oh, I see where this is going. She's talking about our difference in height. She's paraded in front of him to show off how tall she is. She won him over with her height. – Does he have such a high opinion of you because I'm so short? Is that it? So how short am I, you painted barber pole? Tell me. How short am I? I'm not too short to gouge your eyes out with my fingernails.

HELENA

(to LYSANDER and DEMETRIUS) Please don't let her hurt me, gentlemen, however much you want to tease me. I never was much good with insults. I'm not mean and catty like her. I'm a nice shy girl. Please don't let her hit me. Maybe you think that because she's shorter than me I can take her.

HERMIA

'Shorter'! See, she's doing it again!

HELENA

Good Hermia, please don't act so bitter toward me. I always loved you, Hermia, and gave you advice. I never did anything to hurt you – except once, when I told Demetrius that you planned to sneak off into this forest. And I only did that because I loved Demetrius so much. He followed you. And I followed him because I loved him. But he told me to get lost and threatened to hit me, kick me – even kill me. Now just let me go quietly back to Athens. I'll carry my mistakes back with me. I won't follow you anymore. Please let me go. You see how naïve and foolish I've been.

HERMIA

Well, get out of here then! What's keeping you?

HELENA

My stupid heart, which I'm leaving behind here.

HERMIA

What, you're leaving it with Lysander?

HELENA

No, with Demetrius.

LYSANDER

Don't be afraid. She can't hurt you, Helena.

DEMETRIUS

(to LYSANDER) That's right, Hermia won't hurt Helena even if you try to help her.

HELENA
O, when she's angry, she is keen and shrewd!
She was a vixen when she went to school.
And though she be but little, she is fierce.

HERMIA
'Little' again? Nothing but 'low' and 'little'? –
Why will you suffer her to flout me thus?
Let me come to her.

LYSANDER
(*to HERMIA*) Get you gone, you dwarf,
You minimus of hindering knotgrass made,
You bead, you acorn!

DEMETRIUS
You are too officious
In her behalf that scorns your services.
Let her alone. Speak not of Helena.
Take not her part. For if thou dost intend
Never so little show of love to her,
Thou shalt aby it.

LYSANDER
Now she holds me not.
Now follow, if thou darest, to try whose right,
Of thine or mine, is most in Helena.

DEMETRIUS
'Follow'? Nay, I'll go with thee, cheek by jowl.
Exeunt LYSANDER and DEMETRIUS.

HELENA
Oh, when you get her angry, she's a good fighter, and vicious too. She was a hellcat in school. And she's fierce, even though she's little.

HERMIA
'Little' again? Nothing but 'little' and 'short'! – Why are you letting her insult me like this? Let me at her!

LYSANDER
(*to HERMIA*) Get lost, you dwarf, you tiny little weed, you scrap, you acorn!

DEMETRIUS
You're doing too much to defend a woman who wants nothing to do with you. Leave Hermia alone. Don't talk about Helena. Don't take Helena's side. If you continue treating Hermia so badly, you'll pay for it.

LYSANDER
Hermia's not holding onto me anymore. Follow me if you're brave enough, and we'll fight over Helena.

DEMETRIUS
'Follow'? No, I'll walk right next to you, side by side.
DEMETRIUS and LYSANDER exit.

READING

1 Who does Lysander love and who does he hate?

2 Who are Helena and Hermia fighting over?

3 Who does Helena love?

4 What insult does Helena keep using to annoy Hermia?

5 What are Demetrius and Lysander going to have a fight about?

6 What pronouns do the characters use when they are speaking to each other?

7 List four words from this text that you think are retired words. Find out what these words mean.

8 Can you pick out an example of a line inversion from this extract?

9 Can you pick out an example of a contraction from this extract? What is the full word being contracted?

10 Does this scene remind you of any show, film or book you have come across? In what way?

WRITING

Write a short diary entry from the perspective of Hermia. In the diary entry you should talk about who she is in love with, who she is fighting with and why they are fighting. You should use first-person narrative perspective (see page 6) to reveal Hermia's innermost thoughts and feelings.

PERFORMING

Create a speedy mime performance of this scene.

- Divide the class into groups of four.
- Each of you should choose to play one of the characters from the extract above.
- You need to condense the scene into a lightning-quick performance using no dialogue.
- Think about how you could use facial expressions, gestures and movement across the stage to express the plot and the emotions of the characters. It might be a good idea to jot down the plot of the scene first and then decide how you could express this using mime.

A MIDSUMMER NIGHT'S DREAM: Act 3, Scene 2 (pt. 5)

©2018 Mya Lixian Gosling   www.goodticklebrain.com

PROJECT:
Who Was William Shakespeare?

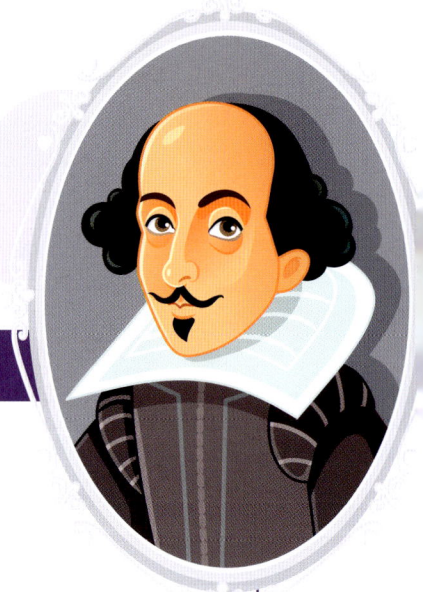

💡 PROJECT BRIEF

Investigate the life and times of William Shakespeare to find out why people still study his works 400 years after his death. Present your research in the form of a report. Assume your audience know nothing about Shakespeare.

To be successful in this project, you will need to:

- investigate and explore relevant sources and summarise these effectively
- write consistently in a clear, informative and formal tone
- use a consistent layout to add meaning and clarity to your report.

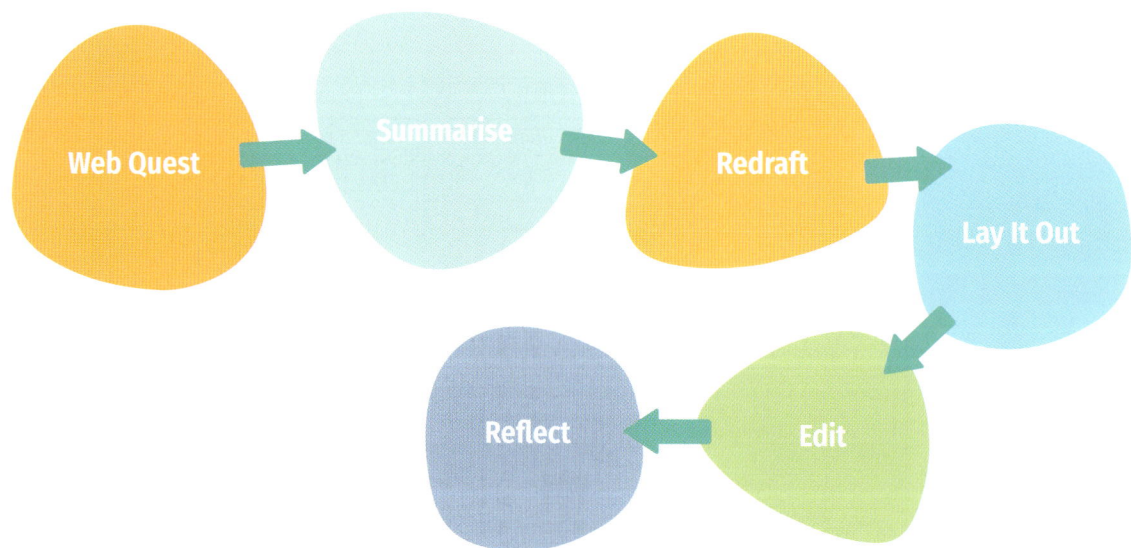

Web Quest → Summarise → Redraft → Lay It Out → Edit → Reflect

Web Quest

The links below will take you directly to websites that will help you answer these research questions. A research question helps you focus your investigations.

1 What was Shakespeare's early life like?
2 What do we know about Shakespeare's adult life?
3 What do we know about Shakespeare's work – his plays and his poems?

edco.ie/g6d7   edco.ie/q9kj   edco.ie/ajx6   edco.ie/92kp

Summarise It

In your activity book (see pages 126–127), record the information that you find, particularly the most important points. Remember that the information should relate to your research questions – do not copy down every fact you find. The best way to record your findings is by summarising the information you find.

How to summarise

What is summarising? It is the ability to identify the most important information and condense it down into one manageable chunk. It is about getting to the heart of the matter and understanding the gist of what you are reading. Here's what to do:

1 Identify the purpose of your summary. What exactly are you looking for?

2 Skim and scan the text. Highlight any key words and phrases.

3 Cut anything unnecessary or anything repeated.

4 Create a summary sentence or two containing the gist of the text and any key ideas and facts.

Look at the examples below, where key words and phrases have been highlighted in the text.

In Shakespeare's time, a stage wasn't just one type of space; plays had to be versatile. The same play might be produced in an outdoor playhouse, an indoor theatre, a royal palace – or, for a company on tour, the courtyard of an inn. In any of these settings, men and boys played all the characters, male and female; acting in Renaissance England was an exclusively male profession. Audiences had their favourite performers, looked forward to hearing music with the productions, and relished the luxurious costumes of the leading characters. The stage itself was relatively bare. For the most part, playwrights used vivid words instead of scenery to picture the scene onstage.	**Purpose:** What was different about theatre in Shakespeare's time? **Summary sentence:** Staging a play in Shakespeare's time was different as only men could be actors, stage sets were bare and plays were performed in a variety of settings, not just in theatres.
The Bard of Avon, as William Shakespeare is also known, was the child of a leather merchant and glover, John Shakespeare. His mother was from a family of landed gentry. In the absence of records detailing Shakespeare's early education, historians guess he attended a nearby school where he learned to read and write English as well as Latin. In 1582, when he was just 18, Shakespeare married Anne Hathaway, a woman eight years his senior. They would have three children, a daughter in 1583 and a set of twins in 1585. They lost their only son, Hamnet, when the boy was 11 years old. Daughters Susanna and Judith would live to be 66 and 77, respectively.	**Purpose:** Find out about Shakespeare's private life. **Summary sentences:** Shakespeare was born to a merchant father and his mother was from gentry. He married Anne Hathaway and they had three children.

Redraft It

Once you have collected and summarised all of the information you need on Shakespeare, you should look at how you will make your report interesting to read. Repeating the same type of sentences over and over again can make your writing less appealing. Using a variety of sentence types can help to make your writing more engaging.

Try redrafting some of your sentences to include a couple of the sentence types from the box below.

Sentence type	The rules	Example 1	Example 2
Rhetorical question	A sentence that asks a question to which no answer is required, used for dramatic effect and to draw the reader's attention	Could Shakespeare be the most impressive writer of all time?	Ever wondered what Shakespeare was like as a child?
Embedded quotation	A sentence that includes evidence from sources	It is said that Shakespeare 'contributed 1,700 words to the English language because he was the first author to write them down'.	Shakespeare is hailed by many as 'not of an age, but for all time'.
List of three	A sentence where three examples are listed	Shakespeare wrote comedies, tragedies and histories.	Shakespeare's most famous plays are *Romeo and Juliet*, *Hamlet* and *Macbeth*.

Lay It Out

The layout of your report is important as it can help fulfil the purpose of your piece of writing: to inform people about Shakespeare and why we study his writing in school. The layout should therefore make the information as clear as possible.

- Title: What are you reporting on?
- Headings and sub-headings: Divide your report up into sections, each with a heading and subheadings so it is easy to navigate.
- Introduction: State the purpose of the report.
- Bullet points and numbered lists: Break up any factual information or statistics and make it easy to read and understand.

- Pictures, diagrams and infographics: Include captions with these to support your explanations.
- Conclusion: Summarise the overall findings of your research.
- Sources: You must back up your research with evidence from legitimate sources and credit any books or websites by naming them at the end of your report under a Sources heading.

Edit It

Scan through your piece of writing looking at your punctuation. Focus on checking the capital letters and full stops.

Here are the rules you should be following:

Use a capital letter at the start of each sentence.	Use a capital letter for the names of people and places.
Use a capital letter for the titles of books and films.	A full stop (or a question mark or exclamation mark) appears at the end of each sentence.

REFLECTION

1 Are you convinced that it is worth studying Shakespeare?
2 Rank the three most important things to consider when researching a topic.
3 Do you think Shakespeare is worthy of the praise he receives?

William Shakespeare

Test Your Knowledge

1 When you are reading a Shakespearean play, how do you know when a sentence ends?

   a) When the text moves onto the next line

   b) When a new character starts to speak

   c) When the punctuation tells you so

   d) When you get to the end of the page

2 **What is a line inversion?**

   a) A line changed into a different language

   b) A line that uses no pronouns

   c) When you change the order of words in a line to fit a particular rhythm or to make a rhyme

   d) When you make up words to make a line sound better

3 **What is a pronoun?**

   a) A descriptive word

   b) A word that describes a verb

   c) A part of speech that replaces a noun in a sentence

   d) A person, place or thing

4 **What is a contraction?**

   a) A line with no pronouns

   b) When you make a word smaller by taking out a letter and replacing it with an apostrophe

   c) When you change the order of the words in a line

   d) A type of punctuation Shakespeare used

5 **Shakespeare used** .... **and** .... **in his plays to entertain and amuse his audience.**

6 **There were no** .... **actors in a theatre during Shakespeare's time.**

7 Match Shakespeare's grammar with the correct explanation.

Grammar	Explanation
Inversions	Shakespeare often cut out syllables and replaced them with an apostrophe to make the rhythm of a line fit better.
Contractions	When Shakespeare was writing his plays, there were more of these in speech than we have today – for example, he regularly uses 'thy', 'thine', 'thee' and 'thou'.
Pronouns	Sometimes Shakespeare changed the order of words in his lines to try fit a particular rhythm or to make a rhyme.

8 Match the method of word invention with the correct example.

Method of word invention	Example
Joining words together	Informal
Changing nouns into verbs	Full-grown
Coining a completely new word	Champion
Adding prefixes and suffixes	Lonely

9 List three differences between the theatre in Shakespeare's time and the theatre now.

10 What was the main difference between the pronouns in Shakespeare's time and the pronouns we use now?

11 Give an example of a word used in Shakespeare's time that has fallen out of use.

12 Name three plays that Shakespeare wrote.

Practise Your Writing Skills

Translate these lines of Shakespearean dialogue into modern English.

- The lady doth protest too much, methinks
- To thine own self be true
- The fool doth think he is wise, but the wise man knows himself to be a fool
- Give every man thy ear, but few thy voice
- Thou know'st 'tis common. All that lives must die,
  Passing through nature to eternity.
- Parting is such sweet sorrow,
  That I shall say good night till it be morrow

Interactive website

Go to **www.edco.ie/touchstones1** for interactive activities based on this unit.

UNIT 6
NON-FICTION

NON-FICTION KNOWLEDGE ORGANISER

Things I need to know

- **Informal letter:** A personal letter usually written between people who already know each other.

- **Formal letter:** Usually written to someone you don't know personally.

- **Cover letter:** A formal letter you send to an employer along with your CV if you are trying to get a job.

- **Email:** An electronic mail, similar to a letter.

- **Travel writing:** Non-fiction writing that describes visits to different places around the globe.

- **Newspaper:** A written record of current events that is printed daily or weekly.

- **Tabloid newspaper:** Reports on celebrity gossip and human-interest stories and uses informal and sensational language.

- **Broadsheet:** Reports on more serious issues, such as politics, the economy and international conflicts.

- **Digital newspaper:** Digital online version of a print newspaper.

- **Journalists:** The people who report the news in newspapers.

- **Masthead:** The name of the newspaper.

- **Byline:** Summary line about the lead story.

- **Biased reporting:** When a journalist deliberately tries to sway the audience toward their point of view.

- **Opinion piece:** An article where a journalist gives their personal opinion on a topic or event that has taken place.

- **Newscast:** A report of the news on television, usually containing a blend of live video footage, live reports and interviews on location, and studio reports and discussion.

- **Speech:** A non-fiction text communicated orally to an audience, often using persuasive language.

- **Advertisement:** A persuasive text, trying to convince people to buy or do something. These are created in different formats – for radio, for television, in print and as digital ads on websites, apps and on social media.

Skills I will develop

- Using the writing process to craft texts: planning, drafting, redrafting and editing
- Learning from model texts to improve my written and oral communication work
- Writing in a variety of text types for different purposes and audiences

Project

- Theme Park: Collaborating with classmates to imagine, create and advertise a unique theme park

What do I know?

Before you begin this chapter, check what you already know about non-fiction text by filling out the non-fiction knowledge download activity in your activity book (see pages 128–129).

What Is Non-Fiction?

PowerPoint

Non-fiction text is writing that deals with real life or facts. In short, non-fiction is anything that is not fiction. You come across non-fiction texts all the time in your everyday life, from the words on the back of your cereal box at breakfast to advertising billboards, from movie reviews to the textbook you are reading right now!

> Writing non-fiction is more like sculpture, a matter of shaping the research into the finished thing.
> **Joan Didion**

> Non-fiction speaks to the head. Fiction speaks to the heart. Poetry speaks to the soul.
> **Ellen Hopkins**

> With non-fiction, the task is very straightforward: do the research, tell the story.
> **Laura Hillenbrand**

> Fiction and non-fiction are only different techniques of story telling.
> **Arundhati Roy, War Talk**

Which of these quotes do you like best? Which quotes do you agree with? Are there any you disagree with?

Non-Fiction Texts

As a student of English, you will encounter many different types of non-fiction texts. Each of these is written for a purpose, perhaps to inform people or to explain something, maybe to persuade someone to do something or to provide entertainment.

It is important, when studying or writing non-fiction, to be aware of the audience of the text. The audience can be specific, for example an email to one person, or wider, for example a speech to your class. The audience you are writing for should have an impact on your choice of tone. For an email to a group of teenagers you might choose an informal tone, but for a letter to your principal you would use a formal tone.

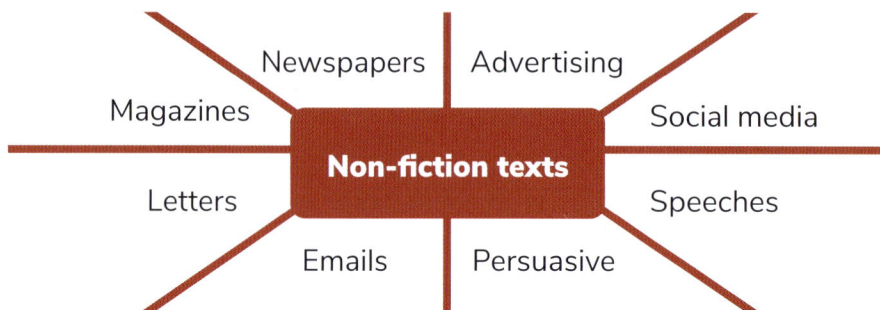

Newspapers   Advertising

Magazines   Social media

Non-fiction texts

Letters   Speeches

Emails   Persuasive

Letters

A letter is a way of communicating using the written word. An informal or personal letter is usually written between people who already know each other. A formal letter is usually written to someone you don't know personally. These two types of letters have many common features but also some clear differences.

Example of an informal letter

Sender's address

Date

Informal greeting

Contains information the sender wants the reader to know

Written in first-person narrative perspective

Informal tone

Informal sign off

> 13 Wayward Avenue
> Nowhere Street
> Co. Clare
>
> 17th March 2021
>
> Dear Cruella,
>
> Hope all is well with you down in Cork. I am just writing to tell you that Spot has had puppies, seven of them. I was wondering if you would like one of them?
>
> They would be able to leave their mother at about twelve weeks old. I know you have always wanted a Dalmatian so now is your chance. There are five males and two females, and you can have your pick of the litter.
>
> Let me know what you think.
>
> All the best,
>
> John

Example of a formal letter

Sender's name and address

Date

Recipient's address

Formal greeting

Written in first-person narrative perspective

Contains information the sender wants the reader to know

Formal tone

Formal sign off

> John Swan
> 13 Wayward Avenue
> Nowhere Street
> Co. Clare
>
> 17th March 2021
>
> Irish Kennel Club
> Barkington Road
> Dublin
>
> Dear Sir/Madam,
>
> I am writing to register the birth of my dog's seven puppies. The dog is registered at the Irish Kennel Club as Spot, under my ownership. Her registration number is: 498398.
>
> Please find enclosed the papers of both the mother and the father of the puppies.
>
> I look forward to receiving their registration papers in due course.
>
> Yours sincerely,
>
> John Swan

Letters of Note

Letters of Note (lettersofnote.com) describes itself as an online museum of correspondence. It is an online collection of letters written by famous people or regarding famous events in history, compiled by Shaun Usher. Some are moving, some are funny and all are brilliant examples of letter writing.

After working in advertising as a copywriter in New York City, Robert Pirosh moved to Hollywood in 1934 with dreams of becoming a screenwriter. Below is a transcript of the cover letter he sent to all of the directors, producers and studio execs he could think of. A **cover letter** is a formal letter you send to an employer along with your CV if you are trying to get a job. Pirosh went on to win an Academy Award for Best Writing (Story and Screenplay) in 1950, so clearly he was as good at screenwriting as he was at writing cover letters.

Dear Sir:

I like words. I like fat buttery words, such as ooze, turpitude, glutinous, toady. I like solemn, angular, creaky words, such as straitlaced, cantankerous, pecunious, valedictory. I like spurious, black-is-white words, such as mortician, liquidate, tonsorial, demi-monde. I like suave 'V' words, such as Svengali, svelte, bravura, verve. I like crunchy, brittle, crackly words, such as splinter, grapple, jostle, crusty. I like sullen, crabbed, scowling words, such as skulk, glower, scabby, churl. I like Oh-Heavens, my-gracious, land's-sake words, such as tricksy, tucker, genteel, horrid. I like elegant, flowery words, such as estivate, peregrinate, elysium, halcyon. I like wormy, squirmy, mealy words, such as crawl, blubber, squeal, drip. I like sniggly, chuckling words, such as cowlick, gurgle, bubble and burp.

I like the word screenwriter better than copywriter, so I decided to quit my job in a New York advertising agency and try my luck in Hollywood, but before taking the plunge I went to Europe for a year of study, contemplation and horsing around.

I have just returned and I still like words.

May I have a few with you?

Robert Pirosh

385 Madison Avenue

Room 610

New York

Eldorado 5-6024

READING

ACTIVITY

1 What does Robert Pirosh claim to like in this letter?

2 What do you think is the purpose of Robert Pirosh's letter?

3 Choose three words from this letter that you have never come across before and complete a word exploration quad for each of them in your activity book (see page 159).

4 What features of letter writing appear in this letter? Complete the quote quest activity in your activity book (see page 130).

5 Do you think this is an example of a formal letter or an informal letter?

6 Do you think this is an interesting letter? Why? Why not?

7 If you were a movie producer and you received this as a cover letter, would you hire Robert Pirosh?

COMMUNICATING

Letters Live is a performance event where an array of well-known performers read a wide variety of letters to the audience. The letters are from all the corners of the world and were written in different time periods, from two hundred years ago to the present day. It is described as a celebration of the letter and was inspired by the Letters of Note website.

1 Choose two letter performances to listen to: edco.ie/hc7c

2 How did you feel after watching the letters being performed? Did you enjoy the performances?

3 Now think about the letter from Robert Pirosh opposite and answer the questions below.

- Who would you cast to read this letter and why? Give three reasons.
- What tone would you use to read this letter?
- Would you use any gestures while reading this letter?

4 Finally, record or perform a reading of the letter live for your class.

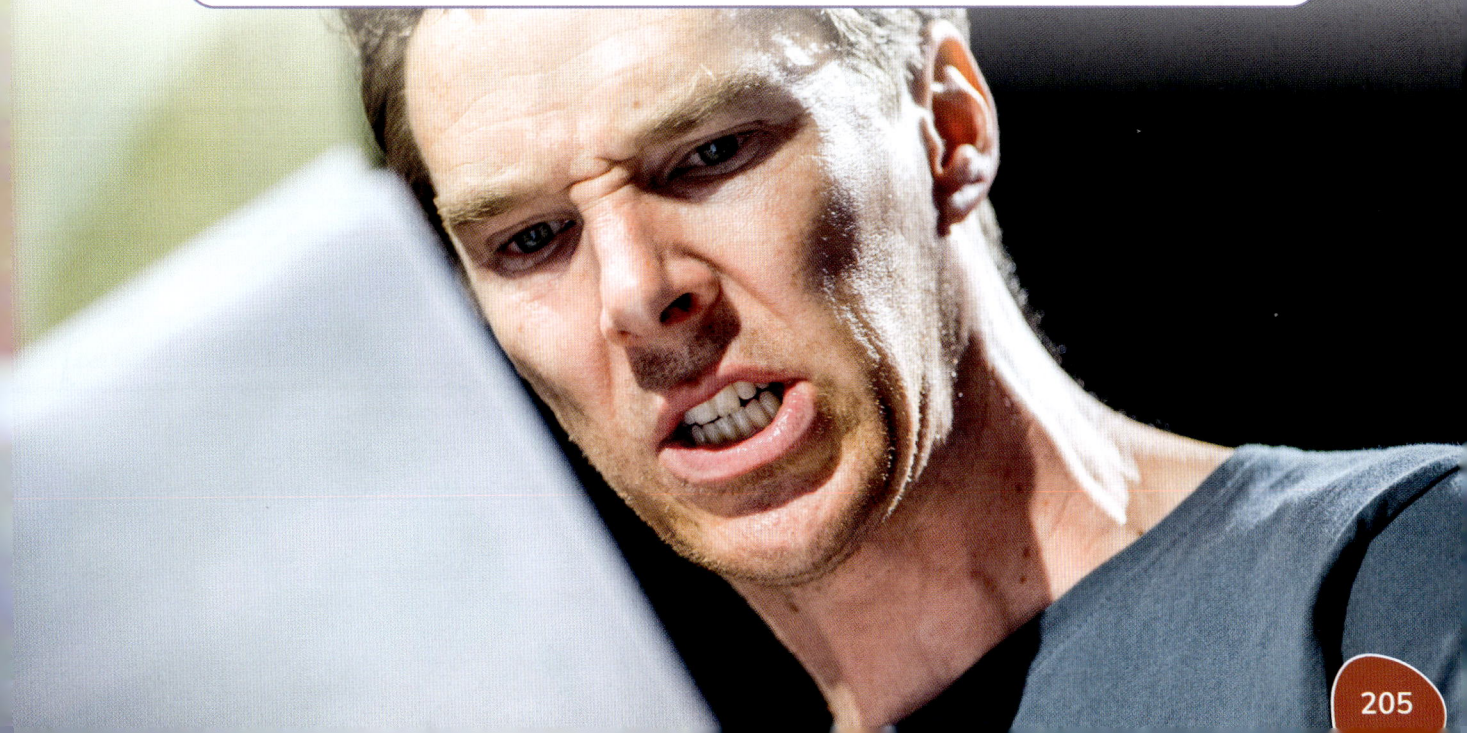

WRITING

You want to apply for one of the following dream jobs that have been advertised in the newspaper. Chose the one that appeals to you the most.

Private tropical island housesitter

Come live on this private tropical island as a caretaker. Spend your days swimming in the crystal-clear seas and walking along white sandy beaches. This private beachfront villa has its own pool, ten bedrooms and six bathrooms. Housesitter needed for at least six months.

Chocolate factory taste tester

Come and work for us as a taste tester. Spend your working day tasting different chocolate treats and offering your expert opinion. Favourable salary and benefits included.

Trainee wizard at Wizarding Academy

Always wanted to know how to fly, become invisible or turn your teacher into a toad? Then a trainee apprenticeship at the National Wizarding Academy is for you. Spend a year learning all the tricks of the trade from master wizards.

Computer game reviewer

Reviewer needed to spend all day testing and playing computer games. We are looking for an expert to offer their opinion of our games and review them for us before they go out to market.

As with Robert Pirosh's letter, you need to make your application letter stand out from the thousands of other applications by using language to impress the reader.

Writing Tips

- Outline your reason for writing clearly.
- Be creative in your description as to why you would be perfect for the job and what makes you stand out from everyone else applying.
- Use the features of a formal letter accurately (see page 203).
- Write convincingly in a formal tone.

Emails

An email is an electronic mail. It is similar to a letter in that it is a form of written communication between two people. You need to have an email address to send or receive an email. An email can be formal or informal depending on who you are sending the email to, just like a letter.

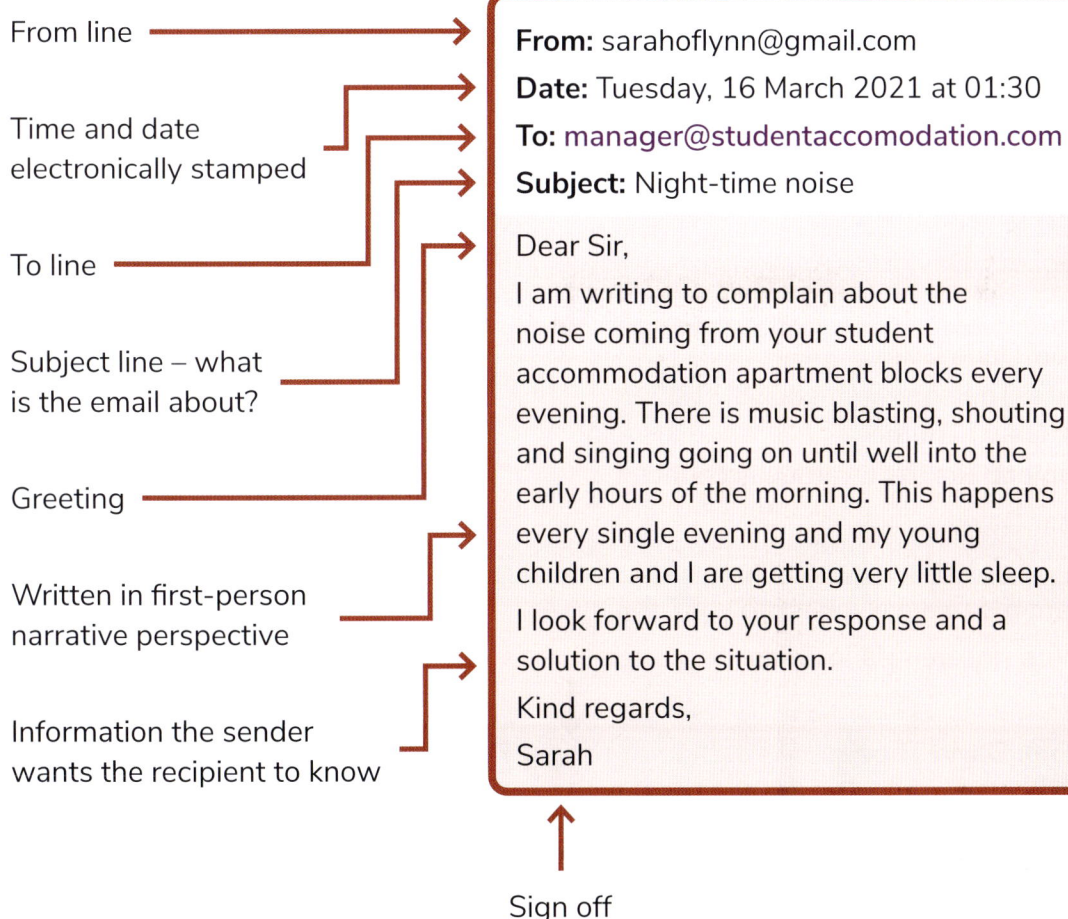

From line →

Time and date electronically stamped →

To line →

Subject line – what is the email about? →

Greeting →

Written in first-person narrative perspective →

Information the sender wants the recipient to know →

From: sarahoflynn@gmail.com
Date: Tuesday, 16 March 2021 at 01:30
To: manager@studentaccomodation.com
Subject: Night-time noise

Dear Sir,

I am writing to complain about the noise coming from your student accommodation apartment blocks every evening. There is music blasting, shouting and singing going on until well into the early hours of the morning. This happens every single evening and my young children and I are getting very little sleep.

I look forward to your response and a solution to the situation.

Kind regards,

Sarah

Sign off ↑

Spider Email Thread

This is a formal email thread between a business owner, Jane Gilles, and a customer, David Thorne, who owes her money. Follow the arrows to read their full conversation.

From: Jane Gilles
Date: Wednesday 8 Oct 2008 12.19pm
To: David Thorne
Subject: Overdue account

Dear David,

Our records indicate that your account is overdue by the amount of $233.95. If you have already made this payment, please contact us within the next 7 days to confirm payment has been applied to your account and is no longer outstanding.

Yours sincerely, Jane Gilles

From: David Thorne
Date: Wednesday 8 Oct 2008 12.37pm
To: Jane Gilles
Subject: Re: Overdue account

Dear Jane,

I do not have any money, so I am sending you this drawing I did of a spider instead. I value the drawing at $233.95 so trust that this settles the matter.

Regards, David

From: David Thorne
Date: Thursday 9 Oct 2008 10.32am
To: Jane Gilles
Subject: Re: Overdue account

Dear Jane,

Can I have my drawing of a spider back then please?

Regards, David

From: Jane Gilles
Date: Thursday 9 Oct 2008 10.07am
To: David Thorne
Subject: Overdue account

Dear David,

Thank you for contacting us. Unfortunately, we are unable to accept drawings as payment and your account remains in arrears of $233.95. Please contact us within the next 7 days to confirm payment has been applied to your account and is no longer outstanding.

Yours sincerely, Jane Gilles

From: Jane Gilles
Date: Thursday 9 Oct 2008 11.42am
To: David Thorne
Subject: Re: Re: Overdue account

Dear David,

You emailed the drawing to me. Do you want me to email it back to you?

Yours sincerely, Jane Gilles

From: David Thorne
Date: Thursday 9 Oct 2008 11.56am
To: Jane Gilles
Subject: Re: Re: Re: Overdue account

Dear Jane,

Yes please.

Regards, David

From: Jane Gilles
Date: Thursday 9 Oct 2008 12.14pm
To: David Thorne
Subject: Re: Re: Re: Re: Overdue account

Attached <spider.gif>

From: David Thorne
Date: Friday 10 Oct 2008 09.22am
To: Jane Gilles
Subject: Whose spider is that?

Dear Jane,

Are you sure this drawing of a spider is the one I sent you? This spider only has seven legs and I do not feel I would have made such an elementary mistake when I drew it.

Regards, David

From: David Thorne
Date: Friday 10 Oct 2008 11.13am
To: Jane Gilles
Subject: Re: Re: Whose spider is that?

Hello, I am back and have read through your emails and accept that despite missing a leg, that drawing of a spider may indeed be the one I sent you. I realise with hindsight that it is possible you rejected the drawing of a spider due to this obvious limb omission but did not point it out in an effort to avoid hurting my feelings.

As such, I am sending you a revised drawing with the correct number of legs as full payment for any amount outstanding. I trust this will bring the matter to a conclusion.

Regards, David

From: David Thorne
Date: Monday 13 Oct 2008 3.17pm
To: Jane Gilles
Subject: Re: Re: Re: Re: Whose spider is that?

I understand and will definitely make a payment this week if I remember. As you have not accepted my second drawing as payment, please return the drawing to me as soon as possible. It was silly of me to assume I could provide you with something of completely no value whatsoever, waste your time, and then attach such a large amount to it.

Regards, David

From: Jane Gilles
Date: Friday 10 Oct 2008 11.03am
To: David Thorne
Subject: Re: Whose spider is that?

Dear David,

Yes, it's the same drawing. I copied and pasted it from the email you sent me on the 8th. David, your account is still overdue by the amount of $233.95. Please make this payment as soon as possible.

Yours sincerely, Jane Gilles

From: David Thorne
Date: Friday 10 Oct 2008 11.05am
To: Jane Gilles
Subject: Out of Office Response

Thank you for contacting me.
I am currently away on leave, traveling through time and will be returning last week.

Regards, David

From: Jane Gilles
Date: Monday 13 Oct 2008 2.51pm
To: David Thorne
Subject: Re: Re: Re: Whose spider is that?

Dear David,
As I have stated, we do not accept drawings in lieu of money for accounts outstanding. We accept cheques, bank cheques, money orders or cash. Please make a payment this week to avoid incurring any additional fees.

Yours sincerely, Jane Gilles

From: Jane Gilles
Date: Tuesday 14 Oct 2008 11.18am
To: David Thorne
Subject: Re: Re: Re: Re: Re: Whose spider is that?

Attached <spider2.gif>

READING

1 Summarise the spider email thread in two sentences.
2 How do you think David felt writing these emails?
3 How do you think Jane felt writing these emails?
4 Which person in this email exchange is using formal language and which is using informal language?
5 Can you pick out a sentence that is an example of formal language?
6 Can you pick out a sentence that is an example of informal language?
7 Complete the features of an email quote quest in your activity book (see page 131).
8 Why is this email exchange humorous?
9 Do you think David actually paid his bill in the end?

PERFORMING

In pairs, perform this email exchange as a short play. You could perform this live in your class or make a video recording and edit it. One of you should take on the character of Jane Gilles and one should be David Thorne. Before you perform the email exchange you should think about the character you are playing and the type of performance you want to give. Consider the points below.

- Should Jane be angry or patient?
- Should Jane lose her cool as the exchange goes on?
- How might you portray David? As a cheeky prankster or as someone oblivious to the ridiculousness of his actions?
- Would you use any sound effects or backing soundtrack to add humour to the performance?
- What props might you use?
- How might you arrange the performers on a stage?

WRITING

Using the spider email thread as an inspiration, write an email exchange between two people. One person should represent a business and the other should be a customer. The customer should try to get out of paying their bill by offering something silly in the place of a cash payment. The business owner should write their emails in a formal businesslike tone, but the customer should write in an informal conversational tone.

Writing Tips

- Let your imagination run wild to create an interesting scenario between the business and the customer.
- Make sure you use a clearly different tone to differentiate between the two people having the email conversation.
- Remember to use all of the features of an email accurately (see page 207).

Travel Writing

Travel writing is a type of non-fiction writing that describes visits to different places around the globe. It can inspire people to visit a new destination or make them conscious of the challenges faced in other parts of the world. Travel writing comes in the form of travel websites, travel guidebooks and travel magazines.

Features of travel writing	Examples
Written mainly in the present tense	I leave my hotel early to hike once more to the top of the hill, to see the sun rise just one more time before I have to depart.
Often interleaved with interviews with locals	Locals tell me that the cave is 'haunted by the spirits of angry ancestors'.
Often written in first-person narrative perspective	I step anxiously onto the shaky bridge.
Often uses personal anecdotes	The woman reminds me of my grandmother, who had always terrified me with her booming voice.
Uses a mixture of imagery and hard-hitting facts	Sitting here on this glorious beach with the crystal-clear water, it's hard to imagine the devastation of the tsunami seven years ago.

National Geographic

National Geographic is the long-standing monthly magazine of the National Geographic Society. It was first published in 1888 and is one of the most widely read magazines of all time. Since 2001, there has also been a National Geographic television channel. The article below is about a visit to Victoria Falls in Africa and is taken from *National Geographic* magazine.

Extreme weather threatens one of Earth's most awe-inspiring waterfalls

Victoria Falls is one of the world's most impressive natural wonders – but what happens as the region gets drier and hotter?

By Amy McKeever

Victoria Falls is one the biggest and most awe-inspiring waterfalls on the planet.

Spanning the width of the Zambezi River – more than a mile across – this legendary waterfall cascades over the lip of a large plateau of volcanic rock and plunges as much as 354 feet. It generate mists that can be spotted from more than a dozen miles away, which is why locals have dubbed it Mosi-oa-Tunya, or 'the smoke that thunders'.

But while the flow has been slicing slowly through this plateau on the national border between Zambia and Zimbabwe for some two million years, extreme swings in rainfall brought on by climate change threaten its future.

Victoria Falls is getting drier and hotter. While the region still sees roughly the same annual rainfall, those rains are compressed into a smaller period of time. Temperatures, too, are rising – in a July 2018 paper, South African researcher Kaitano Dube found that the average daily high temperature in October has warmed 6.8 degrees from 1976 to 2017. Last year, the area suffered its worst drought in a century, bringing the falls to a trickle in December.

This extreme weather threatens not only the majesty of the falls, but also the health of its ecosystem and the local economy. The *Guardian* reports that recent droughts have caused power cuts in both countries, which rely on hydropower from the downstream Kariba Dam.

The mists of Victoria Falls sustain a rainforest-like ecosystem adjacent to the falls and on the opposite cliff that faces them like a dried-up mirror image, thick with mahogany, fig, palm, and other species of vegetation.

The national border between Zambia and Zimbabwe lies midstream, and national parks of both nations exist on either side of the Zambezi. The gorges and cliffs below the falls in these parks are prime territory for raptors, including falcons and black eagles.

Humans have long relied on the falls, too. Stone artifacts from the hominin *Homo habilis* have been identified near the falls and show that early humans may have lived here two million years ago. More 'modern' tools also evidence far more recent – 50,000 years ago – Middle Stone Age settlements at Victoria Falls.

Today, tourism is essential to driving economic growth. Several hundred thousand visitors from around the world trek to the falls each year. Hotels, restaurants, campgrounds, and other tourist businesses have cropped up to cater to them.

The beauty of the falls lies in their natural state, but the area is at some risk of runaway tourism-based development – more resorts, hotels, and even a possible dam below the falls that could flood several park gorges. Operators in the area offer everything from helicopter overflights to bungee jumping, and the management of these activities while preserving a quality visitor experience for all is an ongoing challenge.

READING

1. Where exactly in the world is Victoria Falls located?
2. List four other facts you learn about Victoria Falls from reading this text.
3. Did anything surprise you about the information in this text?
4. Do you think this text contains all of the features of travel writing? Complete the quote quest task in your activity book (see page 132).
5. Would you like to visit Victoria Falls after reading this text? Why? Why not?

COMMUNICATING: GROUP DISCUSSION

YouTube star Drew Binsky has created a series of travel videos while on his quest to visit every single country in the world. His videos are like short travel documentaries telling a unique story about the people, food and culture of different countries. He gives out travel tips, hacks and advice, and his videos have had more than one billion views worldwide.

Watch the video of Drew's trip to Ashgabat, Turkmenistan which he describes as 'the World's Strangest City': edco.ie/2xg9

Now answer the questions below.

1. Go to Google Maps and locate Ashgabat, Turkmenistan, on the map.
2. Describe the city of Ashgabat – the colours, the buildings and the people.
3. What country does Turkmenistan remind Drew of?
4. List three facts you found out about Ashgabat from watching the video.
5. What strange rules and customs has the former dictator of Turkmenistan imposed on his country?
6. Did you enjoy this video? Did you feel you were both informed and entertained?
7. Scroll through the rest of Drew's videos and choose one from another country to watch.

213

WRITING

Imagine you work for *National Geographic* magazine. You have just visited an amazing destination and have been asked to write a piece about the area for the magazine, describing your experience.

Choose one of the three awe-inspiring tourist destinations listed below and create a piece of travel writing about it.

Galápagos Islands, Ecuador	Machu Picchu, Peru	Antarctica

In order to choose your destination, use the internet for some research. Start by watching these *National Geographic* videos to get a sense of the place:

Galápagos Islands, Ecuador edco.ie/b7ya	Machu Picchu, Peru edco.ie/n8zu	Antarctica edco.ie/y5dx

Listen carefully and note down the key facts about the destination and the things you might see there. Look out for anything interesting or unusual that you might like to talk about yourself. There is a table in your activity book (see page 133) to help you organise your ideas.

Writing Tips

- Write with a clear purpose in mind: to inform the reader about the destination.
- Use the features of travel writing creatively (see page 211).
- Check you have used commas correctly. Turn to page 273 to recap on the rules of commas, then pick out any mistakes and correct them.
- Use a variety of sentence types to make your writing interesting (see opposite).

WRITING SKILLS: WRITING BETTER SENTENCES

Look at your piece of writing. Have you used the same type of sentence over and over again? You could make your piece of writing more interesting and engaging by varying the type of sentence you use.

Look at the examples below, which show you how to upgrade a sentence using interesting sentence structures.

Dull sentence ⟶	Upgrading technique ➜	New sentence
Go to visit the Galápagos Islands because they're very beautiful.	Three-part sentence, getting progressively better	The skies are sparkling blue, the sand is glistening gold and the beaches are crawling with beautiful baby turtles.
People who love to explore will love this place.	Three questions and an answer	Feel at home in the wilderness? Love to connect with nature? Have the soul of an explorer? Then the Galápagos Islands are most definitely for you.
On the islands you will find lots of different animals.	Fragments of text in three short sentences	There are hundreds of unique animal species here. Ancient giant tortoises! Spiky marine iguanas! Dancing blue-footed boobies!

Newspaper Articles

A newspaper is a written record of current events that is printed daily or weekly. There are different types of newspapers: **tabloid**, **broadsheet** and **digital**.

A **tabloid newspaper** reports on celebrity gossip and human-interest stories and uses informal and sensational language. It is usually A3 in size.

A **broadsheet** reports on more serious issues, such as politics, the economy and international conflicts. It is usually A2 in size and uses formal and factual language.

A **digital newspaper** is a digital online version of a print newspaper. People generally buy these newspapers by subscription.

The people that report the news in newspapers are called **journalists**. A good journalist should be objective in what they report, which means they should not put their own personal feelings or thoughts into a news report. If a journalist deliberately tries to sway the audience toward their point of view, this is known as **biased reporting**. For example, a reporter may personally be in favour of fox hunting and write a newspaper report promoting it.

A journalist also needs to make sure that what they are reporting is factual and truthful. They do this by fact-checking their sources and the information they find.

In newspapers there are also pieces of writing called **opinion** or **comment pieces**. These are not objective pieces of writing reporting facts; they are a writer's personal opinion on a topic or event that has taken place. These pieces should be clearly signposted as 'opinion' or 'comment'.

Sometimes a newspaper is biased towards a particular political party or viewpoint. These newspapers tend to print opinion or comment pieces in support of that political party.

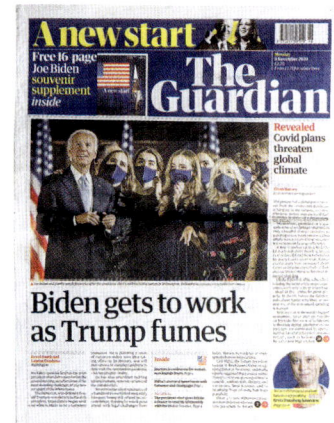

What does a newspaper front page look like?

The front page of a newspaper should grab the reader's attention and make them want to buy the newspaper. It should contain the main story of the day when it is printed.

Features of a newspaper front page	What this means
Masthead	The name of the newspaper
Headline	Summary line about the lead story
Byline	The name of the journalist who wrote the article
Images	Pictures related to the main story
Caption	An explanation of what is in the image
Advertisement	A product or service being promoted or sold
Text in columns	Articles are displayed in column format
Short paragraphs	Just three or four sentences in each paragraph
Lead article	The most important main story
Secondary article	The second most important story
Article menu	A short summary of the most important articles in the paper

Byline

Una Mullally — Crisis will bring out collective best in us — Opinion

Malachy Clerkin — A world with no sport is unimaginable — Sport

Naomi O'Leary — Italians turn to music to persevere in tough times — Page 5

Masthead → THE IRISH TIMES — irishtimes.com

Headline — Pubs asked to close in effort to stem coronavirus

Lead article

Text in columns

Image

Short paragraphs

Image caption

Italy records highest daily death toll of 368

Secondary article

Free Gift

This Mother's Day spend €129 or more & choose a bracelet from a selection*

Ends 22 March

PANDORA

Article menu — Weather | Home News | World News | Business Today | Sports Monday

Advertisement

217

READING

In your activity book, complete the matching activity about newspaper front pages (see page 133).

Writing newspaper articles

To write a good newspaper article, you should try to write like a journalist. Look in the box below for some tips on how to write an article and examples of a sentence that might appear in a newspaper article.

Features of a newspaper article	Example sentence
Headlines summarise the article	Spiderman catches fleeing thieves
The first sentence summarises the entire article	Firemen rescued several cats from the tree in the village square early yesterday morning.
Written in third-person narrative perspective	The criminals were apprehended and jailed immediately.
Written in the past tense	On 4 January, the president's wife gave birth to a baby boy.
The first paragraph addresses the who, what, where, when and why of the story	Two female penguins escaped from London Zoo in the early hours of Saturday 25 August. Zookeepers noticed they were missing at the 9am feeding. A preliminary investigation has revealed a hole had been pecked in the fencing.

Headline should summarise the article →

First sentence should summarise the entire article

First paragraph should address the who, what, where, when and why of the story

Written in the past tense

Paragraphs should be short

Written in the third person

Third heroic rescue by father and son fishermen

A Galway swimmer has been rescued after getting into difficulty off Salthill. Fishermen Patrick Oliver and his son Morgan spotted the man at around 10.30am. Galway RNLI had also been called out.

The two men were fishing off Salthill at the time and spotted the man taking refuge on Palmer's Rock about 200 metres from the shore. They took him on board their boat and brought him back to Galway Docks. The man was taken into the lifeboat station where he received treatment for symptoms of hypothermia until an ambulance arrived. The Galway lifeboat was stood down.

Deputy Launch Authority Seán Óg Leydon says many people who have taken up sea swimming this year during the Covid lockdown may not realise the dangers of winter swimming. 'The sea is a great resource for us but we have to respect it and our limits. Luckily this swimmer made his way to a place he could rest and wait for assistance.'

It is the third rescue by the father and son in the past four months. They famously rescued paddle-boarding cousins Ellen Glynn and Sara Feeney in August, after they spent a whole night at sea. A couple of weeks later, the Olivers again went to the rescue, this time saving a man from the River Corrib.

Donald Trump Rally News Article

This is a newspaper article that appeared in the digital edition of the *London Evening Standard* on 21 June 2020.

Empty seats at Donald Trump rally 'down to TikTok users and K-pop fans'

Donald Trump's campaign rally in Oklahoma was hit by a lower-than-expected attendance because of teenagers on TikTok and fans of Korean pop music, it has been claimed.

The US president, who is looking to secure a second term in November's election, held his first major campaign event since Covid-19 shut down much of the country in Tulsa on Saturday. But images from the rally, which was moved back a day from its original June 19 date, show swathes of empty spaces at the BOK Center, which seats 19,000 people.

The empty seats were blamed on 'radical protesters' and 'apocalyptic media coverage' by Brad Parscale, Mr Trump's campaign director.

But Democratic congresswoman Alexandria Ocasio-Cortez replied, suggesting the low numbers were in fact down to a campaign on video-sharing app TikTok. She tweeted: 'Actually you just got ROCKED by teens on TikTok who flooded the Trump campaign w/ fake ticket reservations & tricked you into believing a million people wanted your white supremacist open mic enough to pack an arena during COVID.

'Shout out to Zoomers. Y'all make me so proud.

'KPop allies, we see and appreciate your contributions in the fight for justice too.'

The efforts to disrupt the rally numbers appear to have been started by Mary Jo Laupp, who on June 11 posted her anger at Mr Trump initially arranging the rally for the day of Juneteenth – a holiday marking the end of slavery in the United States – in a city where a racist massacre took place in 1921.

In her TikTok video, Ms Laupp – described by CNN as a 51-year-old grandmother from Iowa, encouraged people to register for two free tickets to the event on the Trump campaign website but not turn up in an effort to keep the venue as empty as possible.

In response, users – many of them young people, known as Generation Z or Zoomers – posted videos of themselves in front of screens showing they had registered for tickets, while dancing to the Macarena.

The viral effort was amplified by a number of K-pop fan accounts.

Trump officials had expected large numbers to turn out, with Mr Parscale tweeting last week that they had received 800,000 applications for tickets. An overflow area was set up outside the venue, but with many empty spaces inside the arena, it was not needed.

While it is unclear how big a part the online campaign played in keeping seats in Tulsa empty, many online users felt that it was a factor.

READING

1 Why was the attendance at Trump's rally so low?

2 Why was Mary Jo Laupp so angry?

3 Who was involved in sabotaging the rally?

4 Is the tone of this newspaper article formal or informal? How do you know?

5 Complete the quote quest activity in your activity book (see page 134).

WRITING

The Happy News is a newspaper with a twist – it only reports on positive and inspiring news. It features upbeat news stories from around the world about global events and everyday heroes. Articles in the newspaper have covered topics as diverse as the rediscovery of a species of turtle thought to be extinct and the decision to give equal pay to men and women's soccer teams.

Your task is to create your own version of a front page of a newspaper that only reports on the positive and uplifting news from your area. You should include all of the features of a newspaper front page (see page 216). There should be a lead article and a secondary article, and you should use all of the features of a newspaper article in your writing (see page 218). There is a planning tool to help you create your newspaper front page in your activity book (see page 135).

Writing Tips

- Use the features of a newspaper front page accurately (see page 216).
- Use the features of a newspaper article accurately (see page 218).
- Summarise your articles with witty headlines (see page 221).
- Consistently show a clear purpose – to inform and uplift the reader.
- Include quotes from witnesses or the people your articles are about. Go to page 275 to check that you have punctuated these quotes correctly.

Newspaper headlines

A headline should be catchy and snappy in order to grab the reader's attention. You could use a pun in one of your headlines or another form of wordplay to make your headline humorous.

A **pun** is a way of playing with words where a homophone is used to humorous effect. A **homophone** is a word that sounds the same as another word but is actually spelled differently and has a different meaning.

Homophone examples	Wordplay examples
ate – eight	Celebrity Big Blubber (whale swims up the Thames into London)
meet – meat	Threeo Walcott (famous footballer scores three goals)
one – won	Ice Scream! (New York City hit by snow blizzard)
bear – bare	Soda Ban Goes Flat (campaign to ban fizzy drinks is over)
heal – heel	A Whole Latte Trouble (coffee company CEO says he will run for president)

Newscasts

The news is also reported on television in the form of a newscast. A **newscast** is similar to a newspaper in that it is a presentation of the facts of an event. Instead of using the written word, however, it is broadcast on television and usually contains a combination of live video footage, live reports and interviews on location, and studio reports and discussion. Newscasters are filmed as they read out their scripts on a teleprompter.

Features of a newscast	Examples
Newscaster introduces themselves and their location	Good Evening. I'm John Swan and this is the evening news.
Introduces the news topic by summarising it	Businesses rushed to evacuate their premises this evening due to the risk of severe flooding in Cork city centre.
Presents facts and does not offer opinions	The gardai stopped seventeen cars and fined ten motorists for speeding.
Blend of live video footage, live reports and interviews on location, and studio reports and discussion	Let's go live to Marty Moloney outside Government Buildings.
Uses formal language	The criminals were apprehended and will appear before the district court on Monday next.

COMMUNICATING

1 Watch these examples of a newscast from RTÉ News and Fairy Tale News. What features of newscasting were used? Did you feel informed after watching them?
- RTÉ News   edco.ie/ef37
- Fairy Tale News   edco.ie/v29e

2 Choose an event from a children's story that you are familiar with to report on. It could be a well-known fairy tale such as Rapunzel, Snow White or Rumpelstiltskin. You may want to choose an episode from a Harry Potter book or one of the Roald Dahl stories, or a tale from when you were really young like *The Very Hungry Caterpillar* or *The Gruffalo*.

3 Write the script of a newscast using all the features in the box on page 221. You should report on the event you have chosen as if it is a serious news event. Your newscast should be about two minutes long.

4 Finally, record or perform your newscast live for your class.

Speeches

A speech is a type of non-fiction text that is communicated orally to an audience. Sometimes people go to a live event to hear people speak and sometimes people watch speeches online or on TV. Most speeches use persuasive or convincing language to get their message across to their audience. There are many language techniques that speechwriters use to make their speeches interesting and inspiring.

Below is an extract from Malala Yousafzai's speech to the United Nations Youth Assembly in July 2013, on her sixteenth birthday.

Begins by addressing the audience →

Dear friends,

Uses emotion and exaggeration →

On 9 October 2012, the Taliban shot me on the left side of my forehead. They shot my friends too. They thought that the bullets would silence us. But they failed. And out of that silence came thousands of voices. The terrorists thought that they would change my aims and stop my ambitions but nothing changed in my life except this: weakness, fear and hopelessness died. Strength, power and courage was born. I am the same Malala. My ambitions are the same. My hopes are the same. And my dreams are the same …

← **Uses lists of three things**

Addresses the audience directly again →

Dear brothers and sisters, we must not forget that millions of people are suffering from poverty and injustice and ignorance. We must not forget that millions of children are out of their schools. We must not forget that our sisters and brothers are waiting for a bright, peaceful future.

← **Uses facts and statistics**

Use of personal pronoun 'we' to engage with the listener

Greta Thunberg's Speech to the United Nations

Greta Thunberg is a Swedish teenage climate activist. In August 2018, aged 15, she started spending her school days outside the Swedish parliament to call for stronger climate change action by holding up a sign that read 'SCHOOL STRIKE FOR CLIMATE'. Soon, other students engaged in similar protests in their own communities. Together, they organised a school climate change movement under the name Fridays for Future. In 2019, there were multiple coordinated protests in cities all over the world, each one involving over a million students. In September 2019, Greta addressed the United Nations Climate Action Summit in New York about the dangers of climate change.

PRE-READING: COMMUNICATING

Watch Greta Thunberg deliver her speech to the United Nations:
edco.ie/qcdg

1 How did you feel after listening to the speech?

2 How do you think the adults listening to this speech may have felt?

3 Do you think Thunberg is a good public speaker? Why? Why not?

UN Climate Action Summit: Greta Thunberg

My message is that we'll be watching you.

This is all wrong. I shouldn't be up here. I should be back in school on the other side of the ocean. Yet you all come to us young people for hope. How dare you!

You have stolen my dreams and my childhood with your empty words. And yet I'm one of the lucky ones. People are suffering. People are dying. Entire ecosystems are collapsing. We are in the beginning of a mass extinction, and all you can talk about is money and fairy tales of eternal economic growth. How dare you!

For more than thirty years, the science has been crystal clear. How dare you continue to look away and come here saying that you're doing enough, when the politics and solutions needed are still nowhere in sight.

You say you hear us and that you understand the urgency. But no matter how sad and angry I am, I do not want to believe that.

Because if you really understood the situation and still kept on failing to act, then you would be evil. And that I refuse to believe.

The popular idea of cutting our emissions in half in ten years only gives us a fifty per cent chance of staying below 1.5 degrees [Celsius], and the risk of setting off irreversible chain reactions beyond human control.

Fifty per cent may be acceptable to you. But those numbers do not include tipping points, most feedback loops, additional warming hidden by toxic air pollution or the aspects of equity and climate justice. They also rely on my generation sucking hundreds of billions of tons of your CO2 out of the air with technologies that barely exist.

So a fifty per cent risk is simply not acceptable to us — we who have to live with the consequences.

To have a sixty-seven per cent chance of staying below a 1.5 degrees global temperature rise – the best odds given by the [Intergovernmental Panel on Climate Change] – the world had 420 gigatons of CO_2 left to emit back on 1 January 2018. Today that figure is already down to less than 350 gigatons.

How dare you pretend that this can be solved with just 'business as usual' and some technical solutions? With today's emissions levels, that remaining CO_2 budget will be entirely gone within less than eight and a half years.

There will not be any solutions or plans presented in line with these figures here today, because these numbers are too uncomfortable. And you are still not mature enough to tell it like it is.

You are failing us. But the young people are starting to understand your betrayal. The eyes of all future generations are upon you. And if you choose to fail us, I say: we will never forgive you.

We will not let you get away with this. Right here, right now is where we draw the line. The world is waking up. And change is coming, whether you like it or not.

Thank you.

READING

1 Summarise Greta's message in one sentence.
2 Pick out one example of Greta directly addressing the audience in the speech. How do you think her words would affect the audience?
3 Pick out one example of exaggeration in the speech. What is convincing about it?
4 Pick out one example of the use of statistics and facts in the speech. How does this prop up her argument?
5 Do you think overall that Greta succeeds in her purpose – to persuade people to take drastic action on climate change?

WRITING

Try writing your own short persuasive speech. First you should choose a topic to write your speech about. You can choose either a serious topic or a humorous topic, but it should be one you feel passionately about. Select a statement from the list below or come up with an idea of your own.

Aliens live among us.	Robots are better than humans.	Computer games are educational.
Girls and boys should be taught in separate classrooms.	School should start at 11am.	School uniforms should be banned.

Use the writing frame on page 136 of your activity book to help you plan your persuasive speech.

Remember, a speech is meant to be read aloud. Punctuation, especially question marks and exclamation marks, indicate how to deliver each line. Think about how you would read your speech to a crowded room. Add punctuation marks to help the flow and timing of your speech, and to have a persuasive effect on your audience.

Writing Tips

- Choose a speech topic you are already knowledgeable about or keen to research.
- Use the features of speech writing creatively (see page 222).

WRITING SKILLS: WRITING BETTER SENTENCES

Look at your speech. Have you used the same type of sentence over and over? You could make your piece of writing more interesting and engaging by upgrading your sentences and using a variety of sentence structures.

Dull sentence ➝	Upgrading technique ➝	New sentence
You should ban school uniforms. I hate them. They are so itchy.	Three-part sentence, getting progressively better	Without school uniforms, you will have more engaged students, happier staff and better exam results.
Robots can do all the jobs that humans can do.	Three questions and an answer	Want a tidy bedroom? Your homework done? Your favourite snack after school? A robot can do all that for you!
School should start at 11am because I love sleeping.	Fragments of text in three short sentences.	The first bell rings. Everybody is smiling. Nobody is yawning.

COMMUNICATING

Now you know how to write a persuasive speech – but how do you deliver your speech convincingly? How do you perform a speech for maximum effect and impress your audience?

Watch these two short persuasive speeches. They are both famous speeches from well-known films:

- *Remember the Titans*   edco.ie/m9nm
- *Independence Day*   eedco.ie/ctxs

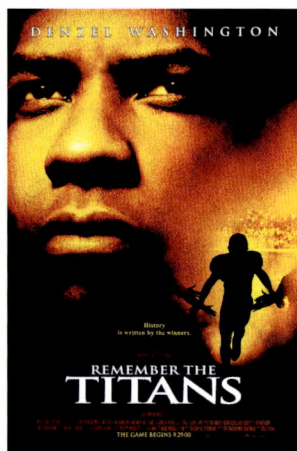	*Remember the Titans* is a film about the racial integration of two schools and their American football teams after the fight for black civil rights in America in the 1970s. In this scene, the coach is trying to bring his football team together after weeks of racist infighting.
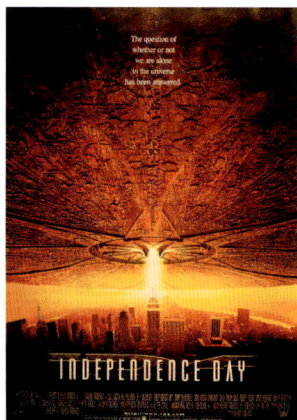	*Independence Day* is a sci-fi film about a devastating alien invasion of earth. In this scene the American president is rallying his troops to fight in the last winner-takes-all battle against the aliens.

ACTIVITY

1 Fill in the table in your activity book (see page 137) as you watch the clips of the two speeches.

2 After watching those two speeches, is there any element of their delivery that you might use in your own speech?

3 Deliver your persuasive speech to your class. To be successful in your speech you should make sure you:

- communicate clearly and fluently
- are convincing and persuasive in your delivery
- engage effectively with your audience.

4 After listening to all of your classmate's speeches, which did you find most convincing or persuasive?

5 Do you think you were most convinced by the content of the speech or the way the person delivered the speech?

Advertisements

A type of persuasive text you come across every day is advertising text. On an ordinary day, the average person comes across about 5,000 ads! We have become so used to them that we don't even notice how many we see in a day. Advertising texts come in different formats – radio advertisements, television advertisements, print ads and digital ads. Each of these ways of advertising includes persuasive techniques and language to convince people to buy or do something. Below is a table showing the basic elements of advertising.

Elements of advertising	Definition	
Target audience	This is the group of people you are targeting, to encourage them to buy whatever you are selling. This could be a very specific group of people, such as girls between the ages of 15 and 20, or a very broad group of people, such as all adults. The audience you are selling to will influence everything you put into your ad, including the colours, images and language you use.	
Colour	Different colours are used in advertising to try to create a specific impression or atmosphere, or to generate a particular emotional response in an audience. For example, if you were selling an environmentally friendly product, you might use the colours green and brown to connect your product with the natural world.	
Copy	These are the words found on advertisements. Ads are a way of persuading people to buy something, so using as much persuasive language as possible in the copy will help sell your product.	
Slogan	A slogan is a short memorable catchphrase used to identify a product or company. Memorable slogans include: Just Do It (Nike) I'm Lovin' It (McDonald's)	JUST DO IT
Logo	A logo is a picture or symbol used to identify a product or company. Some company logos are so well known that an audience will immediately recognise them, such as the Nike swoosh and the adidas three stripes.	
Images	These are the video images, pictures, drawings or photos used to promote a product or idea.	CIRCUS

TV advertisements

A TV advertisement is a way of advertising a product or business on the television. TV ads vary in length and can range from fifteen seconds long to over one minute. They use the elements of film-making to create a short, memorable visual to persuade the target audience to buy something.

Features of a TV ad include:		
A visual message, usually just fifteen to thirty seconds long, aimed clearly at its target audience	Film-making techniques to grab the audience's attention	A mixture of sound effects, dialogue, voice-over and music

COMMUNICATING: GROUP DISCUSSION

ACTIVITY

There are some TV ads that have been so successful that they have not only helped sell a product but also become really popular in their own right.

Watch the following four TV ads and complete the table in your activity book (see pages 137–138):

- Eir   edco.ie/f556
- Esat Digifone   edco.ie/tys3
- Vodafone   edco.ie/9zj4
- Cadbury   edco.ie/rgxf

1 Which was your favourite TV ad and why?
2 Did you think any of the ads were too short or too long?
3 Which TV ad do you think was the most effective in selling its product?
4 Can you think of any other TV ad you have seen that you thought was effective? Describe the ad and why you thought it worked so well.

Radio advertisements

A radio ad is a way of advertising a product or business on the radio. Radio ads are usually between twenty and thirty seconds long. They allow a business to deliver a short, powerful message to its potential customers. As they're on the radio, your audience obviously can't see any images, so it is up to the person making the ad to paint a picture in the listener's mind.

Features of a radio ad include:			
A strong opening hook	A clear repeated message, usually twenty to thirty seconds long, aimed at the target audience	A mixture of sound effects, dialogue, voice-over and music	A special offer or deal to encourage customers

COMMUNICATING: GROUP DISCUSSION

The following are a selection of four radio advertisements. greatirishradioads.com is a website celebrating the creativity of Irish radio ads through the years.

- Flash   edco.ie/tv8z
- Bord Bia   edco.ie/6uz7
- Irish Jobs   edco.ie/5ffd
- Barry's, Christmas   edco.ie/sp95

ACTIVITY

1 Listen to each advertisement and complete the table in your activity book (see page 138).

2 Rank the ads in order of preference. Which did you like best? Which did you like least?

3 Which ads convinced you to buy into their product? Why do you think this is?

4 Which ads put you off their products? Why do you think this is?

5 While the standard length of a radio ad is thirty seconds, the Barry's Tea ad is a minute and a half long. It is one of the most iconic ads on radio and has been playing every Christmas since 1994. Why do you think Irish people enjoy this ad so much?

Digital advertisements & social media

Digital advertising is any advertising that happens online. This can include advertisements on websites, apps or on social media. Social media describes all the ways of communicating using different internet platforms, such as Twitter, Snapchat, TikTok, Instagram and YouTube.

People use social media for different purposes – some use it to connect and communicate with friends, some use it to buy and sell products and some use it to become social media influencers. Social media apps and platforms make most of their money from advertising. Companies pay them to advertise to people on their platforms.

Print advertisements

Print advertisements are ads that appear in newspapers, magazines and on billboards. These types of printed ads are used to sell products or services, but are also used for public health messages and by charities and organisations looking to raise awareness or money.

READING

Look at the four print advertisements opposite.

ACTIVITY

1 Complete the table in your activity book (see page 139).

2 Rank the ads in order of preference. Which did you like best? Which did you like least?

3 Which ads convinced you to buy into their product? Why do you think this is?

4 Which ads put you off their products? Why do you think this is?

WRITING

You have been asked to create an advertising campaign for your favourite book. You could use your First Year class novel or a book you have read at home that you know really well. Your task is to persuade people to buy the book.

Choose one of the forms of advertising you have learned about.

TV advert	radio advert	digital advert	print advert

- Whichever type of advertising you use, make sure to use the features of that type of advertising (see pages 228, 229 and 230).

- Be clear who your target audience is before you start your campaign.

ACTIVITY

- You should use the advertising campaign planning frame in your activity book (see pages 139–140).

SEE THE REALITY BEFORE IT'S TOO LATE

The endangered African penguin needs your help. Act now and help change this picture. **Adopt a penguin** today at www.sanccob.co.za and support SANCCOB and their partners in conservation to save our proudly South African penguins.

SANCCOB™
saves seabirds

GROW OUTSIDE.

Nature Play WA
www.natureplaywa.org.au

Precision Parking.
Park Assist by Volkswagen.

You eat what you touch.

Lifebuoy
HAND WASH

PROJECT:
Theme Park

> ### PROJECT BRIEF
>
> A group of investors have pooled their money and want to create the biggest and best theme park the world has ever seen. It should be unique, attractive and fun for all the family. Your company has a shot at securing the contract to create this theme park. The winning company will be the one that follows the project brief as closely as possible and convinces the board of investors that their theme park is the best.
>
> **1** Create an exciting and engaging multi-modal map of your proposed theme park.
>
> **2** Create a persuasive and factual promotional leaflet for your proposed theme park.
>
> **3** Create a memorable radio advertisement to promote your theme park.
>
> Your teacher may ask you to do one part, two or all three parts of the theme park project.

Research

Before you brainstorm ideas for your park, you should do some research, by browsing the websites and YouTube channels of some successful theme parks all over the world.

Take a look at these ones:

Alton Towers	Tayto Park	Disneyland
PortAventura	LEGOLAND	Chessington World of Adventures

Complete the research task in your activity book by following the guided research questions (see pages 140–142).

You have been asked to imagine a unique theme park that is attractive and fun for all the family. The key words in this line of the project brief are **unique**, **fun** and **attractive**. Keep these in mind as you brainstorm ideas for your theme park.

Use the planning frame in your activity book (see pages 143–144) to record all your ideas as you go.

Deciding On A Theme

Your theme park needs a theme. You may choose to have one unifying theme throughout the park or a number of connected themes and sub-divide your park into separate lands. Whichever you pick, the themes should be maintained in everything you create, from the rides to the restaurants. Possible themes could include:

under the sea	clowns	spies
jungle	space	Wild West
magic	eco-friendly	computer games

Remember the project brief says the investors are looking for something unique, so try not to use something that's been done before.

Imagining Attractions

The minimum number of attractions required in your theme park is sixteen. This doesn't include facilities such as toilets, restaurants and parking. In the project brief, the investors were clear that they wanted to create a theme park that was fun for all the family, so don't forget that both small children and adults need to be entertained.

Possible attractions could include some creative spins on:

teacups	rollercoaster	big drop
chair swing ride	bumper cars	Ferris wheel
carousel	pirate ship	train
water slide	log flume	river rapids
pendulum ride	bouncy castle	bungee jump
go karts	simulator	ghost train

Planning Facilities

Don't forget that people will also need to park, eat and use the bathroom. In your planning you should include parking areas, ticket booths, restaurants, shops and toilets. Try to link these in with your theme to enhance your customers' experience. For example, if your theme park is based on the Wild West, consider laying out your facilities like a frontier town, with a saloon, bank, jail and hardware store.

Choosing A Name

The name of your theme park should sum up the atmosphere and character of your theme park in one or two words. It should be catchy and memorable. Here are some examples of existing theme parks with interesting names.

Adventure City	Carousel Gardens	Dreamland
Enchanted Island	Fort Fun	Galaxyland

Designing A Logo

A logo is a picture or symbol used to identify a product or company. It should represent the theme and atmosphere of the park in a single image. Your logo should be clear, simple and memorable, so that customers immediately link it to your park.

Creating A Slogan

A slogan is a short memorable catchphrase used to identify a product or company. It should have only a few words and should sum up the experience of your theme park. To get some inspiration, look at these examples:

A New Breed Of Speed	A Next-Generation Thrill Ride	A True Giant Among Coasters
Where The Magic Never Ends	Discover The Magic	It's A World Of Adventures!
Face Your Fears	Fast And Full Of Venom	Face Gravity, Face First

Part 1: Creating A Theme Park Map

PROJECT BRIEF

Create an exciting and engaging multi-modal map of your proposed theme park.

To be successful in this project, you will need to:

- create an accurate, informative and appealing representation of your theme park
- communicate your theme park's message through its name, logo and slogan
- balance text and simple visuals to appeal to the reader
- maintain a clear, consistent theme throughout.

Research → Draft → Redraft → Create

Research

Theme park maps are visual representations of the world of the theme park. They have common features that help a potential visitor to the park visualise what the park and its surroundings might look like, help them plan their day and navigate their way around.

Main attractions

Facilities

Main attractions highlighted

Park name

Logo

Pictures or icons or themes

Slogan

Use all your ideas and planning from your initial research to create a list of the features to be shown on your map.

Draft It

Your map should be be at least A3 in size. The first draft should be a rough mock-up in pencil to ensure you have enough room to lay everything out. It might be helpful to draw, very lightly, a grid in the background in pencil.

Be sure to include the following:

Theme park name	Logo	Slogan	A minimum of sixteen attractions	All the main facilities

Redraft It

Check your mock-up map against the success criteria in the project brief box on page 235. Have you left anything out? Is there anything you need to improve?

The names of your rides are one of the best way to persuade people to go on them. Look at the examples below of some successful real-life theme park attraction names and the techniques used to make them sound appealing.

Names that you associate with thrill and risk				
Oblivion	Vampire	Kobra	Temple of Mayhem	Dragon's Fury
Rattlesnake	Endeavour	Power Surge	Nemesis	The Blade

Names that you associate with family fun			
Peter Rabbit Hippity Hop	Bugbie Go Round	Postman Pat Parcel Post	Ladybird Loop

Names that use alliteration		
Tower of Terror	Canopy Capers	Raging River Ride
Tiny Truckers	Viking Voyage	Sky Swinger

Now look at the names for your attractions again. Do you need to upgrade the names of any of your rides to make them sound more exciting?

Create It

Once you are happy with your mock-up version of your map and the upgraded names of your rides, it's time to create your final version. Take time to choose a colour scheme that fits in with your theme. Remember that colour can spark positive or negative emotions, so make sure you think carefully about the emotional reaction you want your customer to have when they see your map. You also want your map to have some resemblance to true-to-life colours so that it's a useful navigation tool.

Part 2: Creating A Promotional Leaflet

PROJECT BRIEF

Create a persuasive and factual promotional leaflet for your proposed theme park.

To be successful in this project, you will need to:

● use a combination of text, pictures and white space to appeal to the eye of the reader

● describe the attractions convincingly using a variety of language techniques

● be clear and include information regarding the practicalities of visiting the theme park.

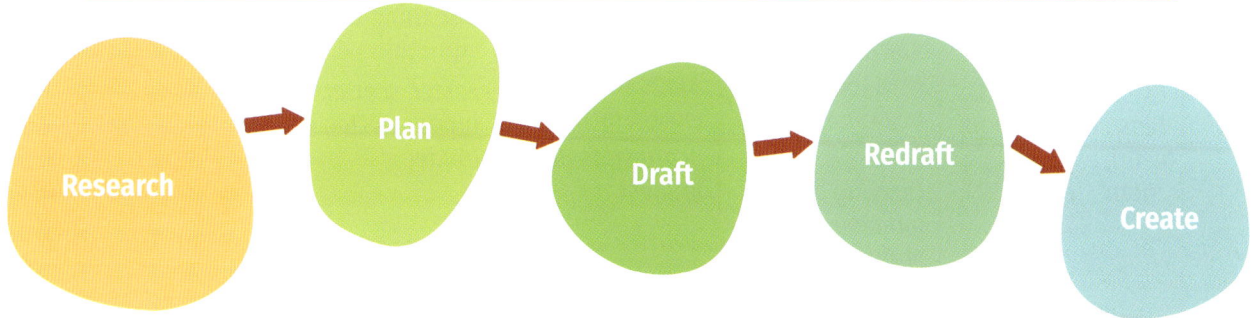

Research → **Plan** → **Draft** → **Redraft** → **Create**

Research

Every year, theme parks spend a large amount of money promoting their parks to persuade people to come and visit them. One of the ways in which they do this is by producing promotional leaflets. A promotional leaflet usually contains a mixture of factual information, such as ticket prices, what facilities are available and directions, and special promotions. They also include positive descriptions of their most exciting or flagship attractions.

See if you can find some promotional leaflets like the one below to look at for inspiration, either on the internet or from previous visits you've made to theme parks.

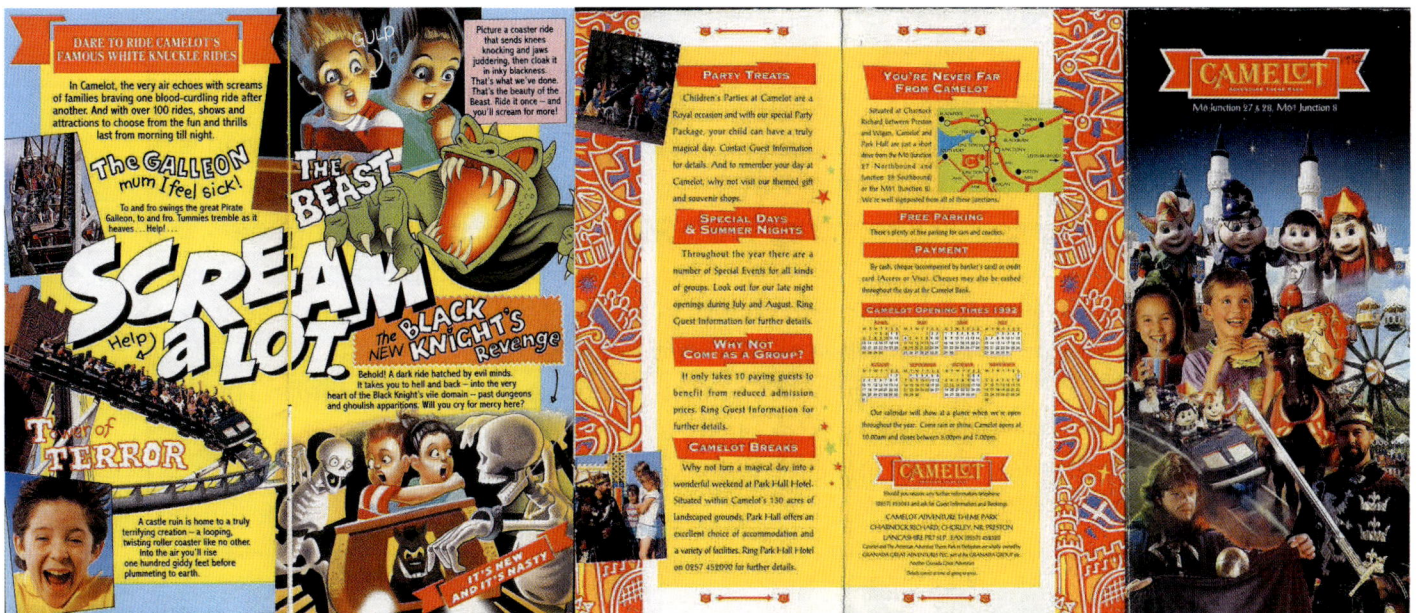

DESCRIBING A THEME PARK ATTRACTION TOOLKIT

The purpose of the descriptions of the most popular rides is to persuade people to want to come and visit the park. Below are some ways a writer could use language to make their descriptions exciting and engaging.

Powerful and exciting verbs	Alliteration	Superlative adjectives	Comparative adjectives	Adverbs
Doing words that suggest power, energy and exhilaration	When two or more words are placed together with the same beginning letter or sound	Tells us that something is the best and tends to be exaggerated	Comparing one thing to something else	Words that describe verbs and usually end in -ly
Blast, dive, swoop, whirl, explode, zoom	*Dizzying drops, ludicrous loops, stupendous speeds*	*Scariest, fastest, loudest*	*Faster, scarier, bigger, better, louder*	*Quickly, slowly*

Take a look at the description below for the Oblivion ride at Alton Towers. See how the toolkit has been used to make this attraction seem appealing.

Alton Towers: Oblivion

The world's first vertical drop rollercoaster

Oblivion beckons you to face your fears. As you're held, overhanging the edge of the world's largest vertical drop rollercoaster, you get a moment to savour slowly what is to come.

You know you shouldn't look, but you won't be able to stop yourself from taking a peek at the colossal vertical 180-foot drop!

Prepare yourself – the dramatic drop into Oblivion is imminent.

Putting your body through an incredibly intense 4.5G drop, Oblivion is amongst the highest G-force rollercoasters in the UK. This iconic thrill ride saw the world's introduction to the Dive Coaster. No ride is faster, scarier and more packed with thrills. This coaster blasts you into oblivion.

Going where no ride has gone before, this is the world's best vertical drop rollercoaster.

Alliteration

Superlative adjectives

Comparative adjectives

Powerful and exciting verbs

READING

Read these attraction descriptions, then answer the questions below.

Alton Towers

GANGSTA GRANNY: THE RIDE

Climb into your royal carriage as Granny and Ben enlist your help to pull off the greatest jewel heist in history! Take a spin through the sewers on a 360° special-effects-laden wild ride to break into the crown jewels vault! Can you grab the jewels and make an explosive escape? Careful, if the Feds catch you, you'll be in a right royal mess! Can you pull off the greatest jewel heist in history?

PortAventura

DRAGON KHAN

An icon for all rollercoasters: 8 loops and more than 110 km/hr of speed will make Dragon Khan a sure temptation as soon as you lay eyes on it. One of PortAventura Resort's most iconic rides.

Tayto Park

THE CÚ CHULAINN

Tayto Park is proud to be the home of Ireland's first rollercoaster and Europe's largest wooden rollercoaster with an inversion, the Cú Chulainn Coaster. With a strong focus on mythological Irish history, the rollercoaster has been named after one of the greatest heroes in Irish history, Cú Chulainn. With the figure of Ireland's greatest mythological warrior emblazoned across the front of the rollercoaster, Cú Chulainn leads his passengers through an epic and thrilling experience like no other. Are you brave enough to join Cú Chulainn on his warrior's quest?

Disneyland

TWIRL IN A TEACUP

Inspired by the Mad Hatter's tea party from Lewis Carroll's classic tale *Alice in Wonderland*, this lively ride promises to be an enchanting experience for all. Celebrate the Mad Hatter's party by whirling around in colourful, larger-than-life teacups!

1 Which of these descriptions persuaded you to go on the attraction? Why?

2 Which attractions were you not persuaded to go on? Why?

3 Choose one attraction description and pick out the language techniques from the toolkit that they used. How do you think the techniques made the ride sound more attractive?

4 Choose one attraction and edit their description to make it sound more appealing by using some additional techniques from the toolkit.

Plan It

Choose at least six flagship attractions that you will describe in your leaflet. Select the rides that are unique to your park and any other particularly exciting ones, but make sure there is a something there for the entire family to enjoy as well.

Remember that the promotional leaflet should also contain information about opening times, ticket prices, facilities, the times of the shows and any special offers. If you have already created a theme park map, you could use this to help you.

Draft It

Write out the important information you need to include on the leaflet and the basic descriptions of the attractions you have chosen.

Redraft It

Check your piece of writing against the success criteria for this task in the project brief box on page 237. Have you left anything out? Is there anything you need to improve?

Redraft your piece of writing using the toolkit on page 238 to make your attractions even more appealing, and take a look at the suggestions below.

EXAMPLE A	EXAMPLE B
The rollercoaster is brilliant and loads of fun.	This rampaging rocket of a rollercoaster will blast you higher than you've ever gone before!

Example A gives a basic description of the experience of the rollercoaster by using simple adjectives.

Example B is a much better description, as it uses alliteration, comparative adjectives and powerful verbs.

The way you structure your sentences can have a big impact on how exciting you make your attractions seem. Look at these two examples and think about which is more effective.

EXAMPLE A	EXAMPLE B
Come have a go on the fastest rollercoaster in the world. It's fun and exciting.	Are you a speed demon? Love to feel the fear? Totally addicted to adrenaline? Then you need to experience the Juggernaut!

Using a variety of sentence types can help to make your writing more engaging. Try redrafting some of your sentences to include a couple of the sentence types from the box opposite.

Sentence type	Example 1	Example 2
Three-part sentence, getting progressively better	Step into the gently flowing stream and float through the forest, then pick up super speed through the raging rapids, before splashing down the gigantic, thunderous waterfall.	Family Funderland is the perfect place to spend quality time together, have heaps of family fun and make some wonderful forever memories.
Three connected short sentences	The fear! The thrill! The total euphoria!	Set sail. Enjoy the sights. Experience another world.
Three leading questions and an answer	Do you just love PAW Patrol? Always wanted to visit Ryder's Lookout tower? Ever imagined yourself driving the PAW Patroller? Then head down to Adventure Bay, where all your PAW Patrol dreams will come true.	Ever wanted to climb 100 metres into the air? Ever thought about how it would feel to drop out of the sky? Ever wondered how brave you truly are? Test your nerve on the Dreadful Drop of Doom!

Create It

To create your final leaflet, stick two blank sheets of A4 paper together, then fold them lengthways into three, to make three columns.

The theme park name, location and contact details should go on the front section. Don't forget to use your theme park logo and slogan that you created earlier.

If you have already created a theme park map, try to match the colour scheme for continuity.

Part 3: Creating A Radio Advertisement

> **PROJECT BRIEF**
>
> Create a memorable radio advertisement to promote your theme park.
> To be successful in this project, you will need to:
> - include the features of a radio ad in a convincing way
> - use convincing and persuasive language to appeal to your audience
> - perform your radio ad fluently and clearly.

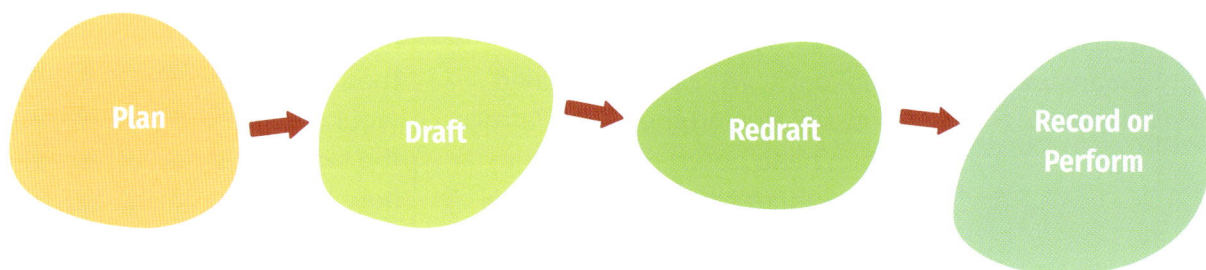

Plan → Draft → Redraft → Record or Perform

Plan It

How are you going to convince people in thirty seconds, with no visuals, to visit your theme park? For information on the features of a radio advertisement, look back at page 228.

Plan your radio ad ideas in your activity book (see pages 145–146).

Draft It

When drafting the script for your radio ad, it is important to make clear when and where you are going to use each sound effect and voice-over and any elements of song. You must also choose in advance what type of accent or tone of voice you want your voice actors to use when performing the script.

Look at the radio ad script opposite, where each element of the ad is clear and sequential.

In your activity book, use the radio ad organiser to draft your script (see page 147).

Order	Voice-over	Sound effects	Music	Text
1	–	–	Intro jingle for 3 seconds – Water Wonderland	–
2	–	Splashing and laughing	–	–
3	Loud excited voice	Fading splashing sound	–	Do you love the water? Brilliant boat rides? Raging rapids? Wondrous waterfalls?
4	–	Big splash and kids laughing	–	–
5	Loud excited voice	Fading giggling sound	–	Do you want a family-friendly day out your kids will be talking about for years to come?
6	–	Joyful scream and big splash	–	–
7	Loud excited voice	–	–	Then come on down to Water Wonderland!

Redraft It

Check your script against the success criteria for this task in the project brief box opposite. Have you left anything out? Is there anything you need to improve? Can you make it more exciting?

Redraft your script, making improvements by referring to the toolkit on page 238.

Record Or Perform It

You can choose to perform your radio ad live to your class or record it using a voice recording app, such as WhatsApp Voice Note or Soundtrap. If you are recording, it is best to do this in a small, quiet room for the best sound quality.

> **REFLECTION**
>
> 1 What was the most enjoyable element of this project? Why?
>
> 2 Describe what the creative process involved. Did you have a very set vision from the start or did your ideas change over time?
>
> 3 What did you learn from this project about how English is used in the real world?

Test Your Knowledge

1 **Which of the following would you not expect to find in a formal letter?**

   a) Text written in first-person narrative perspective

   b) Text written in a formal tone

   c) Formal greeting and sign off

   d) The sender's innermost thoughts and feelings expressed

2 **Which of the following would you not expect to find in an email?**

   a) Subject line

   b) Time and date electronically stamped

   c) Sender's street address

   d) Text written in first-person narrative perspective

3 **Which of the following would you not expect to find in a newspaper article?**

   a) Text written in the future tense

   b) Formal language

   c) A first paragraph addressing the who, what, where, when and why of the story

   d) A headline summarising the article

4 **Which of the following would you not expect to find in a newscast?**

   a) Newscaster introduces themselves and their location

   b) Newscaster uses informal language

   c) Newscaster presents facts and does not offer their opinion

   d) Blend of live video footage, live reports and interviews on location, and studio reports and discussion

5 .... **writing is a type of non-fiction that describes visits to new places.**

6 **A** .... **is a type of text that is communicated orally to an audience.**

7 **Match the features of advertising with their correct definitions.**

Feature	Definition
Copy	A picture or symbol used to identify a product or company
Slogan	The group of people you are aiming your ad at, to get them to buy whatever you are selling
Logo	The words found on advertisements
Target audience	A short, memorable catchphrase used to identify a product or company

8 **Match the features of persuasive language with their correct definitions.**

Feature	Definition
List of three	Information and data to add credibility to your argument
Direct address	Using 'we' and 'us' to convince people we are all in this together
Personal pronouns	Talking directly to the audience
Facts and statistics	List things in groups of three to make your argument more convincing

9 **What are the features of a radio ad?**

10 **What are the features of a TV ad?**

11 **What are the features of a print ad?**

12 **What makes advertising on social media different from other forms of advertising?**

Practise Your Writing Skills

Complete these writing tasks. Each one asks you to write in a specific text type and with a specific purpose.

- Write a letter to a friend from your primary school describing your life at your new secondary school.
- Write an email to someone that inspires you, thanking them for how they help you to achieve your goals.
- Write a short newspaper article describing a local sports event.
- Write a short speech on behalf of your class to your teacher about the amount of homework you have been set.
- Write a short script for a newscast about an extreme weather event.
- Write a short script for a radio advertisement about a circus visiting your local city or town.

Interactive website

Go to **www.edco.ie/touchstones1** for interactive activities based on this unit.

UNIT 7
READING

Why Read?

There are a multitude of reasons why reading is a fantastic use of your time. Reading improves your language skills, develops your mind, helps you learn to listen and can transport you to another time and place.

> We read to know we are not alone.
> **C.S. Lewis in Shadowlands, by William Nicholson**

> The more that you read, the more things you will know. The more that you learn, the more places you'll go.
> **Dr Seuss, I Can Read With My Eyes Shut**

> We read books to find out who we are. What other people, real or imaginary, do and think and feel… is an essential guide to our understanding of what we ourselves are and may become.
> **Ursula K. Le Guin**

> Books are mirrors: you only see in them what you already have inside you.
> **Carlos Ruiz Zafón, The Shadow of the Wind**

Which of these quotes do you like best? Which quotes do you agree with? Are there any you disagree with?

COMMUNICATING: GROUP DISCUSSION

Lots of research has been done on why people read and what the benefits are. Read these six studies that suggest reading is good for you, then discuss the questions below.

Reading reduces stress

In 2009, scientists at the University of Sussex in the UK looked at how different activities lowered stress by measuring heart rate and muscle tension. Reading a book or newspaper for just six minutes lowered people's stress levels by 68 per cent. This was a higher percentage drop in stress than going for a walk at 42 per cent, drinking a cup of tea or coffee at 54 per cent, or listening to music at 61 per cent. According to the authors, the ability to be fully concentrating on what you are reading and therefore not distracted is what makes reading the perfect way to relieve stress.

Reading helps you live longer

A daily dose of reading may lengthen your lifespan. A team of scientists at Yale University followed more than 3,600 adults over the age of 50 for 12 years. They discovered that people who reported reading books for 30 minutes a day lived nearly 2 years more than those who read magazines or newspapers. Participants who read more than 3 and a half hours per week were 23 per cent less likely to die, and participants who read less than 3 and a half hours per week were 17 per cent less likely to die. 'The benefits of reading books include a longer life in which to read them,' the authors wrote.

Reading makes you smarter

In the 1990s, a team of scientists carried out a variety of tests to try to figure out the link between reading and a person's vocabulary and fact-based knowledge. The researchers were surprised that the average result of these studies was that avid readers, as measured by the tests, had around a 50 per cent larger vocabulary and 50 per cent more fact-based knowledge than people that did not read at all.

Reading makes you a nicer person

In 2013, at Harvard University, a group of volunteers either read fiction, popular fiction non-fiction or nothing. Across five experiments, those who read fiction performed better on tasks like predicting how characters would act and identifying the emotions in facial expressions. These results show us that reading improves your ability to read other people's emotions and feelings. Put simply, reading makes you a nicer person.

Reading reduces your risk of dementia

A study published in the journal *Neurology* claimed that reading and similar activities reduced the rate of cognitive (relating to the mental process involved in knowing, learning and understanding things) decline in dementia patients. Researchers questioned 294 patients about their reading habits over the course of 6 years and then examined their brains for dementia in a post-mortem. They found a slower rate of decline in patients who reported more early-life and late-life cognitive activity, such as reading, writing and playing games.

Reading helps you sleep

Creating a bedtime ritual, like reading before bed, signals to your body that it's time to wind down and go to sleep, according to the Mayo Clinic. Reading a real book helps you relax more than zoning out in front of a screen before bed. Screens like e-readers and tablets can actually keep you awake longer and even upset your sleep. That applies to kids too – 54 per cent of children sleep near a small screen, and clock 20 fewer minutes of shut eye on average because of it, according to research. So, reach for the literal page-turners before switching off the light.

1 According to these studies, what can reading improve?
2 According to these studies, what can reading reduce?
3 What was the most convincing statistic in these studies? Why?
4 What research about reading surprised you in these studies? Why?
5 Did these studies change your mind about reading in any way?

The Rights Of The Reader

This is a poster about the rights we all have as readers. You may be familiar with the style of the illustrations. They are by Quentin Blake, the illustrator of all Roald Dahl's books.

The Rights of the Reader
by Daniel Pennac
illustrated by Quentin Blake

1 The right not to read.

2 The right to skip.

3 The right not to finish a book.

I'm keeping some for tomorrow!

4 The right to read it again.

Again! again!

5 The right to read anything.

6 The right to mistake a book for real life.

It's just SO me!

7 The right to read anywhere.

8 The right to dip in.

Try this page — it's fantastic!

9 The right to read out loud.

10 The right to be quiet.

10 rights — 1 warning
Don't make fun of people who don't read — or they never will.

COMMUNICATING: GROUP DISCUSSION

Study the poster opposite, then discuss the questions below.

1 Which of these rights do you agree with?
2 Which of these rights do you disagree with?
3 If you were to take away one of these rights, which would you choose and why?
4 If you were to add another right, what would it be?

Using Your Local Library

You may already be a member of your local library or you may have never stepped through the doors of one. Look at the poem below by children's author Julia Donaldson, which describes the benefits and joys of your local library. You will probably be familiar with Julia Donaldson from the books of your childhood, such as *The Gruffalo*, *Room on the Broom* and *The Snail and the Whale*.

Library Poem by Julia Donaldson

Everyone is welcome to walk through the door.
It really doesn't matter if you're rich or poor.
There are books in boxes and books on shelves.
They're free for you to borrow, so help yourselves.

Come and meet your heroes, old and new,
From William the Conqueror to Winnie the Pooh.
You can look into the *Mirror* or read *The Times*,
Or bring along a toddler to chant some rhymes.

The librarian's a friend who loves to lend,
So see if there's a book that she can recommend.
Read that book, and if you're bitten
You can borrow all the other ones the author's written.

Are you into battles or biography?
Are you keen on gerbils or geography?
Gardening or ghosts? Sharks or science fiction?
There's something here for everyone, whatever your addiction.

There are students revising, deep in concentration,
And school kids doing projects, finding inspiration.
Over in the corner there's a table with seating,
So come along and join in the Book Club meeting.

Yes, come to the library! Browse and borrow,
And help make sure it'll still be here tomorrow.

COMMUNICATING: GROUP DISCUSSION

1 What activities take place in the library?
2 What types of books might you find in the library?
3 What types of texts besides books might you find in the library?
4 What are three pieces of advice about the library you could take from this poem?

COMMUNICATING: GROUP DISCUSSION

Read these six reasons to join the library. Then discuss with your classmates whether there are any other points you would like to add to the list.

Six reasons to join the library	
1	In Ireland, we have public libraries that are completely free to join.
2	The library itself offers a quiet, peaceful space to sit and browse books or read.
3	If your local library doesn't have the book you want, the library will find it and order it in for you – for free!
4	Joining is easy – all you need to do is fill in a form online or in person and get the signature of your parent or guardian.
5	You can renew books or order books online using the library app.
6	You can also read magazines, newspapers and e-books online and listen to audiobooks for free by using library apps, such as PressReader, RBdigital and BorrowBox.

What Type Of Reader Are You?

Many different types of reader exist in the world. You may yourself go through all the types in your lifetime or even in the space of a year. There are times in our life when we are reluctant to read and other times when we can't get enough of reading. The important thing to know is that just because you may not be in love with reading right now, doesn't mean you won't fall in love with a book again sometime in the future. Take the quiz opposite to see what type of reader you are at the moment.

```
        ┌──────────────────────────────────────────┐
        │ Do you consider yourself a good reader?    │
        └──────────────────────────────────────────┘
```

No	Yes

Was there ever a time in your life when you considered yourself a good reader?	How often do you read at home?

No	Yes	Once a week	Most days

Was learning to read a frustrating experience for you?	How long do you read for at home in one sitting?

Yes	No	Under 30 minutes	An hour or more

Reluctant Reader	Hibernating Reader	Regular Reader	Total Bookworm
You are not keen on reading… yet! How about trying an audiobook or podcast to kick-start your reading journey? Or maybe a magazine, a newspaper or a short story might whet your appetite instead?	You once liked reading but have somehow fallen out of the habit. Spend some time browsing and try to match your reading choices and text types to your interests. Would you enjoy a magazine about boxing or cars? Or would you prefer to read about current events in a newspaper?	Well done, you are reading regularly! Try expanding your horizons by checking out some books from genres you don't usually gravitate towards.	Congratulations, you are reaping the rewards of being an avid reader! Keep challenging yourself with books from different genres and a variety of text types.

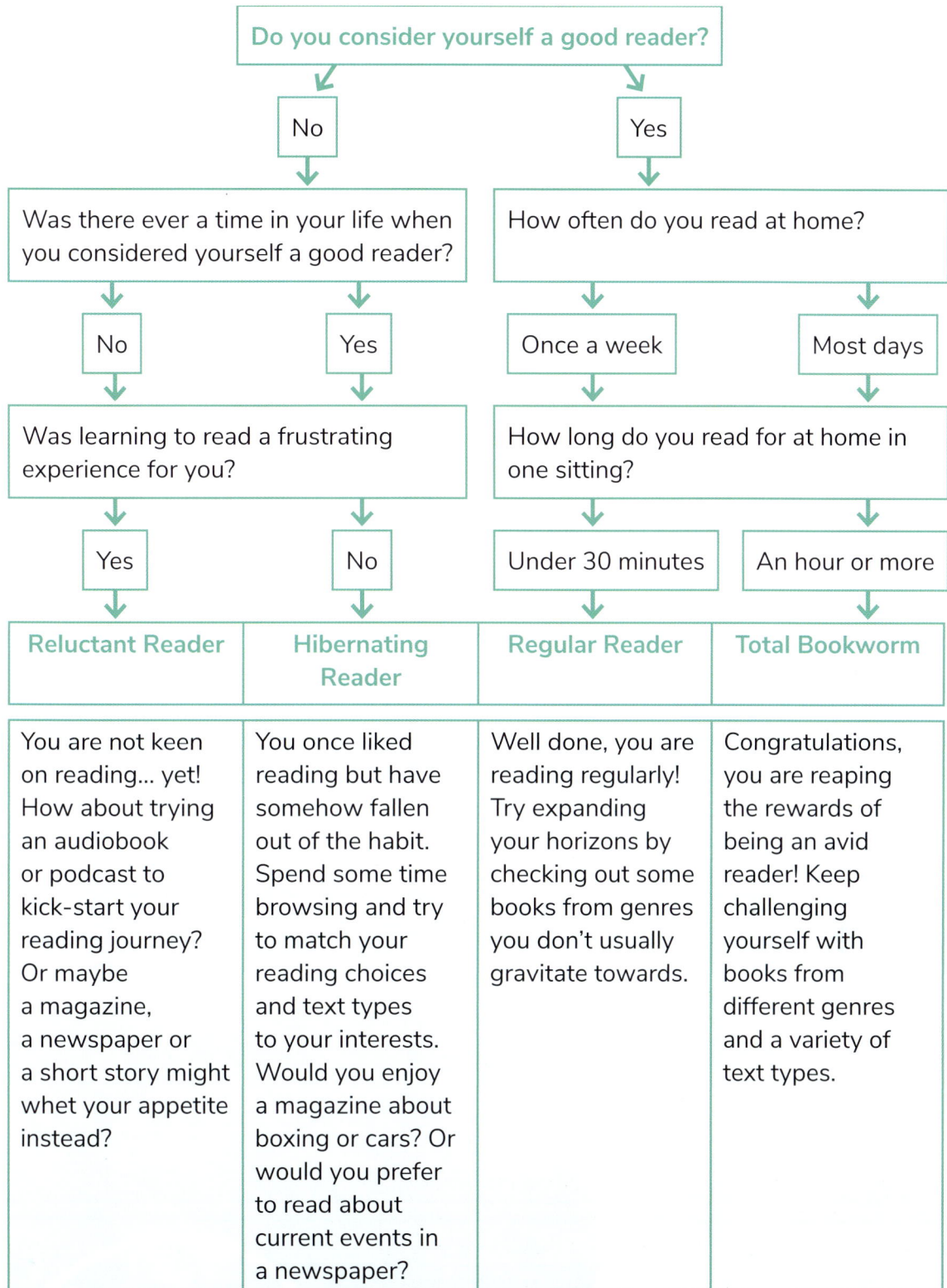

COMMUNICATING: GROUP DISCUSSION

Discuss the questions below in small groups or with your whole class.

1 Which type of reader were you?

2 Which type of reader would you like to be?

3 What advice could you give someone who wanted to read more?

4 What advice might you give someone who doesn't like to read at all?

Finding A Book To Read

1 **Search by genre:** there are lots of different genres of books to choose from – action, adventure, historical fiction, science fiction, mystery, horror. If you have previously read a book of a particular genre and enjoyed it, chances are you will like another book in that same genre. You could do an online search of your chosen genre and see if anything appeals to you.

2 **Search by author:** sometimes people really like the writing style of a particular author. When you finish a book and you have enjoyed it, search online for other books by the same person to see if there is something else you might want to read.

3 **Award-winning books:** every year, a number of book awards are given out to authors whose books are recognised for their brilliance. The CILIP Carnegie Medal, the Newbery Medal, the Waterstones Children's Book Prize, the National Book Awards, the Costa Book Awards and the An Post Book Awards are the most prestigious and well known of these. You could search online for the shortlists and awards winners and browse for something that grabs your interest.

4 **Book trailers:** publishing companies often create online book trailers that offer a preview of what a book is about. There are some great YouTube channels with trailers of interesting young adult reads: try Epic Reads, Walker Books and Penguin Teen.

5 **Good Reads:** this is a community website full of book lovers. You can sign up and create an account that will keep track of all of the books you have read and offer recommendations based on what you like. You can also use the website to search for books, read a book summary, browse community reviews and look up a book's star rating.

6 **Audiobooks:** who doesn't love being read to? Audiobooks are now widely available online. You could subscribe to a service like Audible or Spotify to search for and listen to audiobooks. Alternatively, you can find some audiobooks on YouTube or on the open-source audiobook site LibriVox.

7 **Use an algorithm:** book algorithms use information you input online to create a list of books you might enjoy. Try Whichbook, which offers a book selection based on your preferences in four categories: mood and emotion, world map, characters and plot, and bestsellers.

8 **Best ever book list:** you could also search the 'best ever' book lists that people compile online. There are new lists published all the time; good ones to browse are the best books of the year, the best historical fiction books and the best young adult novels.

9 **Local library:** visit the library in your city or town and browse the book shelves. Libraries are free to join and books are free to borrow. You could always ask the librarian to help you find a book to try.

10 **Bookshops:** take a trip to your local bookshop and leaf through the books in the different sections, or ask the people who work there for their advice on what might be a good read for you.

11 **Teachers' recommendations:** turn to pages 261–268 and read some short reviews and descriptions of popular books for students. Or ask your own teacher for some suggestions.

12 **Fill your bookshelves:** In your activity book (see page 148), jot down the names of some books that have been recommended to you or that have appealed to you in your search to find a book to read.

COMMUNICATING: GROUP DISCUSSION

It's time to get talking to your classmates about reading! Your teacher will assign a number to everyone in the class. Go to the list below, find the number you have been given and read the task. Quiz your classmates until you find someone who can help you fulfil your task.

You could go through multiple rounds of this activity and be given a different number each time by your teacher.

Find someone who:

1 Has read the entire Harry Potter series. Ask them to name all the books.

2 Has read the entire Northern Lights series. Ask them to name all the books.

3 Has read the entire Chronicles of Narnia series. Ask them to name all the books.

4 Likes to read the newspaper. Ask them to tell you what types of articles they read.

5 Likes to read graphic novels. Ask them to name their favourites.

6 Likes to read short stories. Ask them to name their favourites.

7 Has read three Irish legends. Ask them to name them.

8 Likes to read about sport. Ask them to give two examples.

9 Likes to read about real-life events. Ask them to give two examples.

10 Likes to read about history. Ask them to give two examples.

11 Likes to read about the supernatural. Ask them to give two examples.

12 Likes to read books that are funny. Ask them to give two examples.

13 Has read a book from the *Diary of a Wimpy Kid* series. Ask them to describe their favourite character.

14 Has read a book by David Walliams. Ask them to name the book and describe their favourite character.

15 Has read *The Boy in the Striped Pyjamas*. Ask them to describe their favourite character.

16 Has read *Under the Hawthorn Tree*. Ask them to describe their favourite character.

17 Has read *The Secret Garden*. Ask them to describe the plot.

18 Has read *Black Beauty*. Ask them to describe the plot.

19 Has read *Alice's Adventures in Wonderland*. Ask them to describe the plot.

20 Has read a book from the *Skulduggery Pleasant* series. Ask them to describe their favourite character.

21 Has read a book from the *Percy Jackson* series. Ask them to describe their favourite character.

22 Has read five books by Julia Donaldson. Ask them to name them.

23 Has read five books by Roald Dahl. Ask them to name them.

24 Has read five books by Enid Blyton. Ask them to name them.

25 Has read a book by Neil Gaiman. Ask them to name the book and describe their favourite character.

26 Has read a book from the *Artemis Fowl* series. Ask them to describe their favourite character.

27 Has read a book by Anthony Horowitz. Ask them to name the book and describe their favourite character.

28 Has read a book by J.R.R. Tolkein. Ask them to name the book and describe their favourite character.

29 Has read a book that has been turned into a film. Ask them to name the book and choose which they preferred.

30 Has read a book that has been turned into a TV show. Ask them to name the book and choose which they preferred.

COMMUNICATING: GROUP DISCUSSION

Get into groups of four and form a reading circle. Read your chosen book in silence for 20 to 30 minutes. Then use the questions below as prompts for a discussion in your group.

1   What are you reading at the moment?
2   What is the gist of the story?
3   Where and when is the book set?
4   Do you know what narrative perspective the book is written in?
5   Are you enjoying it?
6   Why did you pick that book?
7   Would you recommend the book to someone else?
8   Have you ever read anything like this before?
9   Are the characters in the book interesting?
10 Is the setting of the book similar to anything you've ever read before?
11 If you could ask the author anything about the book, what would it be?
12 Is there any bit in the book that has stuck with you for some reason?
13 If you could get rid of one of the characters in the book, who would it be and why would you get rid of them?
14 If the main character in the story lived next door, would you be friends with them?
15 If you could add a character to the book, who would it be and why would you add them?
16 If you could swap one of the characters in the book for a character from another book, who would it be and why?
17 If you could change the setting of the book, where would you move it to and why?
18 What do you think is going to happen at the end of the book? What makes you think this?
19 Have you learned anything about the world you live in from reading this book?
20 Have you noticed anything in particular about this author's style of writing?

PERFORMING

Below are the famous first lines of ten popular children's classics. The teacher will read the first line out loud to the whole class. The story then moves around the class, with each student adding a new line and acting it out as they speak. The story does not have to follow the plot of the original book, but it does have to make narrative sense. You can do this in small groups if you prefer.

Black Beauty: 'The first place that I can well remember was a large pleasant meadow with a pond of clear water in it.'

Charlotte's Web: '"Where's Papa going with that axe?" said Fern to her mother as they were setting the table for breakfast.'

The Secret Garden: 'When Mary Lennox was sent to Misselthwaite Manor to live with her uncle everybody said she was the most disagreeable-looking child ever seen.'

The Lion, the Witch and the Wardrobe: 'Once there were four children whose names were Peter, Susan, Edmund and Lucy.'

Paddington Bear: 'Mr and Mrs Brown first met Paddington on a railway platform. In fact, that was how he came to have such an unusual name for a bear, for Paddington was the name of the station.'

Harry Potter and the Philosopher's Stone: 'Mr and Mrs Dursley, of number four Privet Drive, were proud to say that they were perfectly normal, thank you very much.'

The Hobbit: 'When Mr Bilbo Baggins of Bag End announced that he would shortly be celebrating his eleventy-first birthday with a party of special magnificence, there was much talk and excitement in Hobbiton.'

The Worst Witch: 'Miss Cackle's Academy for Witches stood at the top of a high mountain surrounded by a pine forest.'

The Curious Incident of the Dog in the Night-time: 'It was seven minutes after midnight. The dog was lying on the grass in the middle of the lawn in front of Mrs Shears' house. Its eyes were closed.'

COMMUNICATING: GROUP DISCUSSION

Can you do the one-minute book challenge? It sounds easy, but talking about something for a full sixty seconds without pausing or stopping is actually quite difficult.

- First choose a book you know really well.
- Then make a list of all the things you could say about the book, making sure you include comments about the plot, characters, setting and style.
- Start a countdown timer and talk for a full sixty seconds about your book.
- You are out of the game if you say 'Um…', pause or run out of things to say.

WRITING

For this blurb-writing activity you will need a stack of at least five novels. Divide into groups of four to compete against each other.

- Choose one book at a time.
- The teacher will read the blurb of the book to the whole class.
- Each group now has to compose a first line to match the blurb of the book. Write it on a slip of paper, then hand it to the teacher. The teacher writes the actual first line on another slip of paper.
- The teacher reads out all the possible first lines (including the actual one).
- Confer with your group and discuss which one you think is the real first line. Each group then reveals their guess to the class.
- The teacher gives points for each correct guess. The winning team is the group with the most correct guesses at the end of the stack of novels.

WRITING

Write a short letter to an author of a book you have enjoyed. Remember to include all the features of a formal letter (see page 203).

- Outline the reasons why you particularly liked reading the book.
- Add any questions you have about the characters or the plot.
- Ask them where they got their ideas from.
- Ask about the process of writing the book. How did they plan the story? How many times did they draft and redraft it?
- Add any other questions you might have. Did they always want to be a writer? What is their favourite thing about writing?
- Finish by asking them to suggest a book for you to read next.

Book Lists

Classic reads

Little Women by Louisa May Alcott

Set in the American Civil War, this book describes the lives of the four March sisters – Meg, Jo, Beth and Amy – who are reared in near poverty by their mother, known as 'Marmee', in their New England home, while their father serves in the war as an army chaplain. The story follows the four girls as they grow from childhood to womanhood. Loosely based on the lives of the author and her three sisters, it is classified as a semi-autobiographical novel.

Treasure Island by Robert Louis Stevenson

The is a rags-to-riches adventure story about a young boy, Jim Hawkins, who goes in search of treasure after finding a treasure map that once belonged to Billy Bones. Jim encounters the pirates Long John Silver and Ben Gunn on his epic adventure, and heroically faces a shipwreck, a pirate mutiny and sword fights, overcoming all the odds in his search for treasure.

The Princess Bride by William Goldman

This book has it all: sword fights, revenge, true love, giants, lies, death and miracles. It is the story of Buttercup, one of the most beautiful women in the world, and her true love, Westley, the farm boy. In their quest to be together, the hero and heroine must battle the evils of their mythical kingdom, escape from the villainous Prince Humperdink and help their companion, the dashing swordsman Inigo Montoya, find the six-fingered man who killed his father.

Around the World in Eighty Days by Jules Verne

This classic adventure novel tells the story of Phileas Fogg of London and his newly employed French valet Passepartout as they attempt to circumnavigate the world in eighty days to win a bet worth £20,000 (roughly €1.9 million today). Their adventures see them travel by boat, train, elephant and sledge to make it around the world as fast as they can.

Charlotte's Web by E.B. White

A young girl named Fern saves the life of the piglet Wilbur, the runt of his litter. Once he's grown into a pig, Wilbur is sold to another farm, where he befriends a spider called Charlotte, who weaves a series of amazing webs to try to save Wilbur from ending up on the Christmas dinner table. This is a tender novel about friendship, love, life and death.

Historical fiction

When the Sky Falls by Phil Earle

Inspired by a true story, this novel is set in London in 1940, during the Blitz in the Second World War. It follows the story of Joseph, who has been packed off to stay with Mrs F, who owns the rundown city zoo. There Joseph meets Adonis, a huge silverback gorilla, who is ferociously strong and dangerous, but Joseph finds he has an affinity with the lonely beast. When the bombs begin to fall, it is up to Joseph to guard Adonis' cage should it be damaged by a blast, and to pull the trigger if necessary…

The Boy in the Striped Pyjamas by John Boyne

Nine-year-old Bruno knows nothing of the Final Solution or the Holocaust. The only thing he knows is that he has been moved from his happy life in Berlin to a house in a desolate area where there is nothing to do and no one to play with. Until he meets Shmuel, a boy who lives a strange parallel existence on the other side of the adjoining wire fence and who, like the other people there, wears a strange uniform of striped pyjamas.

Savage Her Reply by Deirdre Sullivan

This novel is a retelling of the favourite Irish fairy tale *The Children of Lir*. The witch Aife marries Lir, a king who has four children by his previous wife. Jealous of Lir's love for his children, Aife turns them into swans for 900 years. This story is told from Aife's perspective and delves deep into the heart of this children's myth that you thought you knew everything about.

Once by Morris Gleitzman

Set in Poland during the Second World War, this book is about a Jewish boy named Felix who lived hidden in a Catholic orphanage in Poland during the Holocaust. After he sees Nazis burning books, he sets off on a quest to find his bookseller parents. He makes friends and allies along the way, but also encounters and comes to terms with the horrible reality of life outside the orphanage.

Private Peaceful by Michael Morpurgo

Told from the perspective of Private Tommo Peaceful, a soldier at the front during the First World War, this novel spans just twenty-four hours and captures the narrator's memories of his family and his village life – which were by no means as peaceful and idyllic as they appeared. Ultimately, this is a story of buried family secrets, two brothers and the girl that comes between them.

Books to make you laugh

Diary of a Wimpy Kid by Jeff Kinney

This book series follows Greg Heffley, who illustrates his daily life in the form of a diary. Greg describes his attempts to navigate school life, along with his best friend Rowley Jefferson, as well as their quest to become popular. These books combine comic-style drawings with text and are a hilarious and engaging read about growing up.

Adventures of a Wimpy Vampire by Tim Collins

In the first book in the series, Nigel is transformed into a vampire and will now stay the same age forever. The downside is that he became a vampire at the awkward age of fifteen, and must spend eternity coping with spots, a breaking voice and a total inability to talk to girls, which doesn't help him gain the attention of the love of his life, Della Sparrow.

What Not to Do if you Turn Invisible by Ross Welford

Thirteen-year-old Ethel Leatherhead absolutely hates having acne and goes to some pretty drastic measures to cure it. With a combination of obscure Chinese medicine and a second-hand sunbed, Ethel seems to have done the job. However, the plan doesn't quite work the way she expected, as Ethel seems to have given herself the ability to turn herself invisible at will. Despite being fun at first, Ethel's new power fails to wear off one day and she faces being invisible forever.

Millions by Frank Cottrell Boyce

Millions is a funny adventure story about two boys, brothers Damian and Anthony. One day, a massive bag of cash drops from the sky and they only have a few days to spend it before it becomes worthless. Not only is the clock ticking, the people who own the money want it back and these train robbers mean business.

I Am a Genius of Unspeakable Evil and I Want to Be Your Class President by Josh Lieb

Twelve-year-old Oliver Watson's got the IQ of a grilled cheese sandwich. Or so everyone in Omaha thinks. In reality, Oliver's a mad evil genius on his way to world domination, and he's used his great brain to make himself the third-richest person on Earth! But, to prove his dad wrong, he must put his world domination plans on hold to win his school election.

Sci-fi and fantasy

Darkmouth by Shane Hegarty

This book series is about a boy called Finn and his father Hugo who live in a town called Darkmouth. They call themselves legend hunters and Finn is reluctantly training to be one. Every so often a portal opens in their town and evil monsters storm through, intent on destroying Darkmouth. Finn and his father must track them down to stop them ruining their town.

The Dark is Rising by Susan Cooper

The book opens on Midwinter's Eve. It is the day before Will's eleventh birthday – but this will be a birthday like no other. There is an atmosphere of fear in the familiar countryside around him. Will discovers that he has the power of the Old Ones, and that he must embark on a quest to vanquish the terrifyingly evil magic of the Dark. This thrilling and unforgettable book is the second in a five-part series, but you don't need to have read the others to understand and appreciate the power of this one.

Cogheart by Peter Bunzl

Teenager Lily has no idea why her father has worked so hard to keep her identity a secret. But now Lily's life is in mortal danger, her father is missing and silver-eyed men stalk her through the shadows. With her friends Robert, the clockmaker's son, and Malkin, her mechanical fox, Lily is plunged into a murky and menacing world set in Victorian London.

I am Number Four by Pittacus Lore

The first in the Lorien Legacies series, this book is narrated by Number Four (John Smith), the main protagonist in the series. He is, in fact, an alien from the planet Lorien and the story follows his struggle to blend in with the human species. He has moved to Paradise, Ohio, with Henri his Cêpan or guardian, where he befriends Sam Goode and Sarah Hart. Here Number Four develops his 'Legacies' – his mind-blowing powers – and discovers what it means to be human.

His Dark Materials by Philip Pullman

His Dark Materials is a trilogy of fantasy novels by Philip Pullman, consisting of *Northern Lights*, *The Subtle Knife* and *The Amber Spyglass*. The books chart the coming-of-age of Lyra Belacqua and her friend Will Parry, as they wander through a series of parallel universes and to the frozen lands of the Arctic, where witch-clans reign and ice-bears fight. Lyra's extraordinary journey has immeasurable consequences that reach far beyond her own world…

Horror and supernatural

The Graveyard Book by Neil Gaiman

This stunningly original book follows the adventures of Nobody Owens, known to his friends as Bod – raised in a graveyard, by ghosts, with a solitary guardian who belongs neither to the world of the living nor to the world of the dead. There are dangers and adventures for Bod in the graveyard: the strange and terrible menace of the slithering Sleer, a gravestone entrance to a desert that leads to the city of ghouls and a friendship with a teenage witch. However, it is in the land of the living that the real danger lurks, for it is there that the man Jack lives, and he has already killed Bod's family…

Skullduggery Pleasant by Derek Landy

Stephanie Edgley's uncle – a famed horror author – dies mysteriously, leaving 12-year-old Stephanie with his fortune and mansion. Suddenly thrust into a magical underworld full of murderous hunters, vampires, ghosts and monsters that appear to mirror those described in her uncle's books, Stephanie also meets Skulduggery Pleasant, a humorous skeleton brought to life with a special kind of magic. This engaging story follows these two memorable characters as they journey through present-day Ireland, protecting the magical world from crime and learning more about Stephanie's family's truths along the way.

Ghost Boys by Jewell Parker Rhodes

Twelve-year-old Jerome is shot by a police officer who mistakes his toy gun for a real threat. As a ghost, Jerome observes the devastation his death has unleashed on his family and community, in the wake of what they see as an unjust and brutal killing.

Goosebumps by R.L. Stine

This is a teenage horror fiction series, where the stories follow child characters who find themselves in scary situations, usually involving monsters and other supernatural elements. There are now 62 Goosebumps novels to read, so if you like one, there are plenty to keep you going!

The Book of Learning by E.R. Murray

This book is the first in the Nine Lives Trilogy and follows the exciting adventures of Ebony Smart, a 12-year-old girl who discovers she is part of a special tribe of reincarnated people – and that she has just a week to break a terrible curse that threatens the tribe. If she fails, the future of her family, and her people, is at risk.

Award-winning books

The Giver by Lois Lowry

This tale appears to be set in a perfect utopian society. But it's not long before it's revealed to be dystopian. The novel follows a 12-year-old boy named Jonas who lives in a normal, literally colourless, but otherwise pleasant community, with no knowledge of love or pain. It is not until he is given his life assignment as the Receiver of Memory that he begins to understand the dark, complex secrets behind the structures of his fragile world.

The House on Mango Street by Sandra Cisneros

Esperanza Cordero is a 12-year-old Chicana girl growing up in the Hispanic quarter of Chicago. This novel follows Esperanza over the course of one year of her life, as she enters adolescence and begins to face the realities of life as a young woman in a poor and patriarchal community.

The Knife of Never Letting Go by Patrick Ness

This is the first book in the *Chaos Walking* series, which also includes *The Ask and the Answer* and *Monsters of Men*. In the not-too-distant future, Todd Hewitt discovers Viola, a mysterious girl who has crash-landed on his planet, a place where all the women have disappeared and the men are afflicted by 'the Noise' – a force that puts all their thoughts on display. In this dangerous landscape, Viola's life is threatened. As Todd vows to protect her, he will have to discover his own inner power and unlock the planet's dark secrets.

The Bone Sparrow by Zana Fraillon

This novel centres on Subhi, one of the Limbo kids in a permanent Australian immigration detention centre, and the first to be born in the camp after his Maá and big sister Queeny fled violent persecution in Burma. While he's only experienced life within the cruel confines of the camp, Subhi's rich imagination creates a solace-giving, magical world, in which the 'Night Sea' from his Maá's tales brings him treasures from his dad, who he has never met.

Walk Two Moons by Sharon Creech

Thirteen-year-old Salamanca Tree Hiddle is proud of her country roots and the 'Indian-ness in her blood'. As she travels from Ohio to Idaho with her eccentric grandparents, she tells them the story of Phoebe Winterbottom, who received mysterious messages, met a 'potential lunatic', and whose mother disappeared.

Graphic novels

Artemis Fowl: The Graphic Novel by Eoin Colfer

Twelve-year-old Artemis Fowl is a brilliant criminal mastermind. But even Artemis doesn't know what he's taken on when he kidnaps a fairy, Captain Holly Short of the LEPrecon Unit. But these aren't the fairies of bedtime stories; these ones are armed and dangerous. Artemis thinks he's got them just where he wants them. Then they stop playing by the rules…

The Last Kids on Earth by Max Brallier

This graphic novel series has been described as *Diary of a Wimpy Kid* meets *The Walking Dead*. The first book follows an optimistic loner named Jack Sullivan, who finds himself abandoned in a cartoonish end-of-the-world apocalypse. He thrives on freedom, junk food and video games, while training a team of his classmates to fight off Zombies, Winged Wretches and Vine Thingies.

Anya's Ghost by Vera Brosgol

This story centres on Anya, a teenager who hates her life. She's embarrassed by her family, self-conscious about her body and has pretty much given up on fitting in at school. Her life changes when she falls down a well – of all the things she expected to find at the bottom, a new friend was not one of them. Especially not a new friend who's been dead for a century…

Pumpkinheads by Rainbow Rowell

Deja and Josiah are 'seasonal' best friends. Every autumn, all through school, they've worked together at the best pumpkin patch in the whole wide world. But this Hallowe'en is different – this is their last season at the pumpkin patch. Their last shift together. Their last goodbye…

New Kid by Jerry Craft

A semi-autobiographical story, *New Kid* follows Jordan Banks, who loves nothing more than drawing cartoons about his life and dreaming of going to art school. But instead his parents enrol him in a prestigious and highly academic private school, where he is one of the few African-American children in a building bursting with white privilege. As he makes the daily trip from his Washington Heights apartment to the upscale Riverdale Academy Day School, Jordan soon finds himself torn between two worlds – and not really fitting into either one.

Non-fiction

I am Malala by Malala Yousafzai, co-written with Christina Lamb

I Am Malala: The Girl Who Stood Up for Education and was Shot by the Taliban is an autobiographical book about Malala Yousafzai. When the Taliban took control of the Swat Valley in Pakistan, Malala refused to be silenced and fought for her right to an education. She was shot in the head at point-blank range while riding the bus home from school and few expected her to survive. Instead, her miraculous recovery has taken her on an extraordinary journey from a remote valley in northern Pakistan to the halls of the United Nations in New York. At sixteen, she became a global symbol of peaceful protest and the youngest nominee ever for the Nobel Peace Prize.

The Boy who Harnessed the Wind by William Kamkwamba, co-written with Bryan Mealer

William Kamkwamba was born in Malawi, a country where magic ruled and modern science was a mystery. It was also a land withered by drought and hunger. But teenager William had read about windmills, and he dreamed of building one that would bring to his small village luxuries that only two per cent of Malawians could enjoy: electricity and running water. His neighbours called him 'misala' – crazy – but William refused to let go of his dreams.

The Diary of a Young Girl by Anne Frank

This is the diary kept by teenager Anne Frank while she was in hiding for two years with her family during the Nazi occupation of the Netherlands. The family was eventually caught in 1944 and Anne died of typhus in the Bergen-Belsen concentration camp in 1945. The diary was retrieved by Otto Frank, Anne's father, the family's only known survivor, just after the Second World War. Anne's deeply moving and unforgettable diary has since been published in more than 70 languages.

The Reason I Jump by Naoki Higashida

In this unusual and ground-breaking non-fiction book, a Japanese teenage boy shares his extensive personal experience of autism. Naoki Higashida is non-verbal and wrote the book by pointing to letters on an alphabet grid, aged just 13.

Girl Hearts Girl by Lucy Sutcliffe

A real-life memoir about Lucy's life as a young person coming to terms with her sexuality and her 'coming out', as well as her first relationship with girlfriend Kaelyn, this is a positive and upbeat read about being comfortable in your own skin.

PROJECT:
The Ten-Text Challenge

One of the best things about your Junior Cycle English course is that it recognises the importance of reading for pleasure. The ten-text challenge is a way of recording and tracking your progress in the land of reading over the three years of your course.

All you have to do is choose ten texts to read this year, then record your reading progress.

Research

Take some time to choose your texts and find something that interests you. Remember that a text can be a short story, a podcast, a magazine or newspaper article, a non-fiction book or a novel.

- Look through the lists of recommended books in this chapter (see pages 261–268).
- Ask someone you know for a book recommendation.
- Visit your local library or bookshop to browse the shelves and ask for suggestions or find out what is popular.
- Visit goodreads.com to read some reviews.

Reading

Every time you complete a text, record it in the ten-text challenge section of your activity book (see page 149). You will be able to look back at the end of the year and see how much you've completed.

REFLECTION

1 Which of the texts did you enjoy the most? Why?
2 Which of the texts did you enjoy the least? Why?
3 Were there any texts you started and didn't want to finish? Why?
4 Did any of the texts surprise you?
5 Do you think you have changed as a reader this year?
6 What are your reading plans for next year?

UNIT 8

SPELLING, PUNCTUATION AND GRAMMAR

/
Slash

—
Dash

Ful

!
Exclamation mark

&
Ampersa

SPELLING, PUNCTUATION AND GRAMMAR KNOWLEDGE ORGANISER

Things I need to know

- **Etymology:** The history of a word.

- **Morphology:** The different parts of a word.

- **Synonym:** A word that means the same thing.

- **Antonym:** A word that means the opposite.

- **Prefix:** Letters added to the beginning of a word to make a new word with a different meaning.

- **Suffix:** Letters added to the end of a word to make a new word with a different meaning.

- **Root word:** A word in its most basic form, with no prefix or suffix.

- **Dictionary:** A book where you can find the meaning of words, listed in alphabetical order.

- **Thesaurus:** A book where you can find synonyms of words.

Comma

tation mark

Nouns
(page 276)

Verbs And Tenses
(page 277)

Adverbs
(page 277)

Pronouns
(page 277)

Homophones

PowerPoint

Homophones are words that sound the same but have different spellings and meanings. Take a look at the common examples below. If you're unsure which spelling is correct for the word you want to use, always check in a dictionary.

their	your	two	new	right	sun
there	you're	to	knew	write	son
they're		too			

Capital Letters

It is very important to know how to start a sentence properly. Every sentence should start with a capital letter. Capital letters should also be used for specific names and titles of books and films. Take a look at the rules and examples below.

Punctuation	Rules	Example
Capital letter	Use a capital letter at the start of a sentence.	The boy ate a sandwich for lunch.
	Use a capital letter for names of people and places.	Patricia and I went to Nepal to climb Mount Everest.
	Use a capital letter for titles of books and films.	Layla went to the cinema to watch *No Time To Die*.

Try the tasks on page 150 of your activity book to practise using capital letters correctly.

End Punctuation

It is also important to know how to end a sentence. Every sentence should finish with a piece of end punctuation – a full stop, a question mark or an exclamation mark. Take a look at the rules and examples below.

Punctuation	Rules	Example
Full stop	Use a full stop to end a sentence.	Grainne eventually made it to the end of the hiking trail.
Exclamation mark	Use an exclamation mark to end a sentence in surprise or to show feelings or emotions.	We have no homework today!
Question mark	Use a question mark to end a sentence as a question.	Would you like a drink?

Try the tasks on page 151 of your activity book to practise using end punctuation correctly.

Commas

A comma is a punctuation mark that is used to show a pause or to separate adjectives or items on a list.

Punctuation	Rules	Example
Comma	Use to separate adjectives.	The tired, hungry cyclist weaved dangerously through the traffic.
	Use to separate items on a list.	Afra packed her money, keys, books and a drink in her bag.
	Use as a pause between two or more parts of a sentence.	Although she was tired, Cora went to the party.

Try the task on page 151 of your activity book to practise using commas correctly.

Apostrophes

An apostrophe is used to show ownership or to indicate a missing letter.

Punctuation	Rules	Example
Apostrophe	Use to show ownership of one person.	The girl's hair was tangled.
	Use to show ownership of more than one person.	The boys' boots were dumped in the hallway.
	Use to show a missing letter – contraction.	Don't you dare tell me what to do!
	Use to show a missing letter – abbreviation.	Chasing a will-o'-the-wisp at night is not a good idea.

There are two words that can cause confusion because they break the rules! Look at the box below to see these words and their meanings, then learn them carefully so that you always remember them.

Word	Meaning	Example
It's	Means 'it is' or 'it has'	It's been raining all day.
Its	Means 'belonging to it'	Can you see its sharp teeth?

Try the tasks on page 152 of your activity book to practise using apostrophes correctly.

Semi-colons

A semi-colon is a punctuation mark used between two independent clauses that are related.

Punctuation	Rules	Example
Semi-colon	Use to replace a conjunction.	Daisy spent three hours looking in her bedroom; she couldn't find her phone anywhere.
	Do not use a capital letter afterwards, unless the next word is a proper noun.	The bus left early on Tuesday; Evie had to walk to school.

Colons

A colon is a punctuation mark that may be used to introduce a list, a title, a quote or direct speech. You may also use a colon to introduce a definition of something.

Punctuation	Rules	Example
Colon	Use to introduce a list.	There are three things you need to bring to the party: food, drinks and music.
	Use to introduce a quotation.	The author ends the book on a positive note: 'After all, tomorrow is another day.'
	Use to introduce an explanation.	There's one thing I can't stand about the city: the traffic.

Try the task on page 153 of your activity book to practise using colons correctly.

Punctuating Dialogue

Dialogue is when a character in a story is speaking. It is important that the reader knows when the dialogue starts and ends in a story, so correct punctuation of dialogue is essential. Take a look at the rules and examples below.

Punctuation	Rules	Example
Punctuating dialogue	Move to a new line every time there is a new speaker.	'Get out of my house!' screamed Mary.
	Use speech marks to enclose what you want someone to say.	'Over my dead body,' replied Rory calmly.
	Use a comma, question mark, exclamation mark or full stop before closing your speech marks.	
	Make sure it's clear who is saying what.	

'What is this please, Your Majester?' the BFG asked, peering down at the Queen.

'He has never eaten anything except snozzcumbers before in his life,' Sophie explained. 'They taste revolting.'

'They don't seem to have stunted his growth,' the Queen said.

The BFG grabbed the garden spade and scooped up all the eggs, sausages, bacon and potatoes in one go and shovelled them into his enormous mouth.

'By goggles!' he cried. 'This stuff is making snozzcumbers taste like swatchwallop!'

The Queen glanced up, frowning. Mr Tibbs looked down at his toes and his lips moved in silent prayer.

'That was only one titchy little bite,' the BFG said. 'Is you having any more of this delunctious grubble in your cupboard, Majester?'

'Tibbs,' the Queen said, showing true regal hospitality, 'fetch the gentleman another dozen fried eggs and a dozen sausages.'

Try the task on page 153 of your activity book to practise punctuating dialogue correctly.

Parts Of Speech

Every word plays a part in a sentence. These parts are called the parts of speech. The parts of speech are: nouns, verbs, adverbs, adjectives, pronouns, conjunctions, connectives and prepositions.

Part of speech	Explanation	Examples
Noun	A word used to identify a person, place or thing	Sarah, Paris, pencil
Verb	A doing or being word	walked, jumping, enjoys, slept
Adverb	Gives more information about a verb	bravely, deeply, suddenly, quickly
Adjective	Describes a noun	clever, blue, large, cold
Pronoun	Used in place of a noun	he, she, it, them, us, him, her
Conjunction	Joins two similar ideas together in a sentence or begins a subordinate clause	and, because, or, so
Connective	Joins two separate ideas together in one sentence or in two consecutive sentences	however, but, therefore, additionally
Preposition	Tells you where or when something is in relation to something else	at, on, in, from, to, before, behind

Nouns

A noun is a word used to identify a person, place or thing. Take a look at the different types of nouns below.

Type of noun	Explanation	Examples
Common noun	Refers to an object, person or place	cat, drink, girl, school
Proper noun	Refers to a specific object, person or place	McDonald's, Mount Everest, Johnny Sexton
Collective noun	Describes a collection of objects, animals or people	a basket of fruit, a herd of cattle, a crowd of people
Abstract noun	Refers to things that don't have a physical form, such as emotions or ideas	confusion, knowledge, disgust, love

Verbs and tenses

Verbs are words that describe actions or being. Take a look at the three main tenses in the box below.

Tense	Rules	Example
Past	Describes things that have already taken place	I ate
Present	Describes something that is happening at the moment	I eat
Future	Describes an event that hasn't happened yet	I will eat

Adverbs

An adverb is a word that describes a verb, such as slowly or carefully. Most adverbs end in -ly. Adverbs are used to give you more information about the verb being described. This can add impact to your writing and spark the interest of your reader. Look at example A and example B below.

EXAMPLE A	EXAMPLE B
The donkey walked onwards through the deserted village.	The donkey walked reliably onwards through the deserted village.

Example B uses the adverb 'reliably'. This tells us that the donkey is trustworthy and experienced, which is important information for the reader.

Try the tasks on pages 154–155 of your activity book to practise using adverbs correctly.

Pronouns

Pronouns are used instead of a noun to make writing less repetitive. You will already be familiar with pronouns such as I, you, he, she, we, us and they. Look at example A and example B below.

EXAMPLE A	EXAMPLE B
Jennifer cycles to school because Jennifer wants to get really fit for her triathlon.	Jennifer cycles to school because she wants to get really fit for her triathlon.

Example B uses the pronoun 'she' instead of repeating Jennifer's name. This is less repetitive and makes the text flow better.

Try the task on page 155 of your activity book to practise using pronouns correctly.

Interactive website

Go to **www.edco.ie/touchstones1** for interactive activities based on this unit.

Acknowledgements

The publisher would like to thank the following for text material:

p7: *The Hunger Games* by Suzanne Collins, by permission of Scholastic Corporation (US); *The Fellowship of the Ring* by J.R.R. Tolkien; *The Curious Incident of the Dog in the Night-time* by Mark Haddon, by permission of Penguin Random House UK; p8: *Ender's Game* by Orson Scott Card; p9: *The Lion, the Witch and the Wardrobe* by C.S. Lewis by permission of Harper Collins UK; p10: *The Shadow of the Wind* by Carlos Ruiz Zafón by permission of the Orion Publishing Group Ltd.; p15: *Harry Potter and the Philosopher's Stone* by J.K. Rowling by permission of The Blair Partnership; p27: 'The Secret Life of Walter Mitty', *The New Yorker*; p33 'The Three Little Pigs' by Jon Scieszka, by permission of Viking Press; p50: 'Touchscreen' by Marshal Davis Jones, p50, Original quote by Sanober Khan, by permission of Sanober Khan; p52: 'Risk' by Anon; p54: 'The Mummy's Smile' by Anon; p54: 'Love After Love' by Derek Walcott, by permission of Farrar, Straus and Giroux; p56: 'Delicious Dishes' by Anonymous; p58: 'Folsom Prison Blues' by Johnny Cash, Hal Leonard Publishing; p59: *The Gruffalo* by Julia Donaldson, by permission of MacMillan International Ltd.; p64: 'We Real Cool' by Gwendolyn Brooks, the Estate of Gwendolyn Brooks; p66: 'Refugees' by Brian Bilston, by permission of Unbound; pp70, 72: 'Still I Rise' by Maya Angelou, Little, Brown and Company ; p73: 'First They Came' by Martin Niemoller, by permission of Holocaust Memorial Day Trust; p75: 'Back in the Playground Blues' by Adrian Mitchell by permission of United Agents; p77: 'Mid-Term Break' by Seamus Heaney, Faber & Faber; p85: 'The door' by Miroslav Holub, translation by Ian Milner, by permission of Bloodaxe Books; p93: 'My Puppy Punched Me In the Eye' by Kenn Nesbitt, by permission of Sourcebooks Jabberwocky; p94: 'On the Ning Nang Nong' by Spike Milligan, Penguin Books Ltd.; p96: 'The Sound Collector' by Roger McGough, Peters, Frasers & Dunlop (PFD) Literary Agents; p98: 'Base Details' by Siegfried Sassoon, by permission of the Barbara Levy Literary Agency; p105: 'Alphabet Aerobics' by Blackalicious; p158: *Alone it Stands* by John Breen; p161: *Blood Brothers* by Willy Russell, by permission of Negus-Fancey Agents Ltd.; p163: *Frankenstein* adapted by Philip Pullman, by permission of Oxford Publishing Limited (EDUK); pp185, 188: Modern translation of *Romeo and Juliet* by William Shakespeare, by permission of sparknotes.com; pp190, 191, 192: Modern translation of *A Midsummer Night's Dream* by William Shakespeare, by permission of sparknotes.com; p204: www.lettersofnote.com; p212: 'Extreme weather threatens one of Earth's most awe-inspiring waterfalls' by Amy McKeever, printed in *National Geographic*; p218: 'Third heroic rescue by father and son fishermen' by Greg Murphy, printed in the *Irish Examiner*; p219: 'Empty seats at Donald Trump rally 'down to TikTok users and K-pop fans', by Luke O'Reilly, printed in the *London Evening Standard*. By permission of Luke O'Reilly/the Evening Standard; p238: Oblivion: Alton Towers, by permission of Alton Towers; p239: PortAventura; p239: The Cú Chulainn, by permission of Tayto Park; p.248: '7 Scientific Reasons You Should Be Reading More' by B. Piero, published by www.bpiero.com.

The publisher would like to thank the following for photographs:

Adobe Stock Images, Alamy, Pauline Baynes © copyright CS Lewis Pte Ltd 1950, Heidi Bohnenkamp Photography, Chessington World of Adventures, Éditions Gallimard, flaticon.com, Getty Images, © Mya Lixian Gosling, goodticklebrain.com;, *The Guardian*, thehappynewspaper.com, HarperCollins, *The Irish Times*, iStockphotos, *A Single Life* – 2015 – Job, Joris and Marieke; Bo McCready (@BoKnowsData), Nature Play WA, SANCCOB, Royal Shakespeare Company, Scholastic, Shutterstock, *The Sun*, Tayto Park, The UN Refugee Agency, United Agents, Volkswagen and DDB Berlin, Lifebuoy, www.moviral.com, Walker Books.